OCR Religious Ethics for AS and A2

OCR Religious Ethics for AS and A2 is an ideal textbook for students of Advanced Subsidiary or Advanced Level courses, structured on OCR specification. The book covers all necessary topics of the Religious Ethics A level specification in an enjoyable student-friendly fashion, and is split into four parts:

- What is ethics?
- AS Ethics
- A2 Ethics
- Connections in philosophy of religion and religious ethics

Each chapter includes:

- A list of key issues, to introduce students to the topic
- OCR Syllabus checklist
- Explanations of key terminology
- Exam practice questions using actual examples from previous years
- Self-test review questions
- Helpful summaries
- Annotated further reading suggestions.

To maximise students' chances of exam success, the book includes a chapter dedicated to answering examination questions, and extra help on how to approach the synoptic paper. The book comes complete with lively illustrations, a comprehensive glossary and full bibliography.

The author: Jill Oliphant teaches Religious Studies at Angley School, Cranbrook, Kent. She is also an experienced examiner.
The editor: Jon Mayled is Chief Examiner for Religious Studies. He is author and editor of many popular books for the GCSE syllabus

D1078060

Religious Ethics for AS and A2

JILL OLIPHANT

EDITED BY JON MAYLED

Routledge
Taylor & Francis Group

LONDON AND NEW YORK

First published 2007
by Routledge
2 Park Square, Milton Park, Abingdon, Oxon OX14 4RN

Simultaneously published in the USA and Canada
by Routledge
270 Madison Ave, New York, NY 10016

Routledge is an imprint of the Taylor & Francis Group, an informa business

© 2007 Jill Oliphant and Jon Mayled

Typeset in Charter
by Keystroke, 28 High Street, Tettenhall, Wolverhampton
Printed and bound in Great Britain by
MPG Books Ltd, Bodmin

British Library Cataloguing in Publication Data
A catalogue record for this book is available from the British Library

Library of Congress Cataloging in Publication Data
Oliphant, Jill, 1949–
    Religious ethics for AS and A2 / Jill Oliphant, edited by Jon Mayled.
        p. cm.
    Includes bibliographical references and index.
    1. Religious ethics—Textbooks. I. Mayled, Jon. II. Title.
    BJ1188.O45 2007
    205—dc22   2007001591

ISBN10: 0–415–36631–3 (pbk)
ISBN10: 0–203–01897–4 (ebk)
ISBN13: 978–0–415–36631–1 (pbk)
ISBN13: 978–0–203–01897–2 (ebk)

This book is dedicated to Hannah, Lucinda and Miranda.

Contents

PART IV CONNECTIONS IN PHILOSOPHY OF RELIGION AND RELIGIOUS ETHICS 259

List of illustrations

Acknowledgements

I am very grateful to the many people who have helped me prepare this book, particularly to Lesley Riddle of Taylor & Francis for commissioning me to write this text. I much appreciate the support I have received from Taylor & Francis staff, particularly Gemma Dunn's great work in obtaining pictures and copyright permissions. I also wish to thank greatly the people who have read drafts of the book and made so many helpful suggestions, particularly Lesley Riddle, Gemma Dunn, Moira Taylor and Jon Mayled for all their assistance and support, not to mention their patience while waiting for parts of the text.

I am also very grateful to the friends and family members who have supported and encouraged this project. I would like to thank in particular the sixth-form students of Angley School who read early drafts of the book, especially Emma Whittall who did the drawings for the chapter on genetic engineering.

I also wish to express my thanks to the following authors and publishers for permission to use images or quotations from their work:

TEXTS

The scripture quotations contained herein are from The New Revised Standard Version of the Bible, Anglicised Edition, copyright © 1989, 1995 by the Division of Christian Education of the National Council of the Churches of Christ in the United States of America, and are used by permission. All rights reserved.

Extracts from examination papers and specification details are produced by the kind permission of OCR.

IMAGES

We are indebted to the people and archives below for permission to reproduce photographs or original illustrative material. Every effort has been made to trace copyright-holders. Any omissions brought to our attention will be remedied in future editions.

Bridgeman Art Library

Plato
Aristotle
The School of Athens
René Descartes
Thomas Aquinas
David Hume
Sigmund Freud
St Augustine
Detail of a red figure krater
Socrates
Immanuel Kant
Gottfried Wilhelm Leibniz
Nicolaus Copernicus
Jeremy Bentham
Bust of Epicurus
Moses and the Ten Commandments
John Stuart Mill
John Calvin
Benedict Spinoza
John Locke
The Kiss
Martin Luther King Jr.
Bertrand Russell

Getty images

Make Poverty History – wristband
Diane Pretty
Stephen Hawking
Sperm fertilising egg
Ultrasound image of human foetus
Newborn baby
DNA helix
White laboratory rats

How to Use this Book

This book has been written for OCR students but it will be of use to all AS and A2 level Religious Studies students, as well as students taking the Moral Philosophy section of AS/A2 Philosophy and Scottish National Examinations at Higher Level.

The book is designed for students to use in class and at home. Every chapter provides an overview of the major themes and issues of Religious Ethics on the OCR specification for Religious Studies. The following six features are designed to help you make the most effective use of the book:

1 **'The issue' section**
   This highlights the key issue or issues you should think about while studying each chapter.

2 **OCR checklist**
   The box in each chapter about the OCR specification tells you which topics from the AS/A2 Religious Studies course are covered.

3 **Essential terminology box**
   At the beginning of every chapter there is a box listing the key terminology for the chapter. You should be able to use this terminology accurately in examinations.

4 **Examination questions practice**
   At the end of every chapter there is a section about answering examination questions on the topic, along with a sample question.

5 **Review questions**
   The review questions in every chapter are designed to test your understanding of topics discussed in the chapter. Make use of this section as a way to assess your learning about and from the issues in the chapter.

6 **Further reading**
   The reading suggested at the end of each chapter suggests ways of exploring topics in greater depth.

Answering Examination Questions

In order to be successful in Advanced Level Religious Studies you must learn examination techniques. Some advice to guide you is given below, but there is no substitute for practising writing examination questions. There are example questions at the end of the chapters in this book, and your teacher will give you plenty of other questions with which to practise.

Some important aspects to answering examination questions are explained below.

SUBJECT KNOWLEDGE

At both AS and A2 level the majority of marks are given for your demonstration of a good understanding of the topic the question is examining. It is important not only that you learn the work you have studied, but also that you are able to select the knowledge that is relevant to an answer. For example, if the question is (AS level): *Explain how a follower of Natural Law might approach the issue of abortion*, your answer should be focused on the Natural Law approach to abortion, not writing everything you know about Natural Law or abortion.

When preparing for examination questions, it is a good idea to think about not only what a question is asking, but also what material you have studied that is relevant to the question.

Practise writing answers

It is very important that you practise answering questions for Religious Studies examinations by handwriting answers. In an examination you have very little time to write answers and you have to write not type. This takes practise; try to avoid typing answers when you practise doing examination questions at home.

Selecting the correct information

Think about how you would answer the two questions below. Make a list of the topics and information you need to include in any answer. Be specific – for example, do not just say 'Utilitarianism' for question 1.

1   *Explain Mill's approach to Utilitarianism.*
2   *Explain the main strengths of Utilitarianism.*

TIMING

It is very important that you learn how to complete questions in the time available. In an examination the time available is very limited. It is a good idea to practise timing yourself writing answers to examination-style questions. You will get a low mark if a question is incomplete, as this limits the maximum level your answer can reach.

Always try to spend equal amounts of time on each whole question you answer, as each question is worth the same number of marks. However, at AS level there are two parts within a question. In this case you may be expected to spend slightly longer completing the section of each question for which the higher mark is awarded.

UNDERSTANDING THE QUESTIONS

It is very important that you think carefully about what a question is asking you. The table below focuses on some of the common instruction words used in OCR questions and what they mean.

Instruction word	Explanation
Explain as in: '**Explain** *Kant's theory of duty.*'	When a question uses the word **Explain**, it is telling you to demonstrate your knowledge of the topic in the question, and your ability to select and show understanding of relevant information and to use technical terms accurately.
	Thus, in the example question, you would need to demonstrate what you know about Kant's theory of duty, such as the categorical imperative, universalisability and the importance of good will.
Discuss as in: '*People are not free to make moral decisions.*' **Discuss**.	The word **Discuss** in a question is telling you that you should examine the strengths and weaknesses of arguments for and against the statement in the question. You need to consider whether arguments in favour of and against the statement are successful. To do this, you will need to demonstrate an accurate understanding of one or more philosophers' views and the strengths and weakness of these views.
'*Kant's ethical theory is too inflexible.*' **Discuss**.	At **AS level**, you would need to state (not explain in detail) one or more arguments in agreement with the statement, such as Kant's lack of consideration for consequences, the conflict of maxims, and the importance of universal and unchanging principles, and present reasons for and/or against the claim.
	At **A2 level** if a question uses the word **Discuss**, as well as considering arguments for and against the statement in the question, you need to explain accurately and in detail the philosophers' views and ideas to which the statement is referring. At **AS level** you need only to state the views briefly in a **Discuss** question.

Assess as in:
'***Assess*** *a utilitarian approach to the environment.*'

Assess is normally used as an **A2 level** instruction word. By ***Assess*** the examiner means that you should first ***explain*** the issue you are being asked to assess and second you should present arguments for and against the issue you have been asked to assess. Part of your assessment should present reasons analysing the strengths and weaknesses of arguments supporting or disagreeing with the issue. You should finish your answer with a conclusion which presents the result of your assessment.

In the case of the example question, you would need to explain clearly and precisely the anthropomorphism of Utilitarianism and the application of the principle of utility. Second, you should present philosophers' and theologians' arguments for and against a utilitarian approach. You should analyse the strengths and weaknesses of the philosophers' and theologians' arguments concerning a utilitarian approach to the environment.

To what extent as in:
'***To what extent*** *can ethics be considered the product of society, not of religion?*'

The instruction ***to what extent*** commonly appears in the Connections paper. The phrase ***to what extent*** is used in questions where you have to decide the level or extent of something. In order to do this, you need to explain the view suggested in the question, and why some philosophers and theologians might hold this view. Next, you need to assess the strengths and weaknesses of reasons for holding these views and compare the strengths of the different reasons for holding this view with each other. The ***extent*** will be limited or defined by the strongest view you have considered.

In the example question you need to explain the strengths and weaknesses of reasons philosophers and theologians give when discussing the ways moral codes are formed by societies. The extent of the role of society in forming morality will be decided by comparing the different reasons and arguments you present and deciding which one is strongest.

How fair as in:
'***How fair*** *is the claim that moral language is meaningful, even if religious language is not?*'

How fair is another instruction phrase which commonly appears in the Connections paper. To complete a task beginning with ***how fair*** you need to explain reasons why philosophers and theologians support this view and then ***assess*** the strengths and weaknesses of these reasons. The ***fairness*** of the view in the question is decided by comparing the strengths of reasons for and against the view in the question and deciding which reasoning is strongest. The view in the question is only fair if you can demonstrate that the reasoning of the philosophers and theologians in agreement with the view in the question is stronger than that of those who disagree.

In the case of the example question, you would need to explain the reasons why philosophers and theologians might believe moral language is meaningful, even if religious language is not, and consider the strengths and weaknesses of these reasons when compared to the views of people who disagree. The ***fairness*** of the view in the question is decided by considering whether arguments that *moral language is meaningful even if religious language is not* are stronger than views which disagree.

Timeline

Scientists, Ethicists and Thinkers

This timeline gives the names and dates of people whose great ideas are discussed within the book. This list is not a comprehensive list of every important or significant ethicist of Western civilisation.

Timeline markers: 480 BCE, 0, 1100, 1200, 1400, 1500, 1600, 1700, 1800, 1879

Protagoras (c.480–c.411 BCE)
Socrates (c.470–c.399)
Plato (428–347 BCE)
Aristotle (384–322 BCE)
Epicurus (341–270 BCE)
Cicero (106–143 BCE)
Jesus of Nazareth (c.3 BCE–30)
Saul of Tarsus/Paul (9–67)
Eusebius (c.260–c.340)
Ambrose of Milan (c.340–397)
Augustine of Hippo (354–430)
Pelagius (c.360–c.420)
St Francis of Assisi (1182–1226)
Thomas Aquinas (1225–1274)
John Duns Scotus (c.1266–1308)
William of Ockham (1280–1349)
Francisco de Vitoria (1480–1546)
John Calvin (1509–1564)
Francisco Suárez (1548–1617)
Francis Bacon (1561–1626)
Hugo Grotius (1583–1645)
René Descartes (1596–1650)
Baruch Spinoza (1632–1677)
John Locke (1632–1704)
Isaac Newton (1642–1727)
Gottfried Wilhelm Leibniz (1646–1716)
Joseph Butler (1692–1752)
David Hume (1711–1776)
Emerich de Vattal (1714–1767)
Paul-Henri Thiry (Baron) d'Holbach (1723–1789)
Immanuel Kant (1724–1804)
Jeremy Bentham (1748–1832)
Pierre Laplace (1749–1827)
John Henry Newman (1801–1890)
John Stuart Mill (1806–1873)
Charles Robert Darwin (1809–1882)
Søren Kirkegaard (1813–1855)
Henry Sidgwick (1838–1900)
Ivan Pavlov (1849–1936)
Sigmund Freud (1856–1939)
Clarence Darrow (1857–1938)
Pope Pius XI (1857–1939)
H.A. Prichard (1871–1947)
Bertrand Russell (1872–1970)
G.E. Moore (1873–1958)
W.D. Ross (1877–1971)
John B. Watson (1878–1958)
Albert Einstein (1879–1955)

1886

1900

1954

Karl Barth (1886–1968)
Aldo Leopold (1887–1948)
Reinhold Niebuhr (1892–1971)
Jean Piaget (1896–1980)
Pope Paul VI (1897–1978)
Erich Fromm (1900–1980)
Werner Heisenberg (1901–1976)
Alan Marshall (1902–1984)
B.F. Skinner (1904–1990)
Joseph Fletcher (1905–1991)
Jean-Paul Sartre (1905–1980)
Dietrich Bonhoeffer (1906–1945)
Rachel Carson (1907–1964)
C.L. Stevenson (1908–1979)
A.J. Ayer (1910–1989)
Richard Brandt (1910–1997)
Arne Naess (1912–)
Thomas Merton (1915–1968)
Hans Jürgen Eysenck (1916–1997)
J.L. Mackie (1917–1981)
John Hospers (1918–)
Elizabeth Anscombe (1919–2001)
R.M. Hare (1919–2002)
James Lovelock (1919–)
Philippa Foot (1920–)
John Rawls (1921–2002)
Lawrence Kohlberg (1927–1987)
Julia Annas (1928–)
Annette Baier (1929–)
Germain Grisez (1929–)
Martin Luther King Jr. (1929–1968)
Alasdair MacIntyre (1929–)
Judith Jarvis Thompson (1929–)
Bernard Williams (1929–2003)
Richard Holloway (1933–)
Ted Honderich (1933–)
Richard Sylvan (Routley) (1935–1996)
Walter Wink (1935–)
Keith Ward (1938–)
J. Baird Callicott (1941–)
Richard Dawkins (1941–)
Jonathan Glover (1941–)
James Rachels (1941–2003)
Michael Slote (1941–)
Rosalind Hursthouse (1943–)
Roger Scruton (1944–)
Peter Singer (1946–)
Steven Pinker (1954–)

WHAT IS ETHICS?   PART I

Ethics is the philosophical study of good and bad, right and wrong. It is commonly used interchangeably with the word 'morality', and is also known as moral philosophy. The study of ethics requires you to look at moral issues such as abortion, euthanasia and cloning, and to examine views that are quite different from your own. You need to be open-minded, you need to use your critical powers, and above all learn from the way different ethical theories approach the issues you study for AS and A2.

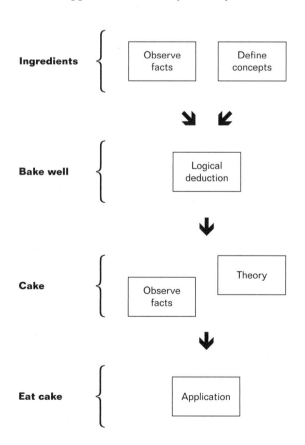

Ethics need to be applied with logic so that we can end up with a set of moral beliefs that are supported with reasons, are consistent and reflect the way we see and act in the world. Ethical theories are constructed logically, but give different weights to different concepts.

However, it is not enough to prove that the theory you agree with is true and reasonable; you must also show where and how other philosophers went wrong.

FALLACIES

With the possible exception of you and me, people usually do not have logical reasons for what they believe. This is especially true for ethical issues. Here are some examples of how not to arrive at a belief. We call them *fallacies*.

Here are some common beliefs and you may recognise your own reasons for holding a particular view:

*   A belief based on the mistaken idea that a rule which is generally true is without exceptions; for example: 'Suicide is killing oneself – killing is murder, I'm opposed to euthanasia.'
*   A belief based on peer pressure, appeal to herd mentality or xenophobia; for example: 'Most people don't believe in euthanasia, so it's probably wrong.'
*   A belief in fact or obligation simply based on sympathy; for example: 'It's horrible to use those poor apes to test drugs, I'm opposed to it.'
*   An argument based on the assumption that there are fewer alternatives than actually exist; for example: 'It's either euthanasia or long, painful suffering.'
*   An argument based on only the positive half of the story; for example: 'Animal research has produced loads of benefits – that's why I support it.'
*   Hasty generalisation: concluding that a population has some quality based on a misrepresentative sample; for example: 'My grandparents are in favour of euthanasia, I would think that most old people would agree with it.'
*   An argument based on an exaggeration; for example: 'We owe all of our advances in medicine to animal research, and that's why I'm for it.'
*   The slippery slope argument: the belief that a first step in a certain direction amounts to going far in that direction; for example: 'If we legalise euthanasia this will inevitably lead to killing the elderly, so I'm opposed to it.'
*   A subjective argument that truth varies according to personal opinion; for example: 'Euthanasia may be right for you, but it's wrong for me.'

- An argument based on tradition: the belief that X is justified simply because X has been done in the past; for example: 'We've done well without euthanasia for thousands of years, we shouldn't change now.'

IS–OUGHT FALLACY

David Hume (1711–1776) observed that often when people are debating a moral issue they begin with facts and slide into conclusions that are normative; that is, conclusions about how things ought to be. He argued that no amount of facts taken alone can ever be sufficient to imply a normative conclusion: the is–ought fallacy.

Ethics looks at what you *ought* to do as distinct from what you may in fact do. Ethics is usually divided into three areas: *meta-ethics, normative ethics* and *applied ethics*.

1 *Meta-ethics* looks at the meaning of the language used in ethics, and includes questions such as: are ethical claims capable of being true or false, or are they expressions of emotion? If true, is that truth only relative to some individual, society or culture?
2 *Normative ethics* attempts to arrive at practical moral standards that tell us right from wrong, and how to live moral lives. These are what we call ethical theories. This may involve explaining the good habits we should acquire, looking at whether there are duties we should follow, or whether our actions should be guided by their consequences for ourselves and/or others.
3 *Applied ethics* is the application of theories of right and wrong and theories of value to specific issues such as abortion, euthanasia, cloning, foetal research, and lying and honesty.

Normative ethics may be further divided into deontological and teleological ethical theories.

- *Deontological ethics*
  Deontological ethical theories claim that certain actions are right or wrong in themselves regardless of the consequences. Examples of deontological theories looked at in this book are: Natural Law, Kantian ethics and Divine Command theory.

- *Teleological ethics*
  Teleological ethical theories look at the consequences or results of an action to decide if it is right or wrong. Examples of teleological theories looked at in this book are: Utilitarianism and Situation ethics.

Ethics is not just giving your own opinion, and the way it is studied at AS and A2 is very like philosophy: it is limited to **facts**, **logic** and **definition**. Ideally, a philosopher is able to prove a theory is true and reasonable based on accurate definitions and verifiable facts. Once these definitions and facts have been established, a philosopher can develop the theory through a process of deduction, by showing what logically follows from the definitions and facts. The theory may then be applied to controversial moral issues.

ETHICAL THEORIES

If we are to have valid ethical arguments then we must have some normative premises to begin with. These normative premises are either statements of ethical theories themselves or statements implied by ethical theories.

The ethical theories that will be examined in this book are:

Utilitarianism:	An action is right if it maximises the overall happiness of all people.
Kantian ethics:	Treat other people the way you wish they would treat you, and never treat other people as if they were merely objects.
Cultural relativism:	What is right or wrong varies according to the beliefs of each culture.
Divine Command:	Do as the creator tells you.
Natural Law:	Everything is created for a purpose, and when this is examined by human reason a person should be able to judge how to act in order to find ultimate happiness.
Situation ethics:	Based on agape which wills the good of others.
Virtue ethics:	Agent-centred not act-centred. Practising virtuous behaviour will lead to becoming a virtuous person and contribute to a virtuous society.

1 Meta-ethics
The Language of Ethics

Essential terminology

Analytic statements
Emotivism
Ethical naturalism/
    ethical cognitivism
Ethical non-
    naturalism/ethical
    non-cognitivism
Intuitionism
Logical positivism
Meta-ethics
Naturalistic fallacy
Normative ethics
Prescriptivism
Synthetic statements

WHAT YOU WILL LEARN ABOUT IN THIS CHAPTER

- How ethical language is used.
- What different philosophers think is meant when people use words such as 'good' and 'bad'.
- Whether morality is a matter of individual feelings or of reason.
- Whether there are any objective moral truths.
- The different theories of meta-ethics.

KEY SCHOLARS

- H.A. Prichard (1871–1947)
- G.E. Moore (1873–1958)
- W.D. Ross (1877–1971)
- C.L. Stevenson (1908–1979)
- A.J. Ayer (1910–1989)
- R.M. Hare (1919–2002)

THE OCR CHECKLIST

Meta-ethics:

- The use of ethical language – the ways in which different scholars have understood how terms such as 'good', 'bad', 'right' and 'wrong' are used when moral statements are made.
- A basic understanding of how meta-ethics differs from normative ethics.
- A basic knowledge of emotivism, intuitionism and prescriptivism, and a consideration of each of these approaches.

From OCR A Level Religious Studies Specification 7877.

WHAT IS META-ETHICS?

Meta-ethics
The analysis of ethical language.

Normative ethics
A term used to describe different moral codes of behaviour; rules by which we make moral decisions (e.g. Utilitarianism, Natural Law, Kantian ethics, virtue ethics).

The word 'meta' in Greek means 'above' or 'beyond'; thus **meta-ethics** goes further than ethical theories to look at what is meant by the terms used in ethics – what does the language mean? Many would say that if we do not know what we are talking about, there is no point to ethical debate.

Meta-ethics differs from **normative ethics**, which decides which things are good and bad and gives us a guide for moral behaviour. The theories of Natural Law, Utilitarianism and Kantian ethics are examples of normative ethics. Meta-ethics is *about* normative ethics and tries to make sense of the terms and concepts used.

In the twentieth century philosophy was occupied almost totally (in 'analytic' anglophone philosophy at least) with an analysis of language and this dominated ethical discussion to the detriment of practical questions. It was even held that one cannot begin to discuss ethical theories without first understanding the terms used.

You often hear people say something is 'good' or 'bad' or 'right' or 'wrong' – but what do they mean? Are they simply expressing opinions or are they stating matters of fact? Can we really tell right from wrong? Many people would answer this by saying that stating what is believed to be right and wrong is essential for any discussion about our behaviour. If this were not the case then we could never have any *meaningful* discussion about morality. Thus for many people ethical language is about *facts* which are either right or wrong (e.g. 'Abortion is murder' may be seen to be either true or false). However, this may need to be qualified, as ethical language in expressing moral facts about the world is also interconnected with beliefs and feelings which often come before (e.g. 'Abortion is murder for Catholics because they believe in the sanctity of life' or 'Abortion is murder for Catholics because they believe the foetus is a person from conception and so abortion goes against Natural Law').

So we can see that ethical statements are not just about observable facts, but are often statements about what we believe should happen and so are not very easy to establish as true or false, as they may be expressions of points of view that are not shared by everyone. Part of the problem is that words such as 'good', 'bad', 'right', 'wrong', 'ought' are used in everyday life and are often just expressing opinions. In ethics, then, do we know something is good, or do we believe it is good and recognise that our belief is subjective? This is the question that philosophers of meta-ethics try to answer – can our ethical statements have any *meaning*?

Thought Point

What do we understand by 'mean' and 'meaning' when we use it in everyday language?

1   I mean to buy her a Valentine card.
2   I mean to win this race.
3   What is the meaning of life?
4   The convict looked really mean.
5   Those dark clouds mean it is going to rain.
6   Does 'good' mean socially approved?
7   Do you understand what I mean?

So, do ethical statements have meaning? The answers to this question vary. Some are *moral realists* and hold that moral facts are objective facts that are out there in the world. Things are good and bad independently of us. Moral values, such as kind and wicked, are real properties of people in the same way that rough and smooth are properties of physical objects. This view is closely related to **cognitive** language. According to **cognitivists**, moral statements describe the world. If I say that murder is wrong, then I have given to murder the property of wrongness – so my statement is *objectively* either true or false.

   Anti-realists, on the other hand, say that moral facts are not out there in the world until we put them there – facts about morality are facts about us. This is linked to **non-cognitive** language. According to **non-cognitivists**, when someone makes a moral statement they are not describing the world, but expressing their feelings or telling people what to do. As non-cognitivists say that moral statements are not descriptive, they cannot be described as true or false – they are *subjective*.

   Meta-ethics is not concerned with what the right or wrong action is in a particular circumstance, but with what it means to be moral.

Ethical naturalism/ethical cognitivism
A theory that moral values can be derived from sense experience.

Ethical non-naturalism/ethical non-cognitivism
A theory that ethical statements cannot be derived from sense experience.

COGNITIVE THEORIES OF META-ETHICS

Cognitivism is the view that we can have moral knowledge. People who hold cognitive theories about ethical language believe that ethical statements are about facts and can be proved true or false.

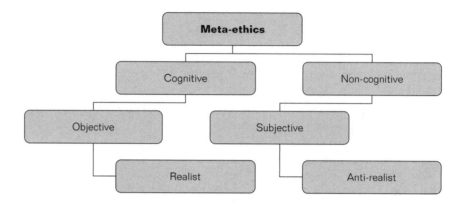

Ethical naturalism

This theory holds that all ethical statements are the same as non-ethical (natural) ones – they are all factual and can, therefore, be verified or falsified. So 'Thomas More was executed for his beliefs in 1535' and 'Thomas More was a good man' can both be proved true or false by looking at the evidence. The first statement is factual, and can be determined by looking at evidence: eyewitness accounts, death certificate and so on. The ethical naturalists would claim that we can do the same for the second statement by establishing if, in his personal behaviour, Thomas More was good, kind, unselfish, caring; or by looking at whether his actions had good consequences. If we find supporting evidence we can conclude that 'Thomas More was a good man' and, if not, then the statement is false. The same holds for any moral issue; if I want to know if euthanasia is right or wrong I simply look at the evidence so that I can *test* the veracity of the statement. Thus I could argue that euthanasia ends the suffering of an individual; therefore euthanasia is right.

Criticisms of ethical naturalism – the naturalistic fallacy

In *Principa Ethica* (1903) G.E. Moore argued against ethical naturalism and called the attempt to identify goodness with a natural quality a mistake. He said that to claim that moral statements can be verified or falsified using evidence is to commit the **naturalistic fallacy**. He based his argument on David Hume, who thinks that to derive an 'ought' from an 'is' is logically invalid:

Naturalistic fallacy
The claim that good cannot be defined.

> I cannot forbear adding to these reasonings an observation, which may, perhaps, be found of some importance. In every system of morality, which I have hitherto met with, I have always remark'd, that the author proceeds for some time in the ordinary way of reasoning . . . when of a sudden I am surpriz'd to find that instead of the usual copulations of propositions, *is* and *is not*, I meet with no proposition that is not connected with an *ought*, or an *ought not*. This change is imperceptible, but is however, of the last consequence. (Hume, *Treatise of Human Nature*, [1740] 2004)

We cannot, he says, infer from a description of how the world *is* to how the world *ought* to be. Moore used what has become known as the 'open question argument'. For any natural property, it always makes sense to ask 'Is it good?' and the fact that we can even ask this question shows that 'good' and 'bad' cannot be the names of natural properties in the way that 'rough' and 'smooth' are. Thus, for instance, if we claim that happiness is a naturally good thing we could always ask 'Is happiness good?', but if happiness is naturally good this question would make no more sense than asking 'Does happiness make people happy?' However, it does make sense and so we have to conclude that goodness is not a property of happiness. If we say 'Mother Teresa helped the dying' or 'Martin Luther King Jr. led the civil rights movement' it is still all right to ask 'Were those actions good?' There is still a possibility of people having different opinions, so moving from a factual objective statement to an ethical statement of values does not work because it leaves an open question that has not been answered.

However, Moore himself did believe there were moral properties and his response to this difficulty was to say that goodness is a 'non-natural' property which is indefinable.

G.E. Moore
(1873–1958)

Moore was a philosopher
and professor whose
approach to ethical
problems and philosophy
made him an important
British thinker. His major
work was the *Principia
Ethica* published in 1903.
He was born into an
evangelical family but
became an agnostic. He
was a leading member of
the Bloomsbury Group,
with John Keynes, Virginia
Woolf and E.M. Forster.
He believed that 'good'
could be understood
directly and became known
as an 'ethical intuitionist'.
He believed that any other
attempt to decide what was
'good' failed because of the
'naturalistic fallacy'.

Intuitionism

A theory that moral truths are
known by intuition.

Intuitionism – G.E. Moore

G.E. Moore said that good is a simple, unanalysable property, just as a primary colour is. Moore adapted a version of Utilitarianism in that he said that right acts are those that produce the most good, but he said that goodness cannot be identified with some natural property such as pleasure: goodness cannot be defined.

> If I am asked 'What is good?' my answer is that good is good, and that is the end of the matter. Or if I am asked 'How is good to be defined?' my answer is that it cannot be defined, and that is all I have to say about it. (Moore, *Principia Ethica*)

Moore said we cannot use our senses to tell whether something is good, but we can use our 'moral intuition' and so we can still say whether a moral statement is true or false. We recognise goodness when we see it – we just know if something is good. Moore called this a 'simple notion' and explained it by saying it is rather like trying to define the colour yellow – just as we cannot explain what 'yellow' is by means of definition, but only by showing someone an example, so likewise we can only explain what goodness is:

> We know what 'yellow' is and can recognise it whenever it is seen, but we cannot actually define yellow. In the same way, we know what good is but we cannot actually define it. (Moore, *Principia Ethica*)

Intuitionism – H.A. Prichard

Prichard discusses the moral claim 'ought' by saying that no definition can be given to this word, but, like Moore's idea about 'good', we all recognise its properties – everyone recognises when we ought to do a certain action, so moral obligations are obvious. Prichard thought there were two types of thinking – reason and intuition. Reason looks at the facts of a situation and intuition decides what to do. In any situation, Prichard thought that intuition would show which particular action was right and where our moral obligation lay.

He did, however, recognise the problem that people's morals were different, but said this was because some people had developed their moral thinking further than others. Prichard does not explain why, nor does he attempt to list any fundamental obligations or moral virtues. Where there is a conflict of obligations he simply says we must look at the situation and decide which obligation is greater. However, according to Prichard, it would seem that intuition would not be something that everyone could use to prove goodness.

> **H.A. Prichard**
> **(1871–1947)**
>
> Prichard was a leading member of the Oxford School of Moral Philosophy. This argued that moral values are ultimate and are known through intuition.
>   His main works were Kant's Theory of Knowledge (1909), Duty and Interest (1928), Moral Obligation (1949), and Knowledge and Perception (1950).

Prichard's intuitionism

- Obligations are as indefinable as good
- Intuition decides what to do in a situation
- Some people's intuition is better developed than others

Intuitionism – W.D. Ross

Ross fleshed out the bare bones of intuitionism found in Prichard, and, while acknowledging his debt to Moore and Prichard and agreeing that 'right' and 'obligatory' are as indefinable as 'good', he was a deontologist, arguing that it was obvious that certain types of actions, which he called prima facie duties, were right. In any particular situation we would come to recognise certain prima facie duties. Ross listed seven classes of prima facie duties:

1   duties of fidelity (e.g. promise-keeping)
2   duties of reparation – when we have done something wrong
3   duties of gratitude
4   duties of justice
5   duties of beneficence – helping others

6   duties of self-improvement
7   duties of non-maleficence – not harming others.

Ross says that when these prima facie duties conflict, we must follow the one we think is right in the situation, and sometimes one prima facie duty will have to give way to another – that is why Ross called them prima facie duties: they are duties at first sight.

However, Ross still does not tell us how we know what a prima facie duty actually is or how to decide which one to obey in cases of conflict. It seems that Ross would say that this depends on a person's moral maturity – they do not know self-evident truths and intuition has deserted them.

**W.D. Ross
(1877–1971)**

Ross was a Scottish philosopher whose most famous work is *The Right and the Good* (1930). Ross agreed with Moore about the naturalistic fallacy but said that Moore's own theories also failed by the same fallacy. He argued that maximising good was just one of the obligations which led to the moral 'ought' in any particular instance. He said that there could never be one true ethical dilemma because one obligation would always outweigh the others.

Ross's intuitionism

Prima facie duties are right

Judgement must be used to decide what to do in any situation

One duty can be rejected in favour of another

Criticisms of intuitionism

This idea of knowing what is good by intuition and not by any empirical evidence is not proved conclusively by Moore – he says you either agree with him or you have not thought about it properly. However, it would seem that if the naturalistic fallacy shows that you cannot infer value judgements from natural facts by means of evidence obtained through the senses, then the introduction of 'non-natural' facts and a special 'intuition' simply shrouds the whole issue in mystery. Some recent philosophers, such as virtue ethicists, say it is our emotions and practical wisdom that give us this intuitive knowledge.

In addition, how can we be sure that intuitions are correct, since people may come to different conclusions, whether using intuition or reason to reach their decisions. As sense experience cannot be used, how can we decide between out intuitions? If they contradict each other, both cannot be right, but they will be right for the person whose intuition tells him what to do. We

Criticisms of intuition

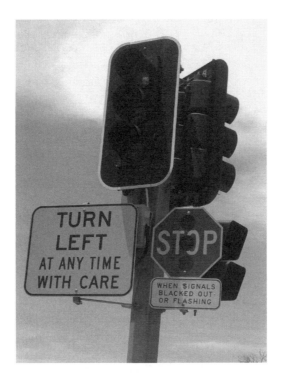

can never know which intuition is true or false, as we do not all recognise goodness intuitively in the same way. Moral intuitions seem to come largely from social conditioning and differ between cultures, so it is hard to see how such intuitions can be a reliable guide to objective ethical truths.

Thought Point

1   According to ethical naturalists how do we know what is good?
2   Explain the naturalistic fallacy.
3   Show how Prichard and Ross build on the work of Moore.
4   Use the intuitionism of Prichard and Ross to argue whether one should give money to a man begging in the street.
5   Does intuitionism mean that there is no absolute idea of what is good?
6   Critically examine the strengths and weaknesses of intuitionism.

Study hint

As you work through this chapter complete the diagram which has been started for you here. Use a large piece of A3 paper and colour code the different ways of looking at meta-ethics.

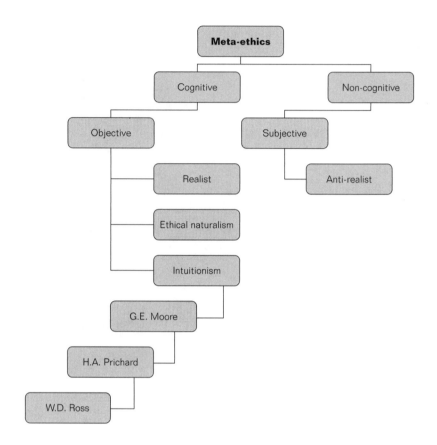

NON-COGNITIVE THEORIES OF META-ETHICS

Non-cognitivism says that there is no ethical knowledge, because ethical statements are not statements that can be proved true or false. Thus to say 'Euthanasia is wrong' is not a statement about facts, but some other kind of saying. Non-cognitivists make a distinction between facts and values.

Emotivism – A.J. Ayer

Emotivists take a completely different view on moral statements and start from the premise that there is no ethical knowledge because ethical judgements are not the kinds of statements that can be true or false. Emotivism will not tell you how to live a moral life, but simply helps us understand moral statements: as action guiding and as conveying certain attitudes. A.J. Ayer said: 'ethical terms do not serve only to express feelings. They are calculated also to arouse feeling, and so to stimulate action.'

However, this view needs to be examined closely: it says that when we talk about 'good' and 'bad', 'right' and 'wrong', we are simply expressing emotional states of approval and disapproval. Any other interpretation of ethical statements is meaningless. Emotivism has its roots in the *Vienna Circle*, a group of philosophers in the 1920s who developed a theory called **logical positivism** which holds roughly that any truth claim must be tested by sense experience (the *verification principle*). Ethical statements cannot be tested by sense experience, so they are not genuine truth claims and can only express feelings.

A.J. Ayer in his book *Language, Truth and Logic*, published in 1935 when he was just 25 years old, stated briefly that there are only two kinds of meaningful statements:

1 **analytic statements** – the truth or falsity of the statement can be determined simply by understanding the terms that occur in them (e.g. 'all bachelors are unmarried men'). Examples of analytic statements are statements of mathematics or logic.
2 **synthetic statements** – the truth or falsity of the statement can be determined by checking to establish the facts either way. Examples of synthetic statements are statements of science, history and ordinary life.

Ethical statements are not verifiable – there are no empirical facts which can be checked to see if any ethical statement is true or false – so they are meaningless. The only way they can be understood is as an expression of feelings. Ayer's theory of ethical language is known as **emotivism**, as it is simply an expression of feeling of approval or disapproval. Emotivism is sometimes known as the *Boo/Hurrah theory* as in saying 'murder is wrong' we are saying 'boo to murder', and in saying 'giving to charity is good' we are saying 'hurrah for giving to charity':

> The presence of an ethical symbol in a proposition adds nothing to its factual content. Thus if I say to someone, 'You acted wrongly in stealing that money,' I am not saying anything more than if I had simply said, 'You stole that money.' In adding that this action is wrong I am not making any further statement about it. I am simply evincing my moral disapproval of it. It is as if I had said, 'You stole that money,' in a peculiar tone of horror, or written it with the addition of some special exclamation marks. (Ayer, *Language, Truth and Logic*)

A word such as 'steal' invokes feelings about what happened – it is an interpretation of the event.

Emotivism does show how the ethical statements we make can depend on our own attitudes, upbringing and feelings, and this can lead emotivism

---

A.J. Ayer (1910–1989)

Ayer first encountered logical positivism while staying in Vienna in 1932.

His most important work was *Language, Truth and Logic* (1936). He developed his ideas from the Vienna Circle and also from the work of Hume, Mill and Moore.

He argued that empirical truth could only be understood through linguistic analysis, and that unverifiable statements were 'nonsense' and without any philosophical significance.

Logical positivism
The view that only those things which can be tested are meaningful.

Analytic statements
Statements which are true by definition.

Synthetic statements
Statements that can be true or false and can be tested using experience or senses.

Emotivism
A theory which says that moral statements are just expressions of feelings.

Make Poverty History –
Wristband

Getty Images (Peter
Macdiarmid)

to be criticised as 'simple subjectivism'. James Rachels said that it can lead to the notion that: 'Where morality is concerned, there are no "facts" and no one is "right".' However, although Ayer does argue that ethical statements have no factual content, he does not believe they have no meaningful function. Emotivism cannot be compared to normative ethical theories, and it does not give any reason why one person's feelings should be any better than another's, or why one person's feelings should stimulate a person to action rather than those of another person. It simply reduces ethical statements to the level of 'I think orange Smarties are best' and so they are simply meaningless.

Emotivism – Ayer

Words like 'good' are meaningless

Ethical statments are just expressions of feelings

Ethical statements cannot be validated

Emotivism – C.L. Stevenson

C.L. Stevenson gave a more detailed version of emotivism in his book *Ethics and Language* (1944). Stevenson did not use the verification principle, but discussed the emotive meaning of words – many moral terms (e.g. 'honesty', 'respect', 'steal', 'murder') are both descriptive and emotive, expressing also what we feel about them. So when an individual is making a moral judgement he is not only giving vent to his feelings, but he is also trying to influence others' attitudes. Emotivism connects 'caring', 'approving', 'disapproving' with the very meaning of the ethical words. This does mean that ethical statements can be based on emotions; however, these are not merely arbitrary, but rather are based on our experience of the world and how we want it to be.

As Stephenson saw ethical statements as not only expressions of emotion, but also the result of attitudes based on fundamental beliefs, ethical disagreements between people are disagreements about fundamental principles.

Emotivism – C.L. Stevenson

Ethical statements are attitudes based on beliefs about the world

Ethical statements are attempts to influence the views of others

Ethical statements are subjective opinions

> **C.L. Stevenson (1908–1979)**
>
> Stevenson was an American. He was a professor at Yale and then at Michigan. He studied in England with Wittgenstein and G.E. Moore. He developed a theory of emotivism which he used as a foundation for his theory of a persuasive definition. He argued that emotivism as a meta-ethical theory marked out the difference between cognitive, scientific language and non-cognitive language. His defence of emotivism is found in *The Emotive Meaning of Ethical Terms* (1937), *Persuasive Definitions* (1938), and *Ethics and Language* (1944).

Criticisms of emotivism

When criticising emotivism, it is important to remember that it does not purport to be an ethical theory, but is simply an analysis of the nature and content of ethical language. It starts from the basis of logical positivism and so removes any factual content from ethical language and does not discuss 'ethical facts'.

However, as Rachels points out, moral judgements appeal to reason; they are not just expressions of feeling. So whereas the statement 'I like orange Smarties' needs no reason, moral judgements do, or else they are arbitrary.

Ayer does suggest that ethical statements are more than simply expressions of feeling, but that they have the intention to stimulate others to act in the way they feel is right. This is developed further by Stevenson, who asks: why should one person's feelings about a matter be any better than those of another? All emotivism can do is draw attention to the reasons why people have different views and then let others decide. It has been shown in history that stimulating people to act through powerful and emotive speeches can have some unfortunate results (e.g. Hitler).

Emotivism may be seen as allowing complete freedom of action on the grounds that everyone's opinion is equally valid and so everyone can do as they like.

Prescriptivism – R.M. Hare

Both Ayer and Stevenson based their views on the distinction between facts and values, which Hume had already claimed made it impossible to deduce a prescriptive statement (an 'ought') from a descriptive statement (an 'is'). Hare attacked this distinction and attempted to show that ethical language is essentially **prescriptive**; the role of ethical statements is to say what *ought* to be done and such prescriptions are moral because they are *universal*.

Hare argues that universal prescriptivism gives a better account of the nature of ethical statements than naturalist, intuitionist or emotivist meta-ethical theories. These theories try to explain what we are doing when we make ethical judgements: are we trying to state truths? If so, what kind of truths? Are we just expressing our emotions? Are we suggesting a course of action? Or are we doing something different? All the philosophers we have looked at saw these questions as closely linked to the meanings of ethical terms. Hare says that although these approaches are useful, universal prescriptivism is superior. It says 'You ought to do this', and means that everyone should do the same in similar situations. Ethical statements are prescriptive, which means they do not state facts and are not true or false, but they express our will or wishes; in other words they are like imperatives.

Hare argues that however we use the word 'good', we always do so in relation to a set of standards:

*   A good chair is one that supports your back, is comfortable and fit for the purpose.
*   A good car again varies, depending on whether it is a family car or a sports car.
*   A good person is someone we should try to emulate.

This means that the word 'good' always has a *descriptive* meaning.

If we use the word 'good' in a moral sense, again we are using a set of standards that apply to a person or an action and we commend that person

---

Prescriptivism

A theory that ethical statements have an intrinsic sense so other people should agree with the statement and follow it.

**R.M. Hare
(1919–2002)**

Hare was influenced by A.J. Ayer and C.L. Stevenson, as well as Wittgenstein, Utilitarianism and Kant. He believed that ethical rules should not be based on utility. He used many ideas from Kant, particularly the idea of universalisability; however, his arguments were still consequentialist rather than those of a deontologist. In *The Language of Morals* and *Freedom and Reason*, Hare outlined a theory that he called universal prescriptivism: moral terms such as 'good', 'ought' and 'right' are universalisable and prescriptive. He argued that the combination of universalisability and prescriptivity led to a form of consequentialism, namely preference utilitarianism.

or that action. This means that the word 'good' also has a prescriptive meaning. This can happen with any words that both commend and describe, such as 'steal' and 'murder'. Hare, like the emotivists, is saying that there is a difference between the descriptive meaning and the prescriptive meaning, and when we use words with an ethical meaning we use them prescriptively: 'Stealing is wrong' really means 'You ought not to steal and neither will I'. Prescriptivism holds that, to achieve consistency in moral judgements, when we say that someone else ought to do something, we ought to do it as well. For prescriptivism we are not only saying 'Boo to stealing'; we can say that stealing is wrong as we would not prescribe it for ourselves.

Prescriptivism – Hare

Ethical statements are expressions of opinion

Ethical statements are also universal

They are not just expressing our views, but prescribing them to others

Criticisms of prescriptivism

If moral judgements are founded on prescriptions, this still does not mean that there is a valid reason for following one person's prescriptions rather than another's. It does not necessarily mean that morals are universal, as one person's preferences may be different from those of another. Hare recognised this problem in Chapter 6 of *Freedom and Reason* (1963), where he admitted that the fanatic who prescribed that all people of a certain race be exterminated could be making a moral judgement according to his theory. The only constraint is that one should put oneself 'in another's shoes' before making the judgement and, as the terrorism and suicide bombings of the twenty-first century show, this does not stop the fanatic.

Prescriptivism says that 'ought' judgements are universalisable prescriptives or imperatives and not truth claims – they are not objective and there is no moral knowledge or moral truth. This goes against the way people approach ethics in their daily lives – in general people do think it is wrong to steal, lie, kill the innocent, rape and so on. According to Hare, we could just as easily choose the opposite if we wished and we could change our moral principles as we choose or as our circumstances alter.

Thought Point

1   What does it mean to say that ethical language is about feelings, not facts?
2   Why does Ayer reject the idea that good is indefinable?
3   How does Stevenson see moral language as influencing action?
4   What is the difference between descriptive and prescriptive meaning?
5   What are the differences between emotivism and prescriptivism?

REVIEW QUESTIONS

Look back over the chapter and check that you can answer the following questions. (You could also use Harry Gensler's web exercises. The address is given at the end of this chapter under Further reading.)

1   What is meant by the word meta-ethics?
2   Explain one cognitive theory of meta-ethics.
3   Explain the views of G.E. Moore.
4   Explain Ross's intuitionism.
5   Explain one non-cognitive theory of meta-ethics.
6   Explain emotivism.
7   What is prescriptivism?
8   Complete the meta-ethics mind map from memory.

Terminology

Do you know your terminology?

Try to explain the following keywords without looking at your books and notes:

* Meta-ethics
* Analytic statements
* Synthetic statements

- Emotivism
- Ethical naturalism
- Intuitionism
- Prescriptivism
- Cognitive
- Non-cognitive

Examination Questions Practice

PAST PAPER QUESTIONS

1 Explain how meta-ethics is different from normative ethics. (OCR AS Level 2760 June 2003 question 3, 33 marks)

- You need to explain that normative ethics expresses moral truths and tells us how to act in ethical dilemmas, whereas meta-ethics is about the language used in ethics.
- To make this clear you would need to give examples of both approaches.
- You could contrast the idea that normative ethics is about finding what the right or wrong thing is, whereas emotivism says that moral statements cannot have objective meaning.
- You could discuss how meta-ethics explores what it means to say that something is right/wrong, good/bad, while normative ethics expresses what is claimed to be right/wrong, good/bad.

2 'Everyone knows what good means.' Discuss. (OCR AS Level 2760 June 2003 question 3, 17 marks)

- You could explore the different meanings of the word 'good', varying from a 'good film' and a 'good meal' to a 'good person' and a 'good action'.
- You could look at how the word is used both subjectively and objectively.
- You could analyse the approaches of some of the different scholars.

SAMPLE AS EXAMINATION QUESTIONS

(a) Explain what scholars mean when they say that ethical statements are no more than expressions of opinion.
(b) How far do you consider these views to be justified?
(OCR AS Level 2760 Specimen question 4)

(a) Examine the different ways 'good' is used in meta-ethics.

(b) 'Anything people approve of must be good.' Discuss.
(OCR AS Level 2760 June 2001 question 3)

(a) Explain the different ways 'right' and 'wrong' are used in meta-ethics.
(b) 'Words such as "right" and "wrong" are meaningless.' Discuss.
(OCR AS Level 2760 January 2004 question 1)

FURTHER READING

Ahluwalia, L. *Foundation for the Study of Religion*, London, Hodder & Stoughton Educational, 2001.

Ayer, A.J. *Language, Truth and Logic*, London, Penguin [1936], 2001.

Gensler, H. *Ethics: A Contemporary Introduction*, New York/London, Routledge, 1998.

Gensler, H., Earl, W. and Swindal, J. *Ethics: Contemporary Readings*, New York/London, Routledge, 2004 (see also his website for good multiple-choice exercises to check understanding and knowledge at www.jcu.edu/philosophy/ gensler/et/).

Hare, R.M. *Freedom and Reason*, London, Clarendon Press, 1963.

Hare, R.M. *The Language of Morals*, Oxford, Oxford University Press, 1952.

Palmer, M. *Moral Problems*, Cambridge, Lutterworth Press, 1991 (see the appendix for meta-ethics).

Pojman, L.P. *Ethics: Discovering Right and Wrong*, Toronto, Wadsworth, 2002.

Ross, W.D. *The Right and the Good*, Oxford, Clarendon Press, 1930.

Stevenson, C.L. *Ethics and Language*, Oxford, Oxford University Press, 1945.

2 Moral Absolutism and Moral Relativism

This chapter introduces some of the main ethical theories that are looked at in more detail in later chapters. You should read this chapter again once you have studied them. You will need moral relativism and cultural relativism for the Foundation paper, and both absolute and relative morality for the AS Ethics paper.

Examination questions on absolute and relative morality may be approached in more than one way:

- looking at normative ethical theories, both absolute and relative
- looking at cultural relativism
- looking at relative meta-ethical theories.

WHAT YOU WILL LEARN ABOUT IN THIS CHAPTER

- What is meant in ethics to call a system relativist.
- Moral relativism as distinct from cultural relativism.
- Situation ethics as an example of relative ethical systems.
- What is meant by moral absolutism.
- Absolute and relative ways of understanding 'right' and 'wrong'.
- The skills to decide whether there are any moral absolutes, or whether morality is completely relative, or whether there is an in-between position.
- The strengths and weaknesses of moral absolutism.
- The strengths and weaknesses of moral relativism.

KEY SCHOLARS

- Socrates (c.470–c.399)
- Aristotle (384–322 BCE)
- Plato (428–347 BCE)
- Joseph Fletcher (1905–1991)

THE OCR CHECKLIST

An introduction to the following concepts within ethical theory:

*   Moral relativism (e.g. Fletcher's Situation ethics).
*   What it means in ethics to call a system 'relativist'; moral relativism as distinct from cultural relativism; an example of a relativist ethical system or system with relativist aspects. Fletcher's Situation ethics is suggested but another system may be studied instead if pre-ferred. A discussion of the strengths and weaknesses of a relativist approach.

In addition, for Unit 2762:

*   An understanding of what is meant by 'absolute' and 'relative' morality; you should be able to give examples.
*   A consideration of the extent to which the ethical systems studied contain elements of absolutism or relativism.
*   A discussion of absolutist and relativist ways of understanding right and wrong.

From OCR A Level Religious Studies Specification 7877.

WHAT IS ETHICAL RELATIVISM?

Moral relativism
There are no universally valid moral principles and so there is no one true morality.

The theory of ethical **relativism** holds that there are no universally valid moral principles. All principles and values are relative to a particular culture or age. Ethical relativism means that there is no such thing as good 'in itself', but if an action seems good to you and bad to me, that is it, and there is no objective basis for us to discover the truth. The problem today is that rela-tivism tends to lead people into thinking that truth depends on who holds it, or that there is only one truth – their own. We often hear people say, 'Well that's your point of view, but it's not mine', and this can actually be a way of stopping thinking. Truth then no longer matters, as everything depends on the community to which one belongs, or one's own perspective. Where there is no agreed set of values, relativism can seem very attractive.

THE ORIGINS OF RELATIVISM

We can trace the origins of Western ethical thinking to the city states of ancient Greece. At the time of Homer (*c*. eighth century BCE), being good meant being a heroic warrior and the type of person you were – noble, courageous, strong – was the most important thing. This became further developed in the ethical theories of Socrates, Plato and Aristotle who looked at the ideas of character and virtue.

However, everything began to change, and by the sixth century BCE there was no longer any moral certainty. Alasdair MacIntyre in his book *A Short History of Ethics* (1985) says this was due to the discovery of other civilisations with different ideas of what it meant to be good and changes within Greek society itself. The discovery of these different cultures led the Greeks to question the absoluteness of their own moral ideas; also, as the city states expanded, it became less clear what a person's role in society was and so more difficult to know how to live a virtuous life.

Eventually a series of wise men, known as Sophists, appeared and argued that all morality was relative – right and wrong varied from place to place, from time to time and from person to person. Protagoras famously said: 'Man is the measure of all things.' All they saw as important was getting on in life, taking part in political life and fitting in – 'truth' was a variable concept. Socrates and later Plato and Aristotle worked on proving this view to be wrong.

Subjectivism

Each person's values are relative to that person and so cannot be judged objectively.

Sophists

This was a name originally applied by the ancient Greeks to learned men. In the fifth century CE, the Sophists were travelling teachers. They concluded that truth and morality were matters of opinion and emphasised skills such as rhetoric.

Protagoras (*c*.480–*c*.411BCE)

Protagoras was a Greek philosopher, born in Thrace. He taught in Athens for money. He said that nothing is absolutely good or bad and that each individual is their own final authority when making decisions.

Like Socrates, he was charged with impiety and fled to Sicily, but drowned on the journey.

Detail of a red figure krater depicting warriors; Rhodes, 13th–12th century BCE (pottery) by Greek

© National Archaeological Museum, Athens, Greece/Lauros/Giraudon/The Bridgeman Art Library

Socrates did not leave
any writings of his own but,
as a Greek philosopher,
he shaped Western
philosophy. His pupil Plato
wrote dialogues which
claim to describe Socrates'
views.

He is also mentioned in
the works of Xenophon and
others.

At the age of 70 he
was tried for impiety and
sentenced to death by
poisoning (probably
hemlock).

Cultural relativism

What is right or wrong depends
on the culture.

Descriptive relativism

Different cultures and societies
have differing ethical systems
and so morality is relative.

Socrates

It is difficult to distinguish between the views of Socrates and Plato, as Socrates left no writings and everything we know about him we know through his pupil Plato. However, Plato's dialogues have Socrates as the main protagonist and he argues that all humans share a common, innate understanding of what is morally good.

Plato

Plato explained how this moral knowledge was acquired with his theory of the Forms – moral knowledge came from the highest of the forms: the Form of the Good. According to Plato, there are objective and universal moral truths – the complete opposite of the view of the Sophists.

Aristotle

Aristotle approached ethics from a completely different angle, and although he thought universal truths could be discovered, he rejected Plato's idea of the world of the Forms, as he thought that understanding of goodness and wisdom could be found in this world. According to Aristotle, we can find out how to be virtuous by looking at virtuous people and by discovering how we can better develop our character.

Socrates, Plato and Aristotle all oppose complete relativism from different angles and ask people not to just blindly follow what everyone else is thinking and doing, to consider what they believe and why they believe it, to dialogue with others and to look for truths that are not limited by their own time and culture.

It cannot be assumed that relativism means the same thing to everyone and this chapter will explore some of the different approaches.

CULTURAL RELATIVISM

You do not need to be an anthropologist to know that throughout the world there are many different ideas about how to behave and there always seem to be clashes of moral codes between one culture and another. To us it seems obscene to chop off a man's hand as punishment for theft or to stone somebody for adultery, yet to many Muslims this is simply the required punishment, and they on their part will condemn what they see as the excessive liberalism and immorality of Western societies.

This is what is known as the *diversity thesis* – because of the diversity across and within cultures there can be no one true morality.

Many other examples of this clash of cultures may be found. Some societies practise polygamy, others monogamy; some have arranged marriages and others are free to make their own choice of spouse; we put our elderly in homes, whereas in other cultures they are valued for their wisdom and have an important place in the family home. For the relativist such differences present no problems – different tribes, different customs. Rules of conduct differ from place to place, as was noted by the ancient Greek historian Herodotus, who recounts an episode in which the King of Persia induced horror on the part of both the Greeks and the Callatians by asking them to adopt each other's funeral practices. What the Greeks took to be right and proper (e.g. burning their dead), the Callatians saw as absolutely abhorrent – Herodotus, implied that since fire burned just as well in Greece as in Persia, moral practices are relative to cultural contexts. By implication there is nothing right or wrong universally. This is what is known as the *dependency thesis* – what is right or wrong depends upon the nature of the society. No one can judge the morality of other cultures, as different cultures create different values, and we cannot be objective about another culture since we are all the product of our own culture.

However, for the absolutist these different forms of behaviour cause a major dilemma. Absolutism implies that forms of behaviour are universally right or wrong – an example of this is that when the nineteenth century British missionaries went to Africa and Asia they imposed their Western **absolutes** as being more right than local customs. Thus, for example, female converts to Christianity were made to cover their breasts – surely more a sign of Victorian prudery (and the cold British climate) than any universal moral code.

Historically we can also find support for the relativist position – forms of behaviour that were condemned in the past are now considered acceptable and vice versa. We no longer allow acts of cruelty for public entertainment as in the Roman games; homosexuals can enter into civil partnerships; unmarried mothers are no longer put in mental institutions; slavery is no longer legal and so on. The attitudes of society have changed on many issues.

Morality then does not exist in a vacuum, and what is considered right or wrong must be considered in context, and morality is seen as just a set of common rules and customs that over time have become socially approved and differ from culture to culture. If all morality is rooted in culture, there can be no universal moral principles valid for everyone at all times.

Plato (428–347 BCE)

Bust of Plato (c.428–347 BCE) (stone) (b/w photo) by Greek

Vatican Museums and Galleries, Vatican City, Italy/Alinari/The Bridgeman Art Library

Plato is one of the most famous philosophers in history. His writings influenced the development of philosophy throughout the Western world and a large number of his books survive. Plato was taught by the first great Western philosopher Socrates. Most of the books he wrote have Socrates as the leading character in them. His early books are about Socrates' philosophy but the later ones present arguments from Plato's own thinking.

Plato wrote about many issues ranging from the existence of the soul and the nature of beauty, to who should run a government. Plato founded his own school of philosophy, like a university, called the Academia, from which we get the word 'Academy' in English. He died in 347 BCE aged 81.

Aristotle
(384–322 BCE)

Aristotle (engraving) (b/w
photo) by French School

Bibliothèque Nationale,
Paris, France/Giraudon/
The Bridgeman Art Library
Nationality/copyright status:
French/out of copyright

Aristotle was born in
Macedonia. At the age of
17 he moved to Athens
where he joined Plato's
academy. In 347 BCE he
moved to Turkey due to the
growing political tensions
between Macedonia and
Athens. He spent his time
there investigating science
and particularly biology. In
341 BCE he moved with his
family back to Macedonia
to become the tutor of King
Philip II of Macedonia's son
Alexander (who would later
become Alexander the
Great). After Alexander
became king, Aristotle
returned to Athens and
founded a school called the
Lyceum. He remained in

continued opposite

Cultural relativism

- Different societies have different moral codes
- No objective standard can judge one culture better than another
- Our own moral code is just one among many
- There are no universal truths
- Moral codes are just right for the society to which they apply
- We cannot judge the conduct of other societies – we need to be tolerant

Thought Point

1   Jesus is quoted as saying: 'The sabbath was made for humankind, and not humankind for the sabbath; so the Son of Man is lord even of the sabbath' (Mark 2: 27b–28).

    Does this mean that all rules are relative in human relationships? Or are there some rules that cannot be broken?

2   Winston Churchill's physician, Lord Moran, once remarked of the French President General de Gaulle: 'He's so stuffed with principles that he has no room for Christian Charity.' How relevant is this comment to the discussion on moral relativism?

3   There are many areas of human behaviour about which attitudes have changed.

    • Add to this list: hire purchase; cockfighting; the role of women in society.

- Are the changes all for the better?
- What accepted practices today do you think people will look back at in horror in the future? (e.g. pollution and gas-guzzling cars; the breeding and slaughter of animals for food; the use of nuclear power for energy)

THE REASONS FOR RELATIVISM

- The decline of religious authority.
- A greater understanding of other cultures.
- The unacceptable effects of interfering with other cultures.
- The influence of meta-ethical analysis – asking what the terms 'ought', 'right' and 'wrong' mean. If there is no agreement about what the words mean then this implies conceptual relativism – what an intuitionist thinks is good is different from what an emotivist thinks.
- The development of competing theories – utilitarian, intuitionist, egoist, emotivist.

THE WEAKNESSES OF RELATIVISM

- It implies that there can be no real evaluation or criticism of practices such as the burning of witches, human sacrifice, slavery, the Holocaust or the torture of the innocent.
- Relativism does not allow societies to progress (e.g. the realisation that slavery was unacceptable was slow to develop – but no one would doubt that we have made progress).
- Relativism seems to give little reason for behaving morally except to be socially acceptable.
- Although relativism is not subjectivism, it is only a step away and may come to this problematic position.
- Some statements are true absolutely (e.g. 'It is wrong to torture innocent people', 'It is right for parents to be responsible for their children'). Just because cultures vary, it does not mean that there is no objective 'good'.
- Ethical beliefs can change when challenged – primitive practices do stop.

Athens teaching until 323, when Alexander the Great died. After Alexander's death it became difficult for Aristotle to stay in Athens, as he was a Macedonian. Worried that he would die like Socrates, Aristotle and his family moved to Chalcis, where he died a year later.

Aristotle was a remarkable person. He tutored students on most traditional subjects that are taught at universities today. He was fascinated with understanding the physical world around him and the universe. His biology books were not superseded by anything better until 2,000 years later. Aristotle also wrote about other areas of study, including drama, rhetoric (public speaking), meteorology, sport and physics.

Absolute
A principle that is universally binding.

Moral objectivism
Truth is objectively real regardless of culture.

NORMATIVE RELATIVISM

Consequentialism

The rightness or wrongness of an act is determined by its consequences.

Normative ethics is where actions are assessed according to ethical theories – it is about what is actually right or good and not simply about cultural diversity and cultural dependency. A relativist will normally hold at least one absolute principle: that it is wrong to impose absolute moral rules.

Both Utilitarianism and Situation ethics are examples of normative theories, but they are different in the way they understand this. Utilitarians recognise 'happiness', 'pleasure' or 'well-being' as the result of good actions, but accept that this may differ from culture to culture. Situationists, like Fletcher, reject the use of words like 'never', 'always' and 'absolute' and adopt a pragmatic approach to decision-making. The only exception is that love should be seen as the absolute. 'Love relativises the absolute.'

Normative relativists reject the principle of objectivity or absolutism and see morality as something which evolves and changes.

Utilitarianism is looked at in more detail in another chapter, so this chapter will focus on Situation ethics.

SITUATION ETHICS

Joseph Fletcher (1905–1991)

Fletcher was an American professor who founded the theory of Situation ethics in the 1960s. He was a pioneer in bioethics and was involved in the areas of abortion, infanticide, euthanasia, eugenics, and cloning.

Fletcher was an Episcopalian priest, but later renounced his belief in God and became an atheist.

Joseph Fletcher developed Situation ethics in the 1960s in reaction to Christian legalism and antinomianism (which is the belief that there are no fixed moral principles, but that morality is the result of individual spontaneous acts).

Fletcher argues that each individual situation is different and absolute rules are too demanding and restrictive. The Bible shows what good moral decisions look like in particular situations, but it is not possible to know what God's will is in every situation. Fletcher says: 'I simply do not know and cannot know what God is doing.' As it is not possible to know God's will in every situation, *love* or *agape* is Situation ethics' only moral 'rule'.

So it is not just the situation that guides what you should do, but the principle of agape and the guiding maxims of the Christian community: 'Do not commit murder', 'Do not commit adultery', 'Do not steal', 'Do not lie'. Situation ethics is midway between legalism and antinomianism, and Fletcher's book, which was published in 1966, reflected the mood of the times – Christians should make the right choices without just following rules and by thinking for themselves.

Christians should base their decisions on one single rule – the rule of agape. This love is not merely an emotion but involves doing what is best for the other person, unconditionally. This means that other guiding maxims could be ignored in certain situations if they do not serve agape; for example, Fletcher says it would be right for a mother with a 13-year-old daughter who is having sex to break the rules about under-age sex and insist her daughter uses contraception – the right choice is the most loving thing and it will depend on the situation. However, the situation can never change the rule of agape which is always good and right regardless of the circumstances.

According to Fletcher's **Situation Ethics**, this ethical theory depends on four working principles and six fundamental principles.

The four working principles

1 *Pragmatism* – what you propose must work in practice.
2 *Relativism* – words like 'always', 'never', 'absolute' are rejected. There are no fixed rules, but all decisions must be relative to agape.
3 *Positivism* – a value judgement needs to be made, giving the first place to love.
4 *Personalism* – people are put in first place, morality is personal and not centred on laws.

The six fundamental principles

1 Love (agape) is the only absolute. It is the only thing which is intrinsically 'good' and 'right', regardless of the situation.
2 This love is self-giving love, which seeks the best interests of others but allows people the freedom and responsibility to choose the right thing for themselves.
3 Justice will follow from love, because 'justice is love distributed'. If love is put into practice, it can only result in justice. Justice is concerned with giving everyone their due – its concern is with neighbours, not just our neighbour.
4 Love has no favourites and does not give those whom we like preferential treatment – it is good will which reaches out to strangers, acquaintances, friends and even enemies.
5 Love must be the final end, not a means to an end – people must choose what to do because the action will result in love, not be loving in order to achieve some other result.
6 The loving thing to do will depend on the situation – and as situations differ, an action that might be right in one situation could be wrong in another. This is quite different from traditional Christian ethics and is far more relativistic, having just one moral rule – agape.

Strengths of Situation ethics

- Situation ethics is easy to understand and can be constantly updated for new problems and issues as they arise, such as genetic engineering and foetal research.
- It is flexible and can take different situations into account, but it is based on the Christian concept of love.
- It focuses on humans and concern for others – agape.
- Situation ethics allows people to take responsibility for their own decisions and make up their own minds about what is right or wrong. Bishop John Robinson called it 'an ethic for humanity come of age'.

Weaknesses of Situation ethics

- This method of decision-making was condemned in 1952 by Pope Pius XII, who said it was wrong to make decisions based on individual circumstances if these went against the teaching of the Church and the Bible.
- It is not possible to determine the consequences of actions – how do we know that the result will be the most loving for all concerned?

Situation ethics has just one moral rule – agape or unconditional love – and it is relative in that it accepts that different decisions will be right or wrong according to the circumstance.

Thought Point

These examples are taken from William Barclay's *Ethics in a Permissive Society* (1971). Barclay wants you to agree with the actions; can you see other ways of acting?

1   Suppose in a burning house there is your aged father, an old man, with the days of his usefulness at an end, and a doctor who has discovered a cure for one of the world's great killer diseases and who still carries the formulae in his head, and you can save only one – whom do you save? Your father who is dear to you, or the doctor in whose hands there are thousands of lives? Which is love?

2   On the Wilderness trail, Daniel Boone's trail, westward through Cumberland Gap to Kentucky, many families in the trail caravans lost their

lives to the Indians. A Scottish woman had a baby at the breast. The baby was ill and crying, and the baby's crying was betraying her other three children and the rest of the party; the party clearly could not remain hidden if the baby continued crying; their position would be given away. Well, the mother clung to the baby; the baby's cries led the Indians to the position, the party was discovered, and all were massacred. There was another such occasion. On this occasion there was a Negro woman in the party. Her baby too was crying and threatening to betray the party. She strangled the baby with her own two hands to stop its crying – and the whole party escaped. Which action is love?

3   What about the commandment that you must not kill? When T.H. Lawrence was leading his Arabs, two of his men had a quarrel and in the quarrel Hamed killed Salem. Lawrence knew that a blood feud would arise in which both families would be involved, and that one whole family would be out to murder the other whole family. What did Lawrence do? He thought it out and then with his own hands he killed Hamed and thus stopped the blood feud. Was this right? Was this action that stopped a blood feud and prevented scores of people from being murdered an act of murder or of love?

4   Ethically, has humanity come of age, as Bishop John Robinson suggested in 1966?

5   To what extent is love compatible with human nature?

6   Why might critics of Situation ethics argue that it is really Utilitarianism under a different name?

7   Explain why some critics have questioned whether Situation ethics is really Christian.

WHAT IS ETHICAL ABSOLUTISM?

An ethical absolute is a command that is true for all time, in all places and in all situations. Certain things are right or wrong from an *objective* point of view and cannot change according to culture. Certain actions are *intrinsically* right or wrong, which means they are right or wrong in themselves.

According to moral absolutism, there are eternal moral values applicable everywhere. This is a popular position for those who believe in a God who establishes moral order in the universe. This approach is deontological. The consequences of an action are not taken into consideration.

This ethical system is easy and simple to apply – a crime is a crime, regardless of circumstances. If we take murder as an example – is it all right to kill someone for no reason? Both the ethical relativist and the ethical absolutist would say no. Now if we assume the murderer is a doctor who could kill one patient to save another – again both the ethical relativist and the ethical absolutist would still say no. However, if we consider killing one person to save many lives, the ethical relativist will feel it is all right to kill, but for the ethical absolutist it is still wrong.

Absolute ethics allows judgements to be made about the actions of others – we can say the Holocaust was absolutely wrong. Absolute ethics allows courts of law to exist and order to be maintained.

Where do these absolute laws come from? For a theist the answer is simple – they come from God. For the agnostic or atheist the answer is more complicated – they just seem a priori in nature. They fit into Plato's world of the Forms, as there are some things we just seem to know are wrong without being taught: do you remember your parents ever telling you not to sleep with your sister? So to some extent moral absolutes can be seen as inherent in the nature of man.

Moral absolutism

There is only one correct answer to every moral problem.

MORAL ABSOLUTISM AND RELIGION

Many religions have moral absolutist positions as they see laws as having been set by the deity or deities. Such a position is seen as unchanging and perfect; for example, the Ten Commandments.

For one person, therefore, non-violence may be considered wrong, even in self-defence; for another homosexuality is considered fundamentally wrong, even when the couple are in a monogamous relationship. Many who make such claims even ignore evolving norms within their own communities, such as the rows about homosexual priests within the Anglican Church. In the past slavery was supported by religious believers, whereas today no religious group would endorse it.

Today many Christians believe there is a hierarchy of absolutes – a view called 'graded absolutism'. If there is a conflict between two absolutes, it is our duty to obey the higher one: duty to God comes first, then duty to others, followed by duty to property. Under this view, Corrie ten Boom (1892–1983) was morally right to lie to the Nazis about the Jews her family was hiding, because protecting lives is a higher moral value than telling the truth to murderers.

NORMATIVE ABSOLUTISM

The two absolutist theories that are dealt with elsewhere in this book are Natural Law, which is a religious theory, and Kantian ethics, which is based on reason.

Strengths of absolutism

- Absolutism gives a fixed ethical code by which to measure actions.
- One culture can judge that the actions of another are wrong (e.g. genocide) and then act on that judgement.
- Absolutism can support universal laws such as the United Nations Declaration of Human Rights.
- Absolutism may often be seen as an impossible ideal.

Weaknesses of absolutism

- Absolutism does not take into account the circumstances of each situation.
- Absolutists can seem intolerant of cultural diversity.
- How do we actually know what absolute morals are, as all sources of morality are open to human interpretation?

REVIEW QUESTIONS

Look back over the chapter and check that you can answer the following questions:

1   In 10 bullet points explain what is meant by cultural relativism, including the difference between the diversity thesis and the dependency thesis.
2   List the main weaknesses of relativism.
3   What is the historical background to Situation ethics?
4   List the principles on which Situation ethics is based.
5   List the strengths of absolutism.

Terminology

Do you know your terminology?

Try to explain the following ideas without looking at your books and notes:

- Consequentialism
- Moral absolutism
- Moral relativism
- Moral objectivism

Examination Questions Practice

When writing answers about absolute and relative ethics, do not just make vague assertions about cultural relativism, but explain what the terms mean using ethical theories and even relative approaches to meta-ethics.

PAST PAPER QUESTIONS

(a) Explain what is meant by moral absolutism. (OCR AS Level 2762 January 2005 question 2, 33 marks)

- You need to explain that moral absolutism considers actions are right or wrong intrinsically – consequences or circumstances have no bearing – and that a moral command is considered objectively and universally true.
- Key elements in your answer could include reference to Divine Command theory, Natural Law or Kant's theory so that you can define different kinds of absolutism.
- To make your answer clearer you could contrast moral absolutism with moral relativism, and use examples to illustrate your answer.

(b) 'Moral absolutism cannot be justified.' Discuss. (OCR AS Level 2762 January 2005 question 2, 17 marks)

In your answer you need to compare different approaches to this question.

- You may point to the need to have a universal truth that transcends cultures and history.
- You may also refer to certain unchanging principles (e.g. 'do not murder', 'do not lie') and the need for a set of absolutes that apply to all people, regardless of where they live.
- However, on the other hand you could consider that moral absolutism cannot take into account the circumstances or consequences of an action and that absolutism may seem intolerant of cultural diversity and the need to accommodate different lifestyles.

SAMPLE AS EXAMINATION QUESTIONS

(a) Explain the main differences between moral relativism and moral absolutism.
(b) 'Moral relativism allows people to do what they like.' Discuss.
(OCR AS Level 2762 January 2004 question 2)

(a) Explain the differences between absolute and relative morality.
(b) 'Relativist theories give no convincing reason why people should bother to be good.' Discuss.
(OCR AS Level 2762 second specimen question 4)

(a) Explain why some people believe that there are no moral absolutes.
(b) 'Issues of genetic engineering need absolute rules; there can be no individual circumstances which allow exceptions to be made.' Discuss.
(OCR AS Level 2762 specimen question 3)

(a) Describe any one absolutist theory of ethics other than that of Kant.
(b) Analyse any possible dilemmas that an absolutist theory might have in relation to fertility treatment.
(OCR AS Level 2762 June 2001 question 3(a)(i) and (ii))

(a) Describe the main features of moral absolutism.

(b) Discuss the claim that an absolutist morality is the best way of preserving the sanctity of life.
(OCR AS Level 2762 June 2002 question 3)

(a) Explain moral relativism.

(b) 'Moral relativism threatens religious ethics.' Discuss.
(OCR AS Level 2762 January 2003 question 3)

SAMPLE A2 EXAMINATION QUESTIONS

(a) 'A relativist approach to morality is far more reliable than simply doing your duty.' Discuss.
(OCR A2 Level 2782 January 2006)

(b) 'Absolutist and relativist approaches to abortion are ethically incompatible.' Discuss.
(OCR A2 Level 2780 June 2002)

(c) Discuss the strengths and weaknesses of a relative approach to ethics.
(OCR A2 Level 2780 June 2004)

FURTHER READING

Ahluwalia, L. *Foundation for the Study of Religion*, London, Hodder & Stoughton Educational, 2001.

Barclay, W. *Ethics in a Permissive Society*, London, Collins, 1971.

Kirkwood, R. 'Ethical Theory', in *Dialogue* (Special Issue).

Thompson, M. *Ethical Theory*, London, Hodder Murray, 2005.

Vardy, P. and Grosch, P. *The Puzzle of Ethics*, London, Fount, 1999.

3 Natural Moral Law

WHAT YOU WILL LEARN ABOUT IN THIS CHAPTER

*   The origins of Natural Moral Law.
*   Aquinas' theory of Natural Moral Law
*   The strengths and weaknesses of Natural Moral Law.
*   How to apply Natural Moral Law to ethical dilemmas.

KEY SCHOLARS

*   Thomas Aquinas (1225–1274)
*   Aristotle (384–322 BCE)

THE OCR CHECKLIST

Natural Law:

*   The basis of Natural Moral Law in Aquinas; his understanding of goodness as fitness for a purpose; his understanding of the role of reason in moral behaviour.
*   A consideration of what 'natural' means in this context.
*   A discussion of the value and usefulness of Natural Law in moral decision-making.

> From OCR A Level Religious Studies Specification 7877.

WHAT IS NATURAL MORAL LAW?

Natural Moral Law includes those ethical theories which state that there is a natural order to our world that should be followed. This natural order is determined by some supernatural power. Natural Law as we understand it originated in the philosophy of the ancient Greeks, especially that of Aristotle, and was developed by Thomas Aquinas. It is an absolute theory of ethics but it is not rooted in duty, or in an externally imposed law, but in our *human nature* and our search for genuine *happiness* and *fulfilment*. Aquinas considered that by using our reason to reflect on our human nature, we could discover our specific end *telos* or purpose and, having discovered this, we could then work out how to achieve it. This understanding of God's plan for us, built into our nature at creation, Aquinas called Natural Law.

- Natural Law is *not* just about 'doing what comes naturally' – it is not about what nature does in the sense of being observed in nature. Natural Law is based on nature interpreted by human *reason*.
- Natural Law is not exactly a law in that it does not give you a fixed law – it is not always straightforward and there is some flexibility in its application.

Deontological ethics
Ethical systems which consider that the moral act itself has moral value (e.g. telling the truth is always right, even when it may cause pain or harm).

THE ORIGINS OF NATURAL LAW

The earliest theory of Natural Law first appeared among the Stoics, who believed that God is everywhere and in everyone. Humans have within them a divine spark which helps them find out how to live according to the will of God, or in other words to live according to nature. Humans have a choice whether to obey the laws that govern the universe but they need to use their reason to understand and decide whether to obey these cosmic laws.

Thomas Aquinas linked this idea of a cosmic Natural Law with Aristotle's view that people, like every other natural object, have a specific nature, purpose and function. Aristotle considered that not only does everything have a **purpose** (e.g. the purpose of a knife is to cut), but that its *supreme good* is found when it fulfils that purpose (e.g. the knife cuts sharply). The supreme good for humans is *eudaimonia*, which is usually translated as happiness but includes the idea of living well, thriving and flourishing with others in society. Aristotle saw this as the final goal for humans but this is to be achieved by living a life of reason. Aristotle saw reason as the highest of all human activities:

Purpose
The idea that the rightness or wrongness of an action can be discovered by looking at whether or not the action agrees with human purpose.

> Reason is the true self of every man, since it is the supreme and better part. . . . Reason is, in the highest sense, a man's self. (*Nichomachean Ethics*)

Purpose

Reason

Aristotle and Plato: detail from the *School of Athens* in the Stanza della Segnatura, 1510–11 (fresco) (detail of 472) by Raphael (Raffaello Sanzio of Urbino) (1483–1520)

Vatican Museums and Galleries, Vatican City, Italy/The Bridgeman Art Library

Nationality/copyright status: Italian/out of copyright

Reason is not just seen as the ability to think and understand, but also how to act: ethics is reason put into practice.

THE NATURAL LAW OF THOMAS AQUINAS

Thomas Aquinas (1225–1274) was very influenced by Aristotle's writings, which had been lost as far as European philosophy was concerned but preserved by Islamic scholars. Aristotle's philosophy had been 'rediscovered' just before Aquinas took up his position at the University of Paris.

Aquinas used the ideas of Aristotle and the Stoics as an underpinning for Natural Law:

1 Human beings have an essential rational nature given by God in order for us to live and flourish – from Aristotle and the Stoics.
2 Even without knowledge of God, reason can discover the laws that lead to human flourishing – from Aristotle.
3 The Natural Laws are universal and unchangeable and should be used to judge the laws of particular societies – from the Stoics.

THE PURPOSE OF HUMAN BEINGS

Like Aristotle, Aquinas concludes that humans aim for some goal or purpose – but he does not see this as *eudaimonia*. Humans, for Aquinas, are above all made '*in the image of God*' and so the supreme good must be the development of this image – *perfection*. However, unlike Aristotle, Aquinas did not think that this perfection, or perfect happiness, was possible in this life. Aquinas sees happiness as beginning now and continuing in the next life. The purpose of morality is to enable us to arrive at the fulfilment of our natures and the completion of all our desires.

In his book *Summa Theologiae*, Aquinas attempts to work out what this perfection actually is by examining the 'reflections' of Natural Moral Law as revealed by:

- **Eternal Law** – the principles by which God made and controls the universe and which only God knows completely. We only know these as 'reflections'; in other words, we only have a partial and approximate understanding of the laws which govern the universe.

Eternal Law

The principles by which God made and controls the universe which are only fully known by God.

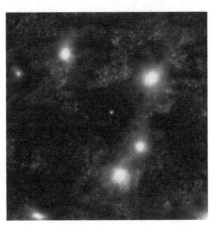

Eternal Law

Divine Law
The Bible – this reflects the Eternal Law.

Natural Law
The theory that an eternal, absolute moral law can be discovered by reason.

- **Divine Law** – this is the Bible, which Aquinas believed 'reflects' the Eternal Law of God. However, this 'reflection' can only be seen by those who believe in God and only if God chooses to reveal it.
- **Natural Law** – this refers to the moral law of God which has been built into human nature; it is also a 'reflection' of the Eternal Law of God. However, it can be seen by everyone as it does not depend on belief in God or God choosing to reveal it – we simply need to use our reason to understand human nature.

Divine Law

Natural Law

Human laws

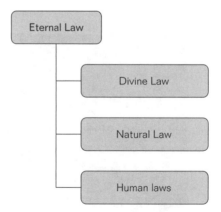

Thought Point

1 How does Aquinas use and change Aristotle's ideas?
2 Explain how Natural Law, according to Aquinas, can lead us to the supreme good.
3 Explain where Natural Law may be found and how it can show us how we ought to behave.

NATURAL INCLINATIONS

Aquinas thought that God had instilled in all humans inclinations to behave in certain ways which lead us to the highest good and, by using our reason, we can discover the **precepts** (laws) which express God's Natural Law built into us.

The most fundamental inclination, according to Aquinas, is to act in such a way as to achieve good and avoid evil. He thought this because we are designed for one purpose – perfection, and so we would not knowingly pursue evil. Aquinas saw that in fact humans do not always behave like this and explained this by saying that we got things wrong and followed **apparent good** – something we think is good but in reality does not fit the perfect human ideal. For example, if someone has an affair they do not do so with the express purpose of hurting their partner but because they think they are 'in love' and this is a good thing to do. In order to work out what is a **real good** and what is an **apparent good** we need to use our reason correctly and choose the right thing to do. There is an 'ideal' human nature that we can all live up to or fall away from and our moral actions determine whether we achieve this or not.

When humans act in accordance with their true nature, they act in accordance with their final purpose, so both the intention (interior act) and the act (exterior act) are important and need to be correct. However, Aquinas did believe that acts were good or bad in themselves and we need to use our reason correctly ('right use of reason' as Aquinas called it) to work out what to do.

So, looked at in this way, Natural Law is not so much a theory or a way of making moral decisions, but rather a way of stressing that our nature is knowable and we need to use our reason to know it and understand it. This becomes clearer as he explains the fundamental primary principles of Natural Law, which he believes are fixed.

Apparent good

Something which seems to be good or the right thing to do but which does not fit the perfect human ideal.

Real good

The right thing to do – it fits the human ideal.

Study hint

Aquinas thought that all humans share a single nature and so there should be a single aim or purpose for all humans. If we do not believe that there is a final purpose for all humans, then Natural Law makes no sense.

Primary and secondary precepts

Primary precepts
The fundamental principles of
Natural Law.

Aquinas saw the **primary precepts** of Natural Law as always true and applying to everybody without exception, as they are a direct 'reflection' of God's Eternal Law. The primary precepts are as follows:

*   the preservation of life
*   reproduction
*   the nurture and education of the young (to learn)
*   living peacefully in society
*   to worship God.

These primary precepts are always true in that they point us in the right direction and are necessary for human flourishing.

Secondary precepts
These are worked out from the
primary precepts.

The **secondary precepts**, on the other hand, are dependent on our own judgements of what actually to do in a given situation and are open to faulty reasoning and may lead to completely wrong choices. The secondary precepts require experience, the use of reason and the exercise of wisdom. Using excellent reason is vital and its role is to guide us towards those 'goods' that will enable us to thrive and flourish as people. You cannot simply read the secondary precepts from the primary precepts like a list of instructions; so, for example, the primary precept of reproduction might need secondary precepts that explain what is acceptable sex and what is an acceptable way to have children (e.g. IVF). You need to apply practical wisdom, which is an ability to work out what is good and what will lead humans to perfection – this needs imagination and creativity, not blanket rules.

The secondary precepts make Aquinas' understanding of Natural Law realistic and quite flexible. It does not imply a body of principles from which we simply work out our moral decisions, but takes account of our human limitations and weaknesses. Natural Law may seem rigid, but the secondary precepts have to be interpreted in the context of the situation and, according to Aquinas, the more detailed you try to make it, the more the general rule allows exceptions.

What is good for us depends on our natures, not on our decisions – this allows for right and wrong decisions as we have to decide what really leads to human fulfilment, and here lies the problem. **Hughes** says that we tend to see human fulfilment through our own life experiences and from what we have learned is human fulfilment, and forget to apply reason – both reason and practical wisdom are necessary.

THE DOCTRINE OF DOUBLE EFFECT

Aquinas saw the primary precepts as objectively true for everyone and he believes that by using our reason we can discover the right action in every situation by following this principle. In this he is **absolutist**.

There are times when we have moral dilemmas in which we cannot do good without a bad consequence. To solve this dilemma the doctrine of double effect was devised, roughly saying that it is always wrong to do a bad act intentionally in order to bring about good consequences, but that it is sometimes all right to do a good act despite knowing that it will bring about bad consequences. However, these bad consequences must only be unintended side-effects – the bad consequences may be foreseen but not intended. So, if a pregnant woman has cancer she could have a hysterectomy, even though this would result in the death of the foetus – but any other pregnancy-related life-threatening condition whereby deliberately killing the foetus is the only way of saving the woman would not be allowed.

Absolutism
An objective moral rule or value that is always true in all situations and for everyone, without exception.

Thought Point

1. The Catholic Church has a number of secondary precepts on issues such as abortion. Would the prohibition of the abortion of a foetus growing in the fallopian tubes represent incorrect reasoning?
2. The biological purpose of sex is procreation, but it may have a secondary purpose of giving pleasure and showing love. Does sex always need to be open to the possibility of procreation? How far should the secondary purpose be considered?
3. The doctrine of double effect is often used in war. Is it possible to bomb a military command base in the centre of a civilian population and next to a hospital if the deaths of the civilians are not intended but simply foreseen?
4. 'All human beings have a common human nature, and homosexuality is against human nature.' Consider arguments for and against this statement.

SUMMARY OF NATURAL LAW

Natural Law underpins the ethics of the Catholic Church, but in reality it attempts to establish a standard for morality which is independent of God's will (see the Euthyphro Dilemma) and does this by claiming:

Intrinsically good
Something which is good in itself, without reference to the consequences.

The universe is controlled by laws of nature (Eternal Laws).

These laws work in harmony in a rational structure.

The laws of nature also express purpose (e.g. eyes fulfil the purpose of seeing).

The laws of nature also express values (e.g. eyes which can see are 'good' and those which cannot are 'bad'). To be good is to follow our in-built purpose – do what is natural (of nature) as it is good and avoid what is unnatural (not of nature) as it is bad.

The laws of nature are rational so we can understand them by using our reason.

Morality then is independent of religion and both the believer and the non-believer have to find out how to live a moral life by listening to reason.

STRENGTHS OF NATURAL LAW

- It allows for a clear-cut approach to morality and establishes common rules.
- The basic principles of preserving human life, reproduction, learning and living in society are common in all cultures and so Natural Law is reasonable.
- Natural Law does not simply dictate what should be done in individual cases from general moral principles.
- Natural Law concentrates on human character and its potential for goodness and flourishing rather than on the rightness or wrongness of particular acts, and so it allows for some measure of flexibility.
- Moral decision-making is not done by reason alone. Aquinas also involves the imagination – the body, the emotions and passions – and practical wisdom.
- All those things that we require for happiness – health, friends – are morally good. The purpose of morality is the fulfilment of our natures.

WEAKNESSES OF NATURAL LAW

- Natural Law finds it difficult to relate complex decisions to basic principles in practice (e.g. should more money be spent on schools than on hospitals?).

- Natural Law depends on defining what is good, but according to **G.E. Moore** this commits the *naturalistic fallacy*. Moore argues that goodness is unanalysable and unnatural, and so cannot be defined by any reference to nature. Aquinas argues that humans are social animals and it is part of our nature to want to live peacefully in the company of others and to care for them. He then goes on to argue that as this 'property' of caring for others is part of our human nature, it must be *good*. Moore criticises this by saying, '*You cannot derive an ought (value) from an is (fact)*' – so it may be a fact that I have within me the natural inclination to care for others, but that does not mean that I *ought* to care for them. In reality we do not make divisions between facts and values in the way we experience the world – because we are moral beings we unite these together.

- Others argue that Natural Law is based on assumptions about the world and the in-built purpose of things that are questioned by modern science. Darwin shows that nature has particular characteristics due to natural selection. The world has no rational system of laws governing it but the laws of nature are impersonal and blind with no intention of moving towards particular purposes. There is no divine purpose – it is simply the way things are.

- **Kai Neilsen** argues against Aquinas' belief in a single human nature common to all societies. Differing moral standards and cultural relativism challenge the idea of a common natural law. Maybe people have changeable natures (e.g. some are heterosexual and some are homosexual), and Natural Law is more complex than Aquinas thought.

- **Karl Barth** thought that Natural Law relies too much on reason, as human nature is too corrupt to be trusted, and not enough on the grace of God and revelation in the Bible.

- Some Catholic scholars also distrust philosophical theories such as Natural Law, and insist it must be supplemented by revelation or by Church teaching – this has led to some rigid interpretations of Natural Law.

- **Vardy** and **Grosch** criticise the way Aquinas works from general principles to lesser purposes and see his view of human nature as unholistic and too simplistic.

APPLICATION OF NATURAL MORAL LAW TO AN ETHICAL DILEMMA – VOLUNTARY EUTHANASIA

Natural Law is nature interpreted by human reason – by observing nature it deduces the final purpose of everything. Acting in keeping with essential nature is right and going against it is wrong. To achieve the final purpose

Natural Law sets out primary precepts as always true and applying to every-body – the first of these is the preservation of innocent life. Natural Law recognises human life as having unique value and sees that each person has a duty to live their life in accordance with God's plan that human life should be fruitful and find its full perfection in eternal life. As a secondary precept, therefore, Natural Law prohibits suicide (and voluntary euthanasia) as this rejects God's final purpose and denies the natural instinct to live. The preservation of life could mean that more resources are put into palliative care, effective pain relief and hospice treatment, and so people's dignity is affirmed and they can die in peace.

Another angle would be to consider the effect on the primary principle of living harmoniously in society. There could be pressure put upon the elderly and terminally ill and their contribution to society could be devalued as today's right to die becomes tomorrow's duty to die. However, **Maguire** argues that though the principle of 'no direct killing of innocent life' is true most of the time, in certain circumstances the principle would have to give way to the principle of achieving a good death. He does agree, however, that making a judgement between conflicting values is not easy and may be mistaken, but he maintains that the whole purpose of ethical reflection and using reason to reach moral decisions is to achieve a finer sensitivity to the conflicting values and make the possible options less arbitrary – thus voluntary euthanasia may sometimes be a good moral choice.

Diane Pretty died from motor neurone disease shortly after she lost a legal battle to claim her right to die.

Picture dated 29 April 2002 of British woman Diane Pretty, AFP (Adrian Dennis) Getty Images

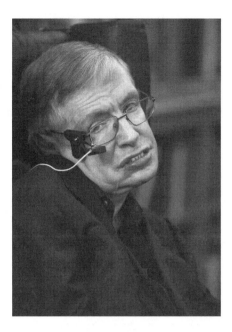

Stephen Hawking has motor neurone disease.

World-famous British scientist
Stephen Hawking,
AFP (Menahem Kahana)
Getty Images

It is also worth looking at the doctrine of double effect and how, though Natural Law forbids any act whose direct effect is death, it is possible to allow actions (such as relief from pain) whose indirect effect may be death. There is no moral problem for Natural Law when death is merely a side-effect.

The main case for voluntary euthanasia rests on the claim that the quality of life does not justify life being allowed to continue and that it is merciful, in the patient's best interests and according to the patient's own wishes that death be assisted. Natural Law, on the other hand, maintains life as an absolute value which no other 'good' can outweigh.

REVIEW QUESTIONS

Look back over the chapter and check that you can answer the following questions:

1   Where did Natural Law come from?
2   What did Aquinas see as the purpose of human beings?
3   How do we discover the primary and secondary precepts and what are they?
4   Make a chart of the strengths and weaknesses of Natural Law.

continued

Terminology

Do you know your terminology?

Try to explain the meaning of the following ideas without looking at your books and notes:

- Apparent good
- Deontological ethics
- Intrinsically good/bad
- Primary precepts
- Secondary precepts

 Examination Questions Practice

Read the question carefully – many candidates know all about the weaknesses of Natural Law, but not so much about its strengths. Answer the question set, not the one you would like to have been set.

PAST PAPER QUESTIONS

(a) Explain the strengths of the Natural Law theory. (33 marks)

At the beginning you should explain how the theory of Natural Law according to Thomas Aquinas is absolutist and depends on the idea that God created everything for a purpose.

You also need to say that human reason is to be used to judge how to act morally and so to follow God's will; ignoring reason is ignoring God's command.

You could consider some of the following strengths:

- It is clear-cut and straightforward to apply.
- All those things that we require for happiness – health, friends – are morally good. The purpose of morality is the fulfilment of our natures.
- You could also consider that Natural Law allows societies to have clear common rules and to organise moral life.
- You could also explain that Natural Law considers the importance of both the intention and the act.
- A more difficult approach is to consider that Natural Law concentrates on human character and its potential for goodness and flourishing, rather than on the rightness or wrongness of particular acts, and so it allows some measure of flexibility in the secondary precepts.

(b) To what extent could a believer in Natural Law accept embryo research?
(17 marks)
- You might consider the nature of the embryo – whether it is a person or not – and God's plan for human life.

- You could point to the link between sex and childbirth.
- You may point out that human beings are led by apparent 'goods' that tempt them away from Natural Law and consider that both intention and act are important.

SAMPLE AS EXAMINATION QUESTIONS

(a) Explain how the principles of Natural Law might be applied to the argument that every woman has the right to a child.

(b) To what extent could a believer in the Natural Law theory accept foetal research?
(OCR AS Level 2762 June 2001 question 3(b)(i) and (ii))

(a) Explain how a follower of Natural Law might respond to issues raised by abortion.

(b) 'A Natural Law approach is the best approach to abortion.' Discuss.
(OCR AS Level 2762 second specimen question 2)

(a) Explain the Natural Law theory.

(b) 'The Natural Law theory has no serious weaknesses.' Discuss.
(OCR AS Level 2762 January 2005 question 3)

FURTHER READING

Aquinas, T. 'Summa Theologiae', in *Basic Writings of Thomas Aquinas*, Pegis, A.C. (ed.), Hackett, Indianapolis, Random House, 1997.

Hughes, G. 'Natural Law', in *Christian Ethics: An Introduction*, Hoose, B. (ed.), London, Cassell, 1998.

Macquarrie, J. and Childress, J. *A New Dictionary of Christian Ethics*, London, SCM, 1986.

Maguire, D. *Death by Choice*, New York, Image Books, 1984.

Pojman, L.P. *Ethics: Discovering Right and Wrong*, Toronto, Wadsworth, 2002.

4 Virtue Ethics

WHAT YOU WILL LEARN ABOUT IN THIS CHAPTER

*   The principles of Virtue ethics from Aristotle.
*   Modern forms of Virtue theory from Anscombe, Foot and MacIntyre.
*   The strengths and weaknesses of Virtue ethics.
*   How to apply Virtue theory to ethical dilemmas.

KEY SCHOLARS

*   Plato (428–347 BCE)
*   Aristotle (384–322 BCE)
*   Thomas Aquinas (1225–1274)
*   Elizabeth Anscombe (1919–2001)
*   Philippa Foot (1920–)

*   Julia Annas (1928–)
*   Annette Baier (1929–)
*   Alasdair MacIntyre (1929–)
*   Michael Slote (1941–)
*   Robert Louden (1953–)
*   Rosalind Hursthouse (1943–)

THE OCR CHECKLIST

Virtue ethics:

*   The basis of Virtue ethics in Aristotle; the concepts of *eudaimonia* and the Golden Mean; the recent revival of interest in Virtue ethics; criticisms of Virtue ethics.
*   A discussion of the value and usefulness of Virtue ethics in moral decision-making.

From OCR A Level Religious Studies Specification 7877.

WHAT IS VIRTUE ETHICS?

Virtue ethics goes back to Plato and Aristotle and does not focus on actions being right or wrong, but on how to be a good person. It looks at what makes a good person and the qualities or virtues that make them good. Virtue ethics is *agent-centred* morality rather than act-centred – it asks 'What sort of person ought I to be?' rather than 'How ought I to act?'

Our word 'virtue' sounds rather old-fashioned and religious, but the Greek word for virtue, *arete*, means excellence. So a virtuous person is one who does things excellently all the time. As we saw in Chapter 3 on Natural Law, a knife has excellence when it cuts sharply – *arete* is not only about people.

Virtue ethics was re-examined and redeveloped in the twentieth century.

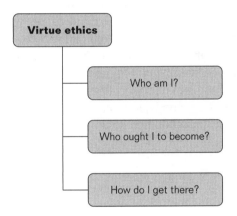

PLATO AND VIRTUE

Plato's moral theory is not one of judging particular actions. It centres around the achievement of man's highest good, which involves the right cultivation of his soul (inner well-being) and the harmonious well-being of his life (**eudaimonia** or happiness). Happiness must be attained through the pursuit of **virtue** and actions are good when they help to achieve this. Plato seemed to consider certain virtues central: temperance, courage, prudence and justice (later called the **Cardinal Virtues**). Plato thought that when these virtues are in balance a person's actions will be good. However, there was not agreement among the Greek philosophers about which virtues were central, and Aristotle gives a very different account of the virtues.

Eudaimonia
The final goal of all human activity – happiness, well-being, human flourishing.

Virtue
Habitually doing what is right – being good requires the practice of a certain kind of behaviour.

Cardinal Virtues
Originated in Plato – prudence, justice, temperance, courage. Added to with three theological virtues of faith, hope and charity.

ARISTOTLE AND VIRTUE

Aristotle sought to give an account of the structure of morality and explained that the point of engaging in ethics is to become good:

> For we are enquiring not in order to know what virtue is but in order to become good since otherwise our enquiry would be of no use. (*Nichomachean Ethics*, Book 1, ch. 2, 1103b27)

Aristotle distinguishes between things which are good as means (for the sake of something else) and things which are good as ends (for their own sake only). He sees one final and overriding end of human activity, one final good – *eudaimonia* or happiness, human flourishing. Aristotle discusses the character traits of a person who is going to achieve *eudaimonia*.

Aristotle's ethical theory is known as **Virtue ethics** or **Aretaic ethics** because at the centre of his description of the good are the virtues which shape human character and ultimately human behaviour. He suggests that human well-being and human flourishing is a life characterised by the virtues. However, this good human life is one lived in *harmony* and *co-operation* with other people, since Aristotle saw people as not only rational beings but also as social beings. We live in groups (e.g. family, school, village) and he saw the well-being of the group as more important than that of a single member.

Aretaic ethics
Another name for Virtue ethics, from the Greek word *arete*, which simply means any kind of excellence or virtue.

Acquiring virtues

Aristotle saw two types of virtues:

1　**intellectual virtues** developed by training and education
2　**moral virtues** developed by habit.

Aristotle compares the virtues to skills acquired through *practice* and *habit*. Aristotle writes:

Intellectual virtues
Characteristics of thought and reason – technical skill, scientific knowledge, prudence, intelligence and wisdom.

Moral virtues
Qualities of character such as courage, friendliness, truthfulness.

> We acquire virtues by first doing virtuous acts. We acquire a skill by practising the activities involved in the skill. For example, we become builders by building, we learn to play the harp by playing the harp. In the same way we become just by doing just acts, temperate by doing temperate acts and courageous by doing acts of courage.

To become virtuous then is rather like playing a musical instrument – it needs teaching and practice before it is possible to play well. We are all capable of being virtuous and need to get into the habit of acting virtuously from childhood so that we enjoy being virtuous. However, Aristotle believed that

Playing a musical
instrument

while all people have the potential to develop moral and intellectual virtues, only a few will actually achieve this – for Aristotle these were the gentlemen philosophers and today we could say that this depends in part on *social factors*: where we are brought up and the environment in which we live.

Aristotle saw that a person who achieved *eudaimonia* was someone who used their **reason** well. He saw reason as the supreme human virtue, but by this he did not only mean an ability to think, but also a moral sense – reason included putting into action what you used your reason to judge as good. Reason is *practical* and involves both *understanding* and *responding*.

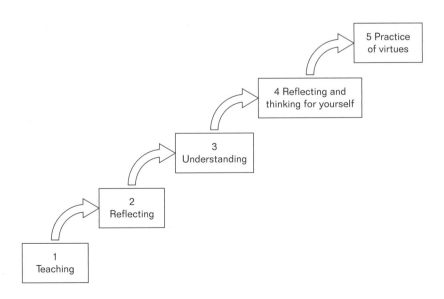

The Golden Mean

Virtue is to be found in the **Golden Mean**, which involves finding the balance between two means – this is the best way to live in society, as extremes of character are unhelpful (people who are too timid or too assertive can cause problems). Aristotle always said that virtue is to be found between two **vices**, each of which involves either an excess or a deficiency of the true virtue (e.g. courage is the mean – a coward does not have enough courage and the foolhardy just runs into danger).

Vice of deficiency	Virtuous mean	Vice of excess
cowardice	courage	rashness
shamelessness	modesty	shyness
malicious enjoyment	righteous indignation	jealousy
servility	proper self-love	arrogance

Aristotle said that the difference between virtue and vice in both emotions and action was a matter of *balance* and extremes. However, the mean is not the same for everyone and depends on circumstance – you need to apply *phronesis* (practical wisdom) to decide on the right course of action in each situation. *Phronesis* is acquired as we grow up and move away from rules and the demands of authority figures to a more autonomous, person-centred and virtue-centred morality.

The example of virtuous people

As virtue is acquired through *doing,* one way to learn how to be virtuous is to follow the example of virtuous people. Most of us learn how to do things by watching others and imitating them. The lives of Socrates, Jesus, Gandhi, Martin Luther King Jr., Nelson Mandela and so on give us possible examples of moral excellence. They are not all 'perfect people' but they challenge us to go beyond the minimum, to aspire to 'moral heights' and to see what can be achieved.

There are many novels and films that show what happens when characters are destructive, such as Darth Vader in *Star Wars* or Dr Octopus in *Spiderman 2*, who sell out to the dark side and warn us of the consequences of losing our own integrity.

Thought Point

1 The following is a list of virtues that lie in the mean between two vices. Write down what you think would be the vice of excess and the vice of deficiency for each one:

- responsible
- honest
- forgiving
- compassionate
- patient

2 What virtues do you think are most important in the world today and what are their corresponding vices?

3 How does Aristotle's approach to ethics differ from other ethical theories you have learnt?

4 Does the Golden Mean imply that Aristotle supports mediocre people who do not take risks?

5 Aristotle implies that being virtuous depends a little on upbringing, environment and so on. Do you agree?

MODERN VIRTUE ETHICS

In the twentieth century there was a revival of interest in Virtue ethics by philosophers who were unhappy with act-centred ethical theories. Modern versions of Virtue ethics argue that the assessment of a person's character is an important aspect of our ethical thought and needs to be included in any ethical theory.

Elizabeth Anscombe
(1919–2001)

Anscombe was a
close friend of Ludwig
Wittgenstein. She taught
at Oxford and Chicago, and
then took the Chair of
Philosophy at Cambridge.
She became a Catholic in
1940.

In analysing actions she
stressed reasons rather
than causes and argued for
a return to Aristotle's idea
of virtue.

Philippa Ruth Foot
(1920–)

Philippa Foot is a British
philosopher, best known
for her works in ethics.
She is one of the founders
of modern Virtue ethics,
showing that it can
compete with modern
deontological and utilitarian
ethics.

She was a tutor at
Somerville College, Oxford,
and later held the position
of Griffin Professor of
Philosophy at the
University of California,
Los Angeles.

Elizabeth Anscombe and Virtue ethics

In 1958 **Elizabeth Anscombe** published a paper called 'Modern Moral Philosophy' and put forward the idea that modern moral philosophy is misguided, asking if there can be any moral laws if there is no God – what do right and wrong mean without a lawgiver? She suggests an answer in the idea of *eudaimonia*, human flourishing, which does not depend on any God.

Both Kantian ethics and Utilitarianism do not depend on God, but they are still act-based and ignore the person who acts. She also thought that act-based ethics does not make sense because it ignores a belief people no longer hold, and in stressing the principle of autonomy it neglects the community aspect of morality.

Philippa Foot and Virtue ethics

Philippa Foot attempted to modernise Aristotle's Virtue ethics while still keeping the Aristotelian understanding of character and virtue. She recognises the importance of the person's own reasoning in the practice of virtue, claims that the virtues benefit the individual by leading to flourishing and stresses that the virtuous person does far more than conform to the conventions of society. Foot argues that a virtue does not operate as a virtue when turned to a bad end (e.g. when someone needs daring to commit a murder). Virtues are good for us and also help us to correct harmful human passions and temptations.

Alasdair MacIntyre and Virtue ethics

In his book *After Virtue*, **Alasdair MacIntyre** claims that ethical theories have simply resulted in ethical disagreements. The result of this, he claims, is that people do not think there are any moral truths and consider one opinion to be as good as any other opinion. MacIntyre argues that most people's attitudes today are based on *emotivism* – moral statements are neither true nor false but simply express the feelings and attitudes of the speaker. He says that people often speak and act as if emotivism was true (racism is wrong: 'boo to racism', tolerance is right: 'hurrah for tolerance'). Do you agree with MacIntyre that 'people now think and act as if emotivism were true'?

MacIntyre looked at what has happened to ethical thought through history and concluded that the Age of Enlightenment, which gave rise to theories such as Utilitarianism and Kantianism, had lost sight of the idea of morality being people achieving their true *telos* – function or purpose. MacIntyre wants to restore the idea that morality should be seen in terms of human purpose, but he thought it would not be possible to restore Aristotle's theory of function and so he attempts to make human function, and so human virtue, depend on community. It is the shared practices of a community which help cultivate virtues. These virtues improve and evolve through time; there is a difference between the Homeric virtues such as strength, courage and honour, the Aristotelian virtues such as courage, justice and temperance, and the Christian virtues outlined by Aquinas. **James Keenan** suggests prudence, justice, fidelity, self-care and mercy. **James Rachels** suggests courage, honesty and loyalty to support friendship. For MacIntyre virtues are 'any virtues which sustain the households and communities in which men and women seek for good together'. MacIntyre opposes much of the individualism of today.

Rosalind Hursthouse and Virtue ethics

Rosalind Hursthouse has a very Aristotelian framework for her Virtue ethics, even though she does not agree with all of Aristotle's conclusions. Hursthouse defends a version of Virtue ethics which claims that virtues are virtues because they help a person achieve *eudaimonia*, and so living a virtuous life is a *good* thing for a human being. Like **Julia Annas** she sees the virtues as shaping the virtuous person's practical reasoning in characteristic ways, and not simply as shaping that person's attitudes or actions. For Hursthouse being virtuous is the most reliable path to flourishing and she seems to think that no other path is as reliable. She also attempts to address the major criticism of Virtue ethics that it provides no guidance in moral dilemmas – not by telling us how a virtuous person would act, but by showing how a virtuous person would think about a moral dilemma.

Michael Slote and Virtue ethics

Michael Slote describes Virtue ethics as being mostly based on our common-sense ideas and intuitions about what counts as a virtue, and prefers to use the word 'admirable' to describe an action, rather than 'good' or 'excellent' which need qualifying and explaining. He sees the opposite as a 'deplorable' action, which can mean both foolish and careless and morally blameworthy actions. He describes virtue as 'an inner trait or disposition of the individual', so a virtue is a kind of balanced caring between those who are close to us, namely family and friends, and people in general. He goes on to say that morally admirable caring could, in some way, copy the sort of

Alasdair MacIntyre (1929–)

MacIntyre is a Scottish philosopher who is best known for his work in moral philosophy. He presents complicated and controversial philosophical arguments in simple narratives, often using ordinary story-telling to address complicated issues in philosophy.

MacIntyre is key to the recent interest in Virtue ethics. He focuses on moral problems in making the most of an entire human life. He emphasises the importance of moral goods rather than ideas such as the obligation of a moral agent or the consequences of a particular moral act.

Rosalind Hursthouse (1943–)

Rosalind Hursthouse is Professor of Philosophy at the University of Auckland, New Zealand, and is known for her work in Virtue ethics. As well as theoretical work on Virtue ethics, she has also written about the ethical treatment of animals in *Ethics, Humans and Other Animals* (2000).

Michael Slote (1941–)

Michale Slote is Professor of Ethics at the University of Miami. He is a leading figure in the field of Virtue ethics and argues that, in a particular form (the ethics of caring), it offers advantages over deontology, Utilitarianism and common-sense morality.

love we have for those to whom we are close and will always express balanced caring. However, Slote's view does seem to allow a wide range of actions by the person facing a moral dilemma, as a wide range of actions could be fitted into a life that showed balanced caring and does not seem to help very much when having to choose between a family member and strangers.

Perhaps the major contribution of Slote to the discussion of Virtue ethics is his explanation of the difference between *agent-focused* and *agent-based* theories. Agent-focused theories understand the moral life in terms of what it is to be a virtuous person, where virtues are inner dispositions – Aristotle's Virtue ethics is an example of this. On the other hand, agent-based theories evaluate actions according to the inner life and motive of the people who do such actions. He says there are many human traits we find admirable such as kindness and compassion, and we can identify these by looking at people we admire. Slote focuses on care and concern for others and empathy – he looks at the motives more than the community aspect of virtues.

Thought Point

1   What virtues do you think are important in the twenty-first century? Do you think they will still be important in the future?
2   Do you think Virtue ethics is worth resurrecting? Why?
3   If we have little control over our personalities, our upbringing or our environment, can we be praised for our virtues or blamed for not possessing virtues?
4   What should someone do when faced with two different possible courses of action, both of which seem to express virtues?
5   How do modern versions of Virtue ethics differ from the Virtue ethics of Aristotle?

Feminism and Virtue ethics

Finally, it is worth looking briefly at one more modern version of Virtue ethics as developed mainly by feminist writers such as **Annette Baier**. They claim that men often think morally in terms of justice and autonomy, which could be seen as 'masculine' traits, whereas women think morally in terms of caring, nurturing and self-sacrifice. Baier advocates a view of ethics that takes account of our natural biases (e.g. the love of a mother for her children and the importance of trust for people in lives and relationships). Writers who discuss the ethics of caring do not always make explicit links with Virtue ethics, but much in their discussion of specific virtues, their relation to social practices, moral education and so on, is central to Virtue ethics.

Annette Baier (1929–)

Annette Baier is a moral philosopher focusing on Hume's moral psychology. She is a well-known feminist philosopher and is strongly influenced by her colleague Wilfrid Sellars.

Virtue ethics

- Virtue is a disposition to act exercised through practical reasoning
- Virtue involves making choices
- A virtuous person does the right thing for the right reasons
- Virtues are developed like learning a skill
- This involves teaching, reflection, understanding and practice
- Virtue involves choice and sensitivity to new situations
- To predict others' actions we need the same practical reasoning

STRENGTHS OF VIRTUE ETHICS

- Virtue ethics avoids having to use a formula (e.g. 'the greatest good for the greatest number') to work out what we ought to do and focuses instead on the kind of person we ought to be.
- Virtue ethics understands the need to distinguish good people from legalists – just because one obeys the law and follows the rules does not make one a good person.
- Virtue ethics stresses the importance of motivating people to want to be good – it stresses the importance of education in showing that good

actions are their own reward. It shows how we acquire and learn virtues by imitating others.

- Virtue ethics tells us how we learn moral principles and involves our entire life, as every moment, even the most mundane, is an opportunity for developing a virtue.
- Virtue ethics enables us to integrate many aspects of life – our emotions, commitments to others, our friends, social responsibilities – into our ethical reflection; it looks at what makes life worthwhile rather than looking at what is right or wrong in a particular situation or particular moment in our lives. It does not reject our emotions but includes them, and so is more in tune with how people naturally react to an ethical dilemma. It relates our ethical choices to the bigger picture.
- Virtue ethics sees it as good to be biased in favour of friends and family, unlike Utilitarianism or Kant which see impartiality as important.
- Virtue ethics does not pretend to be able to tell us what a good person would do in every possible situation but encourages us to be more like such a person so that we will not need an ethical theory to make our decisions for us. It stresses the importance of character – after all, someone who helps the poor out of compassion does seem to be morally superior to someone who does it out of duty.

WEAKNESSES OF VIRTUE ETHICS

- One major difficulty is that of identifying the virtues. Are virtues culturally relative?
- How can Virtue ethics be applied to moral dilemmas? This is the problem raised by **Robert Louden**: Virtue ethics does not help people facing a crisis because it does not give any clear rules for action. It is difficult to work out what is the virtuous response to stem-cell research or abortion. Virtue ethics does not give us any concrete answers and only says it is a matter for the practical wisdom of the person facing the situation.
- Virtue ethics seems to praise some virtues that we might see as immoral (e.g. soldiers fighting unjust wars may be courageous but that does not make them morally good).
- Louden also points out that it is difficult to decide who is virtuous, as acts which appear virtuous on the outside may not necessarily have good motives and vice versa.
- Virtue ethics does not seem to have room for basic concepts such as rights and obligations, so as a theory of ethics it seems incapable of dealing with big issues – Virtue ethics does not always have a view about what makes an act right or wrong.

- Virtue ethics depends on some final end which gives shape to our lives – there may not be one and being virtuous may not affect it anyway.

APPLICATION OF VIRTUE ETHICS TO AN ETHICAL DILEMMA – ABORTION

The issue of abortion usually focuses on the rights of the mother and the rights or status (e.g. sanctity, personhood) of the foetus. Virtue ethics, on the other hand, assesses actions by the type of character which produces and chooses the actions – so in having an abortion in a particular set of circumstances would a woman be behaving virtuously? Would she have good motives?

Hursthouse writes that abortion is part of the spectrum of human life and death, parenthood and family relationships. It is not a decision taken in isolation, nor is it similar to any other operation. Parents care deeply about their children and family relationships are the strongest ties we have – if virtue is linked to human flourishing, and love, relationships and family life contribute to that flourishing, then abortion could be ignoring this.

However, Virtue ethics does not have a single view of abortion or any other moral dilemma and Virtue ethics takes account of the situation; for example, the mother may consider that another child would seriously affect her ability to love and care for the rest of her family, or the pregnancy may threaten her life. What is important in Virtue ethics is not that there is one right or wrong answer but that the decision taken shows that the person has considered the need to be responsible for her own actions and life in relation to parenthood. It should also show that parents have considered the virtues they cultivate in their sexual relationships: rights are perhaps not part of a loving relationship.

Virtue ethics looks at issues such as abortion in a different way from the familiar pro-life, pro-choice arguments, and may also consider the value of relationships and the fact that a person who acts virtuously will always do what is right for the individual within the needs of society. However, it can also be difficult to distinguish between good, virtuous exterior acts which come from doubtful motives. Virtue ethics may also seem to depend on moral absolutes – a virtuous person has a responsibility or duty to act in a certain way. In addition, as well as considering how a virtuous person might act, there is the issue of conflicting virtues.

REVIEW QUESTIONS

Look back over the chapter and check that you can answer the following questions:

1   Where did Virtue ethics originate?
2   What is the difference between Virtue ethics and other normative ethical theories?
3   Explain Aristotle's idea of the Golden Mean.
4   How did Aristotle say we acquired virtues?
5   How can Virtue ethics help us in moral dilemmas?
6   Make a chart of the strengths and weaknesses of Virtue ethics.

Terminology

Do you know your terminology?

Try to explain the following terms without looking at your books or notes:

*   Aretaic ethics
*   *Eudaimonia*
*   Golden Mean
*   *Phronesis*

Examination Questions Practice

Unless the question specifically asks you about Aristotle's Virtue ethics, you do not need to limit your answer just to his approach but may consider more modern approaches also. However, you need to remember the constraints on time in the examination.

PAST PAPER QUESTIONS

(a) Explain Virtue ethics. (OCR AS Level 2762 June 2005 question 4, 33 marks)

- You will probably write about the Virtue ethics of Aristotle and consider modern scholars such as MacIntyre and Foot.
- You will need to explain and discuss how we become virtuous by practising the virtues, and the importance of the Golden Mean and the example of virtuous people.
- You could even discuss whether virtues are culturally defined or absolute.

(b) 'Virtue ethics does not work in practice.' Discuss. (OCR AS Level 2762 June 2005 question 4, 17 marks)

When answering this question it is a good idea to apply Virtue ethics to examples or to ethical dilemmas.

- You may decide people need moral rules or guidelines or you may consider how a virtuous person would behave.
- You may also consider that Virtue ethics does not make it clear how we decide on a particular course of action or what we do when virtues conflict.

SAMPLE AS EXAMINATION QUESTIONS

(a) Explain the theory of Virtue ethics.
(b) To what extent does the 'right to life' clash with the virtue of compassion?
(OCR AS Level 2762 January 2001 question 4)

(a) What is Virtue ethics?
(b) Discuss the view that it is never virtuous to obtain an abortion.
(OCR AS Level 2762 June 2002 question 4)

FURTHER READING

Ahluwalia, L. *Foundation for the Study of Religion*, London, Hodder & Stoughton Educational, 2001.

Crisp, R. and Slote, M. *Virtue Ethics*, Oxford/New York, Oxford University Press, 1997.

Hinman, L. 'Ethics Updates' available at http://ethics.acusd.edu/.

Hursthouse, R. *On Virtue Ethics*, Oxford, Oxford University Press, 1999.

Hursthouse, R. *Ethics, Humans and Other Animals*, London, Routledge, 2000.

Keenan, J. 'Virtue Ethics', in *Christian Ethics: An Introduction*, Hoose, B. (ed.), London, Cassell, 1998.

Lafollette, H. (ed.) *Ethics in Practice – An Anthology*, Oxford, Blackwell, 2002.

MacIntyre, A. *After Virtue*, London, Duckworth, 1985.

Rosenstand, N. *The Moral of the Story* (5th edn), New York, McGraw-Hill, 2006.

Ross, W.D. (trans.) *The Complete Works of Aristotle*, ed. J. Barnes, Princeton, NJ, Princeton University Press, 1984.

Vardy, P. and Grosch, P. *The Puzzle of Ethics*, London, Fount, 1999.

AS ETHICS   PART II

5 Kant

WHAT YOU WILL LEARN ABOUT IN THIS CHAPTER

- Kant's understanding of pure reason, a priori knowledge and objectivity.
- Practical moral reason – the hypothetical and categorical imperatives.
- Kant's ideas of the moral law, good will, duty and the *summum bonum*.
- The strengths and weaknesses of Kant's theory of ethics.
- How to apply Kantian ethics to ethical dilemmas.

KEY SCHOLARS

- René Descartes (1596–1650)
- Gottfried Wilhelm Leibniz (1646–1716)
- David Hume (1711–1776)
- Immanuel Kant (1724–1804)
- W.D. Ross (1877–1971)
- R.M. Hare (1919–2002)

THE OCR CHECKLIST

- An understanding of the nature of the categorical imperative as distinct from the hypothetical imperative in the thinking of Kant; his theory of duty; his understanding of universalisable maxims.
- A consideration of the strengths and weaknesses of Kant's thinking.
  From OCR A Level Religious Studies Specification 7877.

WHAT IS KANT'S THEORY OF ETHICS?

Immanuel Kant believed in an objective right and wrong based on reason. We should do the right thing just because it is right and not because it fulfils our desires or is based on our feelings. We know what is right not by relying on our intuitions or facts about the world, but by using our reason. To test a moral maxim, we need to ask whether we can always say that everyone should follow it and we must reject it if we cannot.

Kant opposed the view that all moral judgements are culturally relative or subjective so that there are no such things as moral absolutes. Kant's approach to ethics was deontological, where the right takes precedence over the good, and basic rights and principles guide us to know which goods to follow.

Modern deontology avoids too close a link with Kant and rejects his absolutism and complete disregard for consequences; however, his moral theory has been and continues to be influential.

KANT'S COPERNICAN REVOLUTION

Kant's main area of study was to investigate the formal structures of pure reasoning, causality, a priori knowledge (knowledge not based on experience) and the question of objectivity. He wrote these ideas in the *Critique of Pure Reason* (1781; 2nd edn 1787). He then went on to demonstrate the formal structure of practical-moral reasoning in the *Critique of Practical Reason* (1788) and to study the conditions of the possibility of aesthetics and religion in the *Critique of Judgement* (1790).

Kant's work was a reaction against the rationalists and empiricists, and he was concerned with the problem of objective knowledge: can I have any knowledge of the world that is not just 'knowledge of the world as it seems to me'? He is asking: 'How do we know what we know and what does it mean to know?'

The views of other philosophers about knowledge

- **Descartes** (1596–1650) – the foundation of knowledge is the knowledge of one's own existence: 'I think therefore I am.' Kant criticised this, as he said it did not tell us what 'I' is, or even that it is.
- **Leibniz** (1646–1716) – thought that we can have knowledge untouched by the point of view of any observer.
- **Hume** (1711–1776) – argued that we cannot have any objective knowledge at all.

**Immanuel Kant
(1724–1804)**

Portrait of Emmanuel Kant (oil on canvas) by German School (eighteenth century)

© Private Collection/The Bridgeman Art Library

Immanuel Kant was born in Königsberg, Prussia, on 22 April 1724. He was educated at the Collegium Fredericianum and the University of Königsberg. He studied Classics and, at university, physics and mathematics. He had to leave university to earn a living as a teacher when his father died. Later, he returned to university and studied for his doctorate. He taught at the university for fifteen years, moving from science and mathematics to philosophy.

He became Professor of Logic and Metaphysics in 1770. He held unorthodox religious beliefs based on rationalism rather than revelation, and in 1792 he was forbidden by the king from teaching or writing on religious subjects.

continued

When the king died in 1797, Kant resumed this teaching and in 1798, the year after he retired, he published a summary of his religious views. He died on 12 February 1804.

Copernican Revolution
Belief that the solar system revolves around the sun.

René Descartes (1596–1650)

René Descartes from 'The Gallery of Portraits', published 1833 (engraving) by English School (nineteenth century)

Private Collection/Ken Welsh/ The Bridgeman Art Library

René Descartes is often called the founder of modern philosophy. He was born in Touraine and was educated at a Jesuit school – La Flèche in Anjou. Here he studied mathematics and scholasticism. He then studied law at Poitiers and later took up a military career.

He went to Italy on pilgrimage in 1623–4 and

continued opposite

Kant is closer to the rationalist views of Descartes and Leibniz and opposed to the empiricist views of Hume, which spurred him to explain his own view. Kant considers that our knowledge is not of the world as it is in itself, but of the world as it *appears* to us. If our sense organs were different, our languages and thought patterns different, then our view of the world would be different. Kant is saying that humans can never know the world as it really is (the thing in itself) because as it is experienced it is changed by our minds – the world we now see is a *phenomenon* (like a reflection in a mirror). Kant argued that various structures or categories of thought (space, time and causality) were built into the structure of our minds – we have been pre-programmed. This means that all we can really know about scientifically are our own experiences and perceptions, which may or may not correspond to ultimate reality.

Kant called this analysis the **Copernican Revolution**, as its implications for us are just as vital as the implications of believing that the solar system revolves around the sun. Science then can never give us any knowledge of objective reality, as it can never move beyond the view of the world given to us by the categories of our mind. But Kant did think that these categories could be described as objective, as they are the objective laws of our mind – this is *pure reason* and tells you what is the case.

KANT'S MORAL THEORY

Practical reason looks at evidence and argument and tells you what ought to be done. This sense of the moral 'ought' is something which cannot simply depend on external facts of what the world is like, or the expected consequences of our actions. Kant saw that people are aware of the moral law at work within them – not as a vague feeling but a direct and powerful experience.

The Copernican Revolution

Portrait of Nicolaus Copernicus (1473–1543) (oil on canvas) by Pomeranian School (sixteenth century)

© Nicolaus Copernicus Museum, Frombork, Poland/Lauros/Giraudon/The Bridgeman Art Library

Two things fill the mind with ever new and increasing admiration and awe the oftener and more steadily we reflect on them: the starry heavens above me and the moral law within me. (*Critique of Practical Reason*)

Kant's moral theory is explained in the *Groundwork of a Metaphysics of Morals* (1785) and tries to show the objectivity of moral judgement and the universal character of moral laws and attempts to base morality on reason as opposed to feelings, inclinations, consequences or religion. He roots his view of morality in reason to the exclusion of everything else, and rejects especially Hume's idea that morality is rooted in desires or feelings. He does not reject desires and feelings, but says that they have nothing to do with morality. Only reason is universal. Kant approached morality in the same way as he approached knowledge (looking at the **a priori** categories through which we make sense of the world) – he looked for the categories we use: what makes a moral precept moral? Kant declared that these were rooted in rationality, were unconditional or categorical, completely unchanging and presupposed freedom.

Freedom

For Kant, if I am to act morally then I must be capable of exercising *freedom* or **autonomy of the will**. The opposite of this is *heteronomy* – that something is right because it satisfies some desire, emotion, goal or obligation. Our reason must not be subservient to something else even if this is the happiness of the majority.

Good will

The idea of a '**good will**' is Kant's starting point for his morality.

> It is impossible to conceive of anything at all in the world, or even out of it, which can be taken as good without qualification, except a good will. Intelligence, wit, judgement and any other talents of the mind we care to name, or courage, resolution, and constancy of purpose, as qualities of temperament, are without doubt good and desirable in many respects; but they can also be extremely bad and hurtful when the will is not good which has to make use of these gifts. . . . Good will, then, like a jewel, it would still shine by its own light, as a thing which has its whole value in itself. Its usefulness or fruitfulness can neither add to nor take away anything from this value. (*Groundwork for the Metaphysics of Morals*)

then, until 1628, he studied philosophy in France. He moved to the Netherlands in 1628 and, in 1637, published his first major work: *Essais Philosophiques* (Philosophical Essays). This book covered geometry, optics, meteors and philosophical method.

He died from pneumonia in 1650.

A posteriori

A statement which is knowable after experience.

A priori

A statement which is knowable without reference to any experience.

Gottfried Wilhelm Leibniz (1646–1716)

Portrait of Gottfried Wilhelm Leibniz (oil on canvas) by German School (eighteenth century)

© Niedersächsisches Landesmuseum, Hanover, Germany/Flammarion/The Bridgeman Art Library

Nationality/copyright status: German/out of copyright

continued

Gottfried Wilhelm Leibniz was a German philosopher, mathematician and statesman. He was born in Leipzig and studied at the universities of Leipzig, Jena and Altdorf.

In 1666 he began work for Johann Philipp von Schönborn, who was archbishop elector of Mainz. In 1673 Leibniz went to Paris. From 1676 until 1716 he was librarian and privy counsellor at the court of Hanover. His work comprised diplomacy, history, law, mathematics, philology, philosophy, physics, politics and theology.

Autonomy

Self-directed freedom, arriving at moral judgement through reason.

Absolute

A principle that is universally binding.

Absolutism

There is only one correct answer to every moral problem.

Good will

Making a moral choice expresses good will.

Duty

A motive for acting in a certain way which shows moral quality.

It is only the 'good will' which counts and which is the starting point for ethics. Abilities, talents and even virtues count for nothing, as do consequences. Only the will is within our control and so only the will can be unconditionally good and can exercise pure practical reason. This will means the total effort involved in making a conscious moral choice.

This is the opposite of Hume's argument that morality is only based on making people happy and fulfilling their desires – it is just a servant of the passions, and morality is founded on our feelings of sympathy for others and depends on our human nature.

Hume

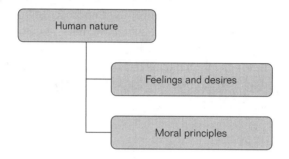

Duty

Duty is what makes the good will good. It is important that duty be done for its own sake and it does not matter whether you or others benefit from your action – our motives need to be pure. Doing duty for any other reason – inclination, self-interest, affection – does not count. The good will chooses duty for duty's sake.

Kant does not rule out pleasure in doing one's duty, but pleasure will not help us to know what duty is or the morality of our actions. According to Kant, there is no moral worth in the feeling of satisfaction we get from doing our duty – if giving to charity out of love for others gives you that warm glow of having helped others, it is not necessarily moral. If I give to charity because duty commands it, then I am moral. So, even though the act of giving to charity has the same result, according to Kant one way is moral and the other is not. *We are not moral for the sake of love but for duty's sake only*. He is arguing against Hume that duty and reason can help us guide our emotions so that we are not dominated and ruled by them.

Duty: a charity
collection box

Kant

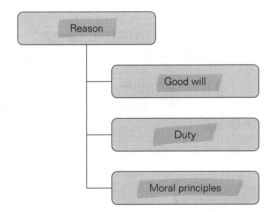

Kant was looking for some sort of objective basis for morality – a way of knowing our duty. Practical reason, therefore, must give the will commands or imperatives. He makes the distinction between two kinds of imperatives – non-moral (**hypothetical**) and moral (**categorical**).

THE HYPOTHETICAL IMPERATIVE

Hypothetical imperatives are not moral commands to the will, as they do not apply to everyone. You only need to obey them if you want to achieve a certain '*goal*' – that is why a hypothetical imperative always begins with the word '*if*'.

David Hume (1711–1776)

David Hume in 1766 by Allan Ramsay (1713–1784)

Scottish National Portrait Gallery, Edinburgh, Scotland/ The Bridgeman Art Library

Nationality/copyright status: Scottish/out of copyright

David Hume was born in Edinburgh on 7 May 1711. He was an historian and philosopher. He influenced the development of scepticism and empiricism.

He worked in an office in Bristol for a short time and then moved to France.

A *Treatise of Human Nature* was published in three volumes between 1739 and 1740. Hume went back to his family home in Berwickshire and worked on *Essays Moral and Political*, published in 1741 to 1742.

Hume moved to Edinburgh in 1751 and became librarian of the Advocates' Library. Hume was a friend of Jean-Jacques Rousseau and brought him to Britain, but

continued

the friendship collapsed due to Rousseau's mental condition. Hume died on 25 August 1776.

Hypothetical imperative
An action that achieves some goal or end.

Categorical imperative
A command to perform actions that are absolute moral obligations without reference to other ends.

Law
Objective principle, a maxim that can be universalised.

Maxim
A general rule in accordance with which we intend to act.

For example: *if* I want to lose weight I ought to go on a diet and exercise more. A hypothetical imperative depends on the results and aims at personal well-being.

THE CATEGORICAL IMPERATIVE

Categorical imperatives, on the other hand, are *moral commands* and do not begin with an 'if', as they tell everyone what to do and do not depend on anything, especially desires or goals. According to Kant these categorical imperatives apply to everyone (like the categories of pure reason which apply to everyone) because they are based on an *objective a priori law of reason* which Kant calls the **categorical imperative**. This is a test to judge whether an action is in accordance with pure practical reason.

There are a number of different forms of this, but they are variations on three basic ones.

1 Act only according to that maxim whereby you can at the same time will that it should become a universal law

Kant calls this the **Formula of the Law of Nature**. This first formulation of the categorical imperative asks everyone to universalise their principles or **maxims** without contradiction. In other words, before you act ask yourself whether you would like everyone in the same situation to act in the same way. If not, then you are involved in a *contradiction* and what you are thinking of doing is wrong because it is against reason.

Kant always wants to universalise rules, as he wants everyone to be free and rational, and if rules are not universalisable then others will not have the same freedom to act on the same moral principles as I use. However, Kant does not claim that everyone should be able to do the same thing as I choose to do in order for it to be moral – but rather everyone should be prepared to act on the same maxim.

Kant uses promise-keeping as an example. I cannot consistently will that promise-breaking for my own self-interest should be a universal law. If I try to make a universal law of the maxim 'I may always break my promises when it is for my benefit', the end result will be that there is no point in anyone making promises – this is inconsistent and so cannot be a moral imperative.

To make his argument as clear as possible Kant uses four examples, including the one of promise-keeping:

• A man feels sick of life as a result of a series of misfortunes that have mounted to the point of despair, but he is still so far in possession of his reason as to ask himself whether taking his own life may be contrary to his duty to himself. He now applies the test 'Can the maxim of my action really become a universal law of nature?' His maxim is 'From self-love I make it my principle to shorten my life if its continuance threatens more evil than it promises pleasure'. The only further question to ask is whether this principle of self-love can become a universal law of nature. It is then seen at once that a system of nature by whose law the very same feeling whose function is to stimulate the furtherance of life should actually destroy life would contradict itself, and consequently could not subsist as a system of nature and is therefore entirely opposed to the supreme principle of all duty.

- Another finds himself driven to borrowing money due to need. He well knows that he will not be able to pay it back; but he sees too that he will get no loan unless he gives a firm promise to pay it back within a fixed time. He is inclined to make such a promise; but he still has enough conscience to ask: 'Is it not unlawful and contrary to duty to get out of difficulties in this way?' Supposing, however, he did resolve to do so; the maxim of his action would be: 'Whenever I believe myself short of money, I will borrow and promise to pay it back, though I know that this will never be done.' Now this principle of self-love or personal advantage is perhaps quite compatible with my own entire future welfare; only there remains the question 'Is it right?' I therefore transform the demand of self-love into a universal law and frame my question thus: 'How would things stand if my maxim became a universal law?' I then see straight-away that this maxim can never rank as a universal law of nature and be self-consistent, but must necessarily contradict itself. For the universality of the intention not to keep it would make promising, and the very purpose of promising, itself impossible, since no one would believe he was being promised anything, but would laugh at utterances of this kind as empty shams.

- A third finds in himself a talent whose cultivation would make him a useful man for all sorts of purposes. But he sees himself in comfortable circumstances, and he prefers to give himself up to pleasure rather than bother about increasing and improving his fortunate natural aptitudes. Yet he asks himself further: 'Does my maxim of neglecting my natural gifts, besides agreeing in itself with my tendency to indulgence, agree also with what is called duty?' He then sees that a system of nature could indeed always subsist under such a universal law, although (like the South Sea Islanders) every man should let his talents rust and should be bent on devoting his life solely to idleness, indulgence, procreation and, in a word, to enjoyment. Only he cannot possibly will that this become a universal law of nature or should be implanted in us as such a law by a natural instinct. For as a rational being he necessarily wills that all his powers should be developed, since they serve him, and are given to him, for all sorts of possible ends.

• Yet a fourth is himself flourishing, but he sees others who have to struggle with great hardships (and whom he could easily help); and he thinks: 'What does it matter to me? Let everyone be as happy as heaven wills or as he can make himself; I won't deprive him of anything; I won't envy him; only I have no wish to contribute to his well-being or to support in distress!' Now admittedly, if such an attitude were a universal law of nature, mankind could get on perfectly well – better no doubt than if everyone prates about sympathy and good will and even takes pains on occasion to practise them, but on the other hand cheats where he can, traffics in human rights, or violates them in other ways. But although it is possible that a universal law of nature could subsist in harmony with this maxim, yet it is impossible to will that such a principle should hold everywhere as a law of nature. For a will which decided in this way would be in conflict with itself, since many a situation might arise in which the man needed love and sympathy from others, and in which by such a law of nature sprung from his own will he would rob himself of all hope of the help he wants for himself. (*Groundwork of the Metaphysics of Morals*)

Kant's followers disagree about how to apply this universal law test. **Hare** suggests an alternative approach to test a proposed moral maxim:

• Try to understand the consequences of following it on affected individuals.
• Try to imagine yourself in the place of these individuals.
• Ask yourself whether you want the maxim to be followed regardless of where you imagine yourself in the situation.

The challenge then is to distinguish right maxims from wrong ones. This is the role of reason in choosing only maxims that can be universalised.

2 So act as to treat humanity, whether in your own person or in that of any other, never solely as a means but always as an end

Kant calls this the **Formula of End in Itself**. He means that we should not exploit others or treat them as things to achieve an end, as they are as rational as we are. To treat another person as a means is to deny that person the right to be a rational and independent judge of his or her own actions. It is to make oneself in some way superior and different. To be consistent we need to value everyone equally.

Kant saw the first two formulations as two expressions of the same idea. He summed this up as follows:

> Principles of action are prohibited morally if they could not be universalised without contradiction, or they could not be willed as universal laws. (*Groundwork of the Metaphysics of Morals*)

The third formulation follows from the other two.

3 Act as if a legislating member in the universal Kingdom of Ends

This he calls the **Formula of a Kingdom of Ends**. Everyone should act as if every other person was an 'end' – a free, autonomous agent. Kant believed that each person is autonomous and moral judgements should not be based on any empirical consideration about human nature, human flourishing or human destiny. However, this idea of the autonomy of the individual does not mean that everyone can just decide their own morality, but rather that each individual has the ability to understand the principles of pure practical reason and follow them. Pure practical reason must be impartial and so its principles must apply equally to everyone.

Kingdom of Ends
A world in which people do not treat others as means but only as ends.

4 Any action that ignores the individual dignity of a human being in order to achieve its ends is wrong

The categorical imperative
- The universal law
- Humans as ends not as means
- A Kingdom of Ends

Thought Point

1   Why does Kant believe that the 'good will' is the only thing that is good without qualification? Can you think of anything else that is good without qualification? What are Kant's supporting reasons? Do you agree with him?

continued

2   How would Kant suggest that where there is a clash of duties, we know what takes precedence by following the categorical imperative. Does this work? Discuss the following:

   (a) It is your turn to make a presentation in class and you are running late. On the way you witness a car crash and are asked to wait to make a statement to the police.
   (b) If only actual persons are ends in themselves, how would a Kantian approach a student who accidentally becomes pregnant and decides to have an abortion so as to continue her studies?
   (c) 'If I had to choose between betraying my country and betraying my friend I hope I should have the guts to betray my country.' E.M. Forster. Do you agree?

THE THREE POSTULATES OF PRACTICAL REASON

Apart from making the individual the sole authority for moral judgement, Kant's theory of ethics seems to grant freedom to do anything that can be consistently universalised. This morality sets limits but does not give direct guidance; therefore, in order for it to make sense Kant has to postulate the existence of *God*, *freedom* and *immortality*.

Kant's ethical theory could, in fact, be said to be a religious morality without God but he seems to take for granted God as lawgiver and he argues that there must be a God and an afterlife, as there has to be some sort of reward.

Kant has already explained that happiness is not the foundation or reason for acting morally, but he claims that it is its reward. Kant's ideas seem to be really twisted with regard to happiness. In the *Groundwork for the Metaphysics of Morals* he writes:

> The principle of personal happiness is the most objectionable not merely because it is false and because its pretence that well-being always adjusts itself to well-doing is contradicted by experience; not merely because it contributes nothing to morality (since making a man happy is quite different from making him good) but because it bases morality on sensuous motives.

However, he also says that we have a duty to make ourselves happy, not because we want to be happy but because it is necessary for us to do our other duties. Kant seems to put duty in a sort of vacuum, totally separate from our everyday lives.

To solve this dilemma Kant looks at the postulates of *God* and *immortality*: after death, in the next world, there is no conflict between 'duty' and 'happiness', as 'duty' is part of the natural harmony of purposes created by God. Kant thought that our aim in acting morally is not to be happy but to be worthy of being happy. The **summum bonum** or highest good is a state where happiness and virtue are united – but for Kant it is the virtuous person who has a 'good will' which is vital for morality; happiness is not guaranteed. The *summum bonum*, however, cannot be achieved in this life and so there must be life after death where we can achieve it – thus for Kant, morality leads to God.

Summum bonum
The supreme good that we pursue through moral acts.

STRENGTHS OF KANT'S THEORY OF ETHICS

* Kant's morality is very straightforward and based on reason.
* There are clear criteria to assess what is moral.
* The moral value of an action comes from the action itself.
* Kant's categorical imperative gives us rules that apply to everyone and command us to respect human life.
* It makes clear that morality is about doing one's duty and not just following feelings or inclinations. This means that we cannot assume that what is good for us is morally good and so good for everyone else. This is Kant's equivalent of the Golden Rule of Christian ethics.
* It aims to treat everyone fairly and justly and so corrects the utilitarian assumption that the minority can suffer so long as the majority are happy.
* Kant sees humans as being of intrinsic worth and dignity as they are rational creatures. Humans cannot be enslaved or exploited. This is the basis of the Declaration of Human Rights.

WEAKNESSES OF KANT'S THEORY OF ETHICS

* Kant's theory is abstract and not always easily applied to moral situations – it tells you what *types* of actions are good, but it does not tell you what is the right thing to do in particular situations. As Alasdair MacIntyre points out, you can use the **universalisability** principle to justify practically anything:

Universalisability
If an act is right or wrong for one person in a situation, then it is right or wrong for anyone in that situation.

> all I need to do is to characterise the proposed action in such a way that the maxim will permit me to do what I want while prohibiting others from doing what would nullify the action if universalised. (Alasdair MacIntyre, *A Short History of Ethics*)

- Kant's emphasis on duty seems to imply that an action is made moral by an underlying **intention** to do one's duty. However, it is not always possible to separate 'intentions' from 'ends', as intentions are closely linked with what we do (e.g. intending to come to the help of a friend who is being beaten up is not the same as actually doing so). In addition, our motives are not always pure and people seldom act from pure practical reason; we more often help others because we like them or we feel sorry for them. Some philosophers think that putting duty above feeling is cold and inhuman. Kant's theory severs morality from everyday life and everyday feelings and emotions.
- Many people would consider that thinking about the result of an action is an important part of ethical decision-making, and if the outcome hurts another person, most people would feel guilty.
- Kant's system only seems to work if everyone has the same view of the final purpose and end of humans. It depends on some notion of God to justify this rationally ordered world. We do not all even have the same views on life and obeying the moral law could put one at a real disadvantage when dealing with people who are wicked, amoral or simply less rational.
- Kant is clear when explaining the conflict between duty and inclination but he does not help us understand the conflict between different duties, each of which could be justified.
- In addition, though Kant tells us in general terms to respect others and not treat them as ends, this does not tell us what to do in individual cases. What about the terminally ill patient who wants help to die? What about protecting the innocent victim from murderers? What about stealing a drug to help a loved one to live? What about conscription in time of war? Kant's theory here seems to lead either to a position where no decision can be made or to a situation where I may consider doing my duty as just plain wrong.

THE THEORY OF W.D. ROSS

These problems with Kant's theory of ethics led **W.D. Ross** to make certain changes. He argued that exceptions should be allowed to Kant's duties – Ross called these *prima facie duties* (first sight duties). These duties are conditional and can be outweighed by a more compelling duty (e.g. 'Never take a life' could be outweighed by 'Never take a life except in self-defence').

Ross lists seven prima facie duties:

1   fidelity or promise-keeping
2   reparation for harm done
3   gratitude

4   justice
5   beneficence
6   self-improvement
7   non-maleficence.

These stress the personal character of duty. The first three duties look to the past and the last four to the future, but they do not need to be considered in any particular order, but rather as to how they fit the particular situation. For example, who should I save from drowning: my father or a famous doctor? A utilitarian would save the doctor because he could help more people. Ross says we have a special duty of gratitude to our parents which outweighs any duty to a stranger.

Ross shows that there are possible exceptions to any rule and these exceptions depend on the situation in which I do my duty, the possible consequences of doing my duty and the personal relationships involved.

Problems with Ross's theory

*   How do we know what a prima facie duty is?
*   How do we know which one is right where there is a conflict between them?

Ross says that we simply **know** which acts are right by consulting our deepest moral convictions, but is this an adequate response? Can we be sure that Ross's list of duties is correct?

APPLICATION OF KANTIAN ETHICS TO AN ETHICAL DILEMMA – GENETIC ENGINEERING

Genetic engineering includes cloning, research on embryonic stem cells, so-called designer babies and genetically modified organisms (GMOs).

Kant says that humans should never be thought of as a means but always as an end. This second formulation of the categorical imperative is often used to protect human dignity. Creating a human life (embryo) for the purpose of obtaining cells which could be used as therapeutic material would not be protecting the dignity of that particular human life. The idea of using individuals to help others in this way is sometimes referred to as 'instrumentalisation', and if Kant is applied too rigidly his ethical theory could also prohibit blood transfusions – as the patient needing the transfusion knows nothing of the anonymous donor and is using the person's blood simply as a means to an end. It is standard practice in IVF treatment to create spare embryos – are these created instrumentally?

However, Kant's principle states: '*Act in such a way that you always treat humanity, whether in your own person or in the person of any other, never simply as a means but always at the same time as an end*'; this is rather vague and may be interpreted selectively according to one's point of view.

We also need to consider what the moral status of a human embryo is – is it the same as a born human and does Kant's principle, or indeed any other principle about persons and personhood, apply to embryos? Some people will think that an embryo is a full member of the moral community with all the rights that humans possess and cite the sanctity of life to support their position.

On the other hand, is it possible to apply Kantian ethics to the idea of attempting to conceive a child to get a 'son and heir'? Is this any different from the idea of selecting an embryo as a genetic match for curing a sibling? Others will consider that it is too simplistic to apply Kant's categorical imperative to any form of genetic engineering and that it is better to do some good than to do no good, and from an ethical point of view it cannot be good to waste spare embryos produced from IVF when they could be used for therapeutic purposes – after all, they were not produced simply as a means.

When applying Kant's categorical imperative to difficult modern ethical dilemmas such as genetic engineering, it is important not to be too dogmatic but to look at the question from different angles.

One must also consider the question of genetically modified organisms – is it better to view this as a means to feed the hungry, or do we again treat people (small farmers) as a means to an end by putting them in thrall to the multinationals?

These are some of the questions that need to be considered and discussed when applying Kantian ethics to genetic engineering in its many forms.

REVIEW QUESTIONS

Look back over the chapter and check that you can answer the following questions:

1   What did Kant mean by 'good will'?
2   Why is duty important to Kant?
3   Spider diagram or mind map the categorical imperative, with examples.
4   Make a chart of the strengths and weaknesses of Kantian ethics.

Terminology

Do you know your terminology?

Try to explain the following terms without looking at your books and notes:

- The categorical imperative
- The hypothetical imperative
- Duty
- Good will
- The Kingdom of Ends
- Maxim
- The *summum bonum*
- Universalisability

Examination Questions Practice

It is a good idea always to use examples to explain the categorical imperative. Do not use phrases like 'a priori' if you cannot remember what they mean.

PAST PAPER QUESTIONS

(a) Give an account of Kant's ethical theory. (33 marks)

- At the beginning you need to set the scene and explain that Kant's theory of ethics is deontological and focused on the idea of a moral law.
- You might explain that moral statements are a priori synthetic.
- You could also explain Kant's understanding of good will and duty and show that they are linked.
- Most importantly you need to explain the categorical imperative and its universalisability; that

people must be considered as ends in themselves and that people work towards a Kingdom of Ends.
- A good answer would include examples, preferably Kant's own.

(b) 'Kant's ethical theory is a good approach to euthanasia.' Discuss. (17 marks)

You can argue this both ways.

- You may refer to the quality of life and compassionate love, or you could take an absolutist view and point to the importance of not treating people as means to an end and how this second formulation of the categorical imperative is often used to protect human dignity.

- However, this formulation is rather vague and may be interpreted selectively according to one's point of view.

- You may also consider the idea of universalisation and the problems involved in making euthanasia a universal maxim.

- On the other hand, you could also contrast Kant's approach with that of a more relative ethical theory, such as Situation ethics.

SAMPLE AS EXAMINATION QUESTIONS

(a) Give an account of Kant's theory of ethics.
(b) How helpful would this theory be when faced with the problem of dying without dignity?
(OCR AS Level 2762 January 2001 question 2)

(a) Describe Kant's reasons for defending the need for the categorical imperative.

(b) How useful are Kantian ethics for drawing conclusions about the right to life?
(OCR AS Level 2762 June 2001 question 2)

(a) Explain Kant's concept of universalisability.
(b) Assess the view that it is always right to keep one's promises.
(OCR AS Level 2762 June 2003 question 4)

FURTHER READING

Kant, I. 'Groundwork of a Metaphysics of Morals', in *The Moral Law*, Paton, H.J. (trans.), London, Routledge, 2005.
MacIntyre, A. *A Short History of Ethics*, London, Routledge, 1968.
Norman, R. *The Moral Philosophers*, Oxford, Oxford University Press, 1998.
Pojman, L.P. *Ethics: Discovering Right and Wrong*, Toronto, Wadsworth, 2002.
Scruton, R. *Kant*, Oxford, Oxford University Press, 1982.
Ward, K. *The Development of Kant's View of Ethics*, Oxford, Blackwell, 1972.

6 Utilitarianism

Essential terminology

Act Utilitarianism
Consequentialist
Hedonic calculus
Hedonism
Preference
  Utilitarianism
Principle of utility
Qualitative
Quantitative
Rule Utilitarianism
Teleological
Universalisability

WHAT YOU WILL LEARN ABOUT IN THIS CHAPTER

*   The principle of utility, the hedonic calculus, Act and Rule Utilitarianism.
*   Classical forms of Utilitarianism from Bentham, Mill and Sidgwick; modern versions from Hare and Singer.
*   The strengths and weaknesses of Utilitarianism.
*   How to apply Utilitarianism to ethical dilemmas.

KEY SCHOLARS

*   Jeremy Bentham (1748–1832)
*   John Stuart Mill (1806–1873)
*   Henry Sidgwick (1838–1900)
*   W.D. Ross (1877–1971)
*   Richard Brandt (1910–1997)

*   R.M. Hare (1919–2002)
*   John Rawls (1921–2002)
*   Bernard Williams (1929–2003)
*   Peter Singer (1946–)

THE OCR CHECKLIST

Utilitarianism, the views of Bentham and Mill:

*   An understanding of the 'greatest happiness principle'.
*   The main similarities and differences between the thinking of Bentham and that of Mill.
*   The distinction between Act and Rule Utilitarianism suggested by some scholars, and the extent to which either of these labels might be appropriate for Bentham or Mill.
*   The strengths and weaknesses of Utilitarianism.

From OCR A Level Religious Studies Specification 7877.

continued opposite

Teleological

Moral actions are right or wrong according to their outcome or *telos* (end).

Consequentialist

Someone who decides whether an action is good or bad by its consequences.

Jeremy Bentham (1748–1832)

Jeremy Bentham: Embalmed body as exhibited at University College

© University College Museum, London, UK/The Bridgeman Art Library

Jeremy Bentham was born in London on 15 February 1748. He could read scholarly works at 3, played the violin at 5, and studied Latin and French at 6. At age 12 he went to Oxford and trained as a lawyer.

Bentham was the leader of the Philosophical Radicals who founded the *Westminster Review*. He died in London on 6 June

WHAT IS UTILITARIANISM?

You have probably heard someone justify their actions as being for the greater good. Utilitarianism is the ethical theory behind such justifications.

Utilitarianism is a **teleological** theory of ethics. It is the opposite of *deontological* ethical theories that are based on moral rules, on whether the action itself is right or wrong. Teleological theories of ethics look at the consequences – the results of an action – to decide whether it is right or wrong. Utilitarianism is a **consequentialist** theory.

The theory of Utilitarianism began with **Jeremy Bentham** as a way of working out how good or bad the consequence of an action would be. Utilitarianism gets its name from Bentham's test question: 'What is the use of it?' He thought of the idea when he came across the words 'the greatest happiness of the greatest number' in Joseph Priestley's *An essay on the first principles of government; and on the nature of political, civil, and religious liberty* (1768). Bentham was very concerned with social and legal reform and he wanted to develop an ethical theory which established whether something was good or bad according to its benefit for the majority of people.

Bentham called this the **principle of utility**. Utility here means the *usefulness* of the results of actions. The principle of utility is often expressed as 'the greatest good of the greatest number'. 'Good' is defined in terms of *pleasure* or *happiness* – so an act is right or wrong according to the good or bad that results from the act and the good act is the most pleasurable. Since it focuses on the greatest number, Bentham's theory is **quantitative**.

THE ORIGINS OF HEDONISM

The idea that 'good' is defined in terms of pleasure and happiness makes utilitarianism a **hedonistic** theory. The Greek philosophers who thought along similar lines introduced the term *eudaimonia,* which is probably best translated as 'well-being'. Both Plato and Aristotle agreed that 'good' equated with the greatest happiness, while the Epicureans stressed 'pleasure' as the main aim of life. The ultimate end of human desires and actions, according to Aristotle, is happiness and though pleasure sometimes accompanies this, it is not the chief aim of life. Pleasure is not the same as happiness, as happiness results from the use of reason and cultivating the virtues. It is only if we take pleasure in good activities that pleasure itself is good. This idea of Aristotle's is taken up by John Stuart Mill, as we will see later.

JEREMY BENTHAM'S APPROACH

Jeremy Bentham developed his ethical system around the idea of pleasure and it is based on ancient hedonism, which pursued physical pleasure and avoided physical pain. According to Bentham, the most moral acts are those that maximise pleasure and minimise pain. This has sometimes been called the 'utilitarian calculus'. An act would be moral if it brings the greatest amount of pleasure and the least amount of pain.

Pain vs. pleasure

Bentham said: 'The principle of utility aims to promote happiness which is the supreme ethical value. Nature has placed us under the governance of two sovereign masters, *pain* and *pleasure*. An act is right if it delivers more pleasure than pain and wrong if it brings about more pain than pleasure.'

By adding up the amounts of pleasure and pain for each possible act we should be able to choose the good thing to do.

Happiness = pleasure minus pain

The hedonic calculus

To help us choose the good thing to do and work out the possible consequences of an action, Bentham provided a way of measuring. This is the **hedonic calculus**.

It has seven elements:

1   the intensity of the pleasure (how deep)
2   the duration of the pleasure caused (how long)
3   the certainty of the pleasure (how certain or uncertain)
4   the remoteness of the pleasure (how near or far)
5   the chance of a succession of pleasures (how continuous)
6   the purity of the pleasure (how secure)
7   the extent of the pleasure (how universal).

This calculus gave Bentham a method of testing whether an action is morally right, in that if it was good it would result in the most pleasurable outcome, having weighed up all the elements. Whatever is good or bad can be measured in a **quantitative** way.

1832. His body was dissected and his clothed skeleton is in a glass case in University College, London.

Bentham advanced his theory of Utilitarianism as the basis for general political and legal reform.

Principle of utility
The theory of usefulness – the greatest happiness for the greatest number.

Hedonism
The view that pleasure is the chief 'good'.

Epicurus
(341–270 BCE)

Bust of Epicurus (stone) by Greek

© Museo Capitolino, Rome, Italy/Giraudon/The Bridgeman Art Library

Epicureans are followers of Epicurus.

continued

The quantity of happiness

Epicurus (341–270 BCE) was born on the island of Sámos. In 322 he began teaching in Colophon. In 311 he founded a philosophical school in Mitilíni on the island of Lésvos and then became head of a school in Lampsacus. He returned to Athens in 306 and taught his group of followers there.

Epicurus developed a system of ethics but later thinkers have used his philosophy as an equivalent to hedonism teaching that pleasure or happiness is the chief good, which people should aim to achieve.

Hedonic calculus
Bentham's method for measuring the good and bad effects of an action.

Quantitative
Looking at the quantity of the happiness.

Act Utilitarianism
A teleological theory that uses the outcome of an action to determine whether it is good or bad.

Hedonism

Bentham's Utilitarianism is a universal hedonism – the highest good is the greatest happiness for the greatest number. Actions are judged as a *means to an end*. What is right is that which is calculated to bring about the greatest balance of good over evil, where good is defined as pleasure or happiness.

Bentham's view is described as **Act Utilitarianism**.

Bentham argued that we should be guided by the principle of utility and not by rules. However, it may be necessary to use rules of thumb based on past experience, especially if there is no time to work out the consequences.

Thought Point

1   What would be the problems if everyone acted as an Act utilitarian all the time?
2   Are all actions only good because they have good results?

3   Suppose a rape is committed that is thought to be racially motivated. Riots are brewing that may result in many deaths and long-term racial antagonism. You are the police chief and have recently taken a man into custody. Why not frame him? He will be imprisoned if found guilty and this will result in peace and safety. Only you, the innocent man and the real rapist (who will keep quiet), will know the truth. What is the morally right thing to do? Look at all the consequences of any action.

4   Suppose a surgeon could use the organs of one healthy patient to save the lives of several others. Would the surgeon be justified in killing the healthy patient for the sake of the others?

5   You are an army officer who has just captured an enemy soldier who knows where a secret time bomb is planted. If it explodes it will kill thousands. Will it be morally permissible to torture the soldier so that he reveals the bomb's location? If you knew where the soldier's children were, would it also be permissible to torture them to get him to reveal the bomb's whereabouts?

JOHN STUART MILL'S APPROACH

Mill was also a hedonist and accepted that happiness is of the greatest importance. He stressed happiness rather than pleasure.

The Greatest Happiness Principle

Mill said: 'The Greatest Happiness Principle holds that actions are right in proportion as they tend to promote happiness, wrong as they tend to produce the reverse of happiness. By happiness is intended pleasure, and the absence of pain; by unhappiness, pain and the privation of pleasure.'

The quality of pleasure

Having affirmed his agreement with the principle of utility, Mill then modifies Bentham's approach, especially the quantitative emphasis. He says: 'Some kinds of pleasures are more desirable and more valuable than others, it would be absurd that while, in estimating all other things, quality is not also considered as well as quantity.'

According to Mill, quality of pleasure employs the use of the higher faculties. Here he is answering the objection to Bentham's approach that

Qualitative
Looking at the quality of the pleasure.

The quality of happiness

utilitarians are just pleasure-seekers. For example, consider the case of the Christians and the Romans: many Romans get a lot of pleasure from seeing a few Christians eaten by lions – here the greatest happiness (that of the Romans) is produced by an act (Christians being eaten by lions) that is surely quite wrong. Mill says that the quality of pleasure that satisfies a human is different from that which satisfies an animal. People are capable of more than animals, so it takes more to make a human happy. Therefore, a person will always choose higher quality, human pleasures, and reject all the merely animal pleasures. As Mill puts it:

> Few human creatures would consent to be changed into any of the lower animals for a promise of the fullest allowance of the beast's pleasures. . . . It is better to be a human being dissatisfied than a pig satisfied; better to be Socrates dissatisfied than a fool satisfied. And if the fool or the pig are of a different opinion, it is because they only know their side of the question.

So since the Romans are only enjoying 'animal' pleasure, it does not matter that they are getting a lot more of it than the Christians – it is the quality not the quantity of the pleasure that really counts. For Mill, it is intellectual pleasures (e.g. reading poetry or listening to music) that really count and are more important than such pleasures as eating, drinking or having sex.

Happiness, he argues, is something that people desire for its own sake, but we need to look at human life as a whole – happiness is not just adding up the units of pleasure but rather the fulfilment of higher ideals.

A pig . . .

Universalisability

Mill next develops the argument that in order to derive the principle of the greatest good (happiness) for the greatest number we need the principle of **universalisability**. He says: 'Each person's happiness is a good to that person, and the general happiness, therefore, is a good to the aggregate of all persons.' This means:

Universalisability

What is right or wrong for one person in a situation is right or wrong for all.

Each person desires his own happiness

Therefore each person ought to aim at his happiness

Therefore everyone ought to aim at the happiness of everyone

As you can see, the last proposition does not follow logically from the previous one. To move from each person to everyone is a fallacy. Mill makes this move because he wants to justify 'the greatest number'. This can mean that Utilitarianism demands that people put the interests of the group before their own interests, and Mill compares this to 'the Golden Rule of Jesus of

Nazareth'. Mill has a positive view of human nature and thinks that people have powerful feelings of empathy for others which can be cultivated by education and so on.

Mill also separates the question of the motive and the morality of the action. There is nothing wrong with self-interest if it produces the right action.

Rule Utilitarianism

Rule Utilitarianism

Establishing a general rule that follows utilitarian principles.

Another aspect of Mill's approach is the idea that there need to be some moral *rules* in order to establish social order and justice – but the rules should be those which, if followed *universally*, would most likely produce the greatest happiness. Mill has been seen as a **Rule utilitarian** in contrast to Bentham's Act Utilitarianism – though Mill never discussed Act or Rule Utilitarianism in these terms.

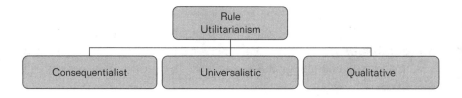

Comparing Bentham and Mill

Bentham	Mill
'The greatest good [*pleasure*] for the greatest number'	'The greatest *happiness* for the greatest number'
Focused on the *individual* alone	We should protect the common good, *universalistic*
Quantitative – hedonic calculus	*Qualitative* – higher/lower pleasures
Act Utilitarianism	*Rule Utilitarianism*
In search of maximisation of happiness	
Consequentialist	Consequentialist

HENRY SIDGWICK'S APPROACH

Another important utilitarian was **Henry Sidgwick**. In *The Methods of Ethics* he argues that the balance of pleasure over pain is the ultimate goal of ethical decisions. His argument is closer to Bentham than to Mill, as he questions how it is possible to distinguish between higher and lower order pleasures, and how we can distinguish one higher order pleasure from another. However, Sidgwick does argue that the process of deciding is *intuitive* – we make self-evident judgements about what we ought to do.

Justice

Sidgwick was concerned with justice in society and, like Mill, he had a positive view of human nature, hoping that the future would bring a growth in human empathy and moral motivation. He argued that justice is the similar and injustice the dissimilar treatment of similar cases: 'whatever action any of us judges to be right for himself, he implicitly judges to be right for all similar persons in similar circumstances'. It cannot be right for Jack to treat Tom in a manner in which it would be wrong for Tom to treat Jack, simply on the grounds that they are two different individuals and without there being any difference in their circumstances or their natures. This argument that we must act according to just laws raises the issue of which laws are just, and the whole issue of justice seems to sit uncomfortably with the principle of utility and the Act utilitarian position.

SIDGWICK AND BENTHAM

There are obvious differences between Bentham and Sidgwick, but both may be described as Act utilitarians – moral actions are not only judged by their consequences, but also by how they benefit the welfare of people. The act that brings happiness to the greatest number is a right act.

Sidgwick's approach to Utilitarianism is the starting point for modern-day approaches to this ethical theory.

ACT AND RULE UTILITARIANISM

Before looking at modern approaches to Utilitarianism, it is important that you fully understand the two variations – Act Utilitarianism and Rule Utilitarianism.

The distinction is to do with what the principle of utility is applied *to*.

**Henry Sidgwick
(1838–1900)**

Sidgwick was born in Skipton, Yorkshire. He became Professor of Moral Philosophy at Cambridge in 1883. The requirement for him to subscribe to Anglican Christianity before taking the post was waived because he was unable to do so on conscientious grounds. He concentrated on ethical problems and thought that many could be resolved by appeal to a god, but he could not himself subscribe to this view. He could not accept that the maximising of human pleasure could be aligned with an idea of 'universal values'.

Sidgwick supported higher education for women and was a founder of Newnham College, Cambridge. He was the first President of the Society for Psychical Research. His principal works include *The Methods of Ethics* (1874), *Principles of Political Economy* (1883) and *Elements of Politics* (1891).

- According to Act Utilitarianism the principle is applied directly to a particular action in a particular circumstance.
- According to Rule Utilitarianism the principle is applied to a selection of a set of rules which are in turn used to determine what to do in particular situations.

ACT UTILITARIANISM

You must decide what action will lead to the greatest good in the particular situation you are facing and apply the principle of utility directly. You need to look at the consequences of a particular act and what will bring about the greatest happiness.

Flexibility

Since the same act might in some situations produce the greatest good for the greatest number, but in other situations not, Utilitarianism allows moral rules to change from age to age, from situation to situation.

There are no necessary moral rules except one: that we should always seek the greatest happiness for the greatest number in all situations.

Act Utilitarianism is linked to Bentham's form of Utilitarianism.

Weaknesses of Act Utilitarianism

- It is difficult to predict the consequences.
- There is potential to justify any act.
- There is difficulty in defining pleasure.
- There is no defence for the minorities.
- It is impractical to say that we should calculate the morality of each choice.

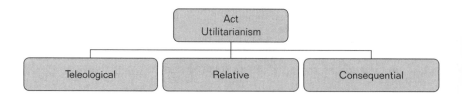

- *Teleological* – aims for a maximisation of pleasure for the majority. It has an end aim or goal.

- *Relative* – no notion of absolute right/wrong. No external source of truth. Nothing in itself is right or wrong.
- *Consequential* – the consequences of an act alone determine its rightness/wrongness.

RULE UTILITARIANISM

Rule utilitarians believe that rules should be formed using utilitarian principles for the benefit of society. Your action is judged right or wrong by the goodness or badness of the consequences of a rule that everyone should follow in similar circumstances. Rule Utilitarianism enables us to establish rules which will promote the happiness of humanity and will generally be right in most circumstances (e.g. telling the truth, keeping your promises).

Strong Rule utilitarians believe that these derived rules should never be disobeyed.

Weak Rule utilitarians say that although there should be generally accepted rules or guidelines, they should not always be adhered to indefinitely. There may be situations where the better consequence might be achieved by disregarding the rule (e.g. where it might be better to tell a lie).

Rule Utilitarianism is commonly linked with Mill.

Weaknesses of Rule Utilitarianism

- It is difficult to predict the consequences.
- It is difficult to define what constitutes happiness.
- There is no defence for the minorities.
- To invoke rules means that the approach becomes deontological not teleological.
- Followers of Rule Utilitarianism can either be strict rule-followers or rule-modifiers, but neither seems satisfactory. Strict rule-followers can be irrational: obeying the rule even when disobeying it will produce more happiness. Rule-modifiers can end up being no different from Act utilitarians.

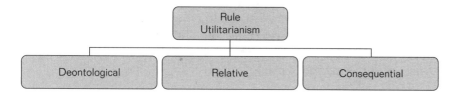

- *Deontological* – rules take priority.
- *Relative* – what is right/wrong is established as the maximisation of pleasure for the particular community/society within which it operates.
- *Consequential* – the overall consequences determine its rightness/ wrongness.

Thought Point

1. Suppose that you were God, and because you are onmibenevolent, you want your creatures to be as happy as possible across time (i.e. you believe in Utilitarianism). If you were choosing a moral code to teach your created people that would make them all happy, what code would you teach them?

2. Explain the distinction between Act and Rule Utilitarianism and why Rule Utilitarianism came about.

3. The country is threatened with drought, so people are urged to conserve water and hose-pipe bans are in force. Joe lives in an isolated part of the country and nobody ever drives past his house. The water company has forgotten Joe exists and so he is never billed for his water. Joe knows about the hose-pipe ban, but he really wants a green lawn. His lawn is tiny, so he knows he will not be harming anyone if he waters it and the small amount he uses will not affect the drought. Joe continues to use water. What would an Act Utilitarian say about this? What would a Rule Utilitarian say? Give reasons.

PREFERENCE UTILITARIANISM

Preference Utilitarianism
Moral actions are right or wrong according to how they fit the preferences of those involved.

Preference Utilitarianism is a more recent form of Utilitarianism and is associated with **R.M. Hare**, **Peter Singer** and **Richard Brandt**.

An Act utilitarian judges right or wrong according to the maximising of pleasure and minimising of pain, a Rule utilitarian judges right or wrong according to the keeping of rules derived from utility, but a Preference utilitarian judges moral actions according to whether they fit in with the preferences of the individuals involved. This approach to Utilitarianism asks: 'What is in my own interest? What would I prefer in this situation? Which outcome would I prefer?' However, because Utilitarianism aims to create the greatest good for the greatest number, it is necessary to consider the preferences of others in order to achieve this.

R.M. Hare's approach

Hare argues that in moral decision-making we need to consider our own preferences and those of others. He says that 'equal preferences count equally, whatever their content'. People are happy when they get what they prefer, but what we prefer may clash with the preferences of others. Hare says we need to 'stand in someone else's shoes' and try to imagine what someone else might prefer. We should treat everyone, including ourselves, with impartiality – he also argues for universalisability.

Peter Singer's approach

Singer also defends Preference Utilitarianism and suggests that we should take the viewpoint of an *impartial spectator* combined with a broadly utilitarian approach. He says that 'our own preferences cannot count any more than the preferences of others' and so, in acting morally, we should take account of all the people affected by our actions. These have to be weighed and balanced and then we must choose the action which gives the best possible consequences for those affected. For Singer, the 'best possible consequences' means what is in the *best interests* of the individuals concerned – this is different from Bentham, Mill and Sidgwick, as he is not considering what increases pleasure and diminishes pain.

This principle of equal consideration of preferences or interests acts like a pair of scales – everyone's preferences or interests are weighed equally. So, in Singer's view, killing a person who prefers to go on living would be wrong and not killing a person who prefers to die would also be wrong. Racism is wrong, as it goes against the principle of acknowledging other people's interests or preferences and gives greater value to the preferences of one's own race.

Richard Brandt's approach

Richard Brandt was one of the leading utilitarian philosophers of the twentieth century. He defended a version of Rule Utilitarianism, but later, in his book *A Theory of the Right and the Good* (1979), he talks about the preferences you would have if you had gone through a process of cognitive psychotherapy and explored all the reasons for your preferences and rejected any you felt were not true to your real values. He argued that the morality you would then accept would be a form of Utilitarianism – with your preferences free from any psychological blocks and you in full possession of all the facts. Such a person would not, therefore, be influenced by advertising.

STRENGTHS OF UTILITARIANISM

- It is straightforward and based on the single principle of minimising pain and maximising pleasure and happiness. A system which aims to create a happier life for individuals and groups is attractive.
- It relates to actions which can be observed in the real world (e.g. giving to charity promotes happiness for poor people and is seen to be good, whereas an act of cruelty is condemned as bad).
- Its consequentialism is also a strength, as when we act it is only natural to weigh up the consequences.
- Utilitarianism's acceptance of the universal principle is essential for any ethical system. It is important to go beyond your own personal point of view.
- The idea of promoting the 'well-being' of the greatest number is also important – this is the basis of the health care system: care is provided to improve the health of the population and if more money is spent on the health service, people are healthier and therefore happier.
- Preference Utilitarianism also gives us the valuable principle of being an impartial observer or, as Hare puts it, 'standing in someone else's shoes'. It is important to think about others' interests or preferences as long as one also includes behaving justly.

WEAKNESSES OF UTILITARIANISM

- It is good to consider the consequences of our actions, but these are difficult to predict with any accuracy.
- Utilitarianism can also be criticised because it seems to ignore the importance of *duty*. An act may be right or wrong for reasons other than the amount of good or evil it produces. The case of the dying millionaire illustrates this. The millionaire asks his friend to swear that on his death he will give all his assets to his local football club. The millionaire dies and his friend sets about fulfilling his last wishes, but he sees an advertisement to save 1,000,000 people who are dying of starvation. Should

he keep his promise or save 1,000,000 people? However, some promises may be bad and should not be kept. Duty does not stem from self-interest and is non-consequential – is motive more important than outcomes? Should promises be kept, the truth told and obligations honoured? **W.D. Ross** thought that the role of duty had some importance and advocated prima facie duties as more acceptable.

- Utilitarianism can also advocate injustice, as in the case above where the innocent man is unjustly framed for rape to prevent riots.
- Another weakness is the emphasis on pleasure or happiness. If I seek my own happiness it is impossible for me to seek general happiness and to do what I ought to do. The qualitative and quantitative approaches also pose problems, as all we can really do is guess the units of pleasure – how do we measure one pleasure against another? Should we try to maximise the average happiness or the total happiness (e.g. should the government give tax cuts for the minority with the lowest income or spread the cuts more thinly across all tax payers?). Bentham would allow an evil majority to prevail over a good minority and the exploitation of minority groups – does this not go against what we would consider ethical behaviour?
- Utilitarianism does not consider motives and intentions and so rejects the principle of treating people with intrinsic value. Utilitarianism does not take any notice of personal commitments but only considers the consequences of an action. **Bernard Williams** said that we should not ignore integrity and personal responsibility for moral actions, and he uses the story of Jim and the Indians to illustrate this and argues that people need to retain their integrity even if this leads to unwelcome consequences.
- **John Rawls** also argues that Utilitarianism is too impersonal and does not consider the rights of individuals in its attempt to look for the 'greater good'.

Utilitarianism has some major weaknesses as far as duty, justice, motives, intentions and consequences are concerned, and the principles of 'the greatest good for the greatest number' and 'treating people as a means to an end' are rather dubious moral principles. The principles of seeking to act in a benevolent way, trying to apply universality and a consideration of consequences (even if only estimated) are principles that may be used with other, more deontological principles such as duty and integrity. Perhaps we need to combine the best principles from both the teleological and deontological approaches to ethics.

Sir Bernard Williams (1929–2003)

Bernard Williams was born in Southend-on-Sea and studied at Balliol College, Oxford. In 1967 he was made Knightbridge Professor of Philosophy at the University of Cambridge. In 1988 he moved to the USA. He was Professor at Berkeley, California, and White's Professor of Moral Philosophy at Oxford until his retirement in 1996.

He was very interested in politics and sat on several government committees, including those on gambling, drugs and pornography.

John Rawls (1921–2002)

John Rawls was known for his theory of 'justice as fairness'. He taught at Cornell University and Massachusetts Institute of Technology, then moved to Harvard.

He is known for *A Theory of Justice* (1971) and *Political Liberalism* (1993).

APPLICATION OF UTILITARIANISM TO AN ETHICAL DILEMMA – ABORTION

Utilitarianism has little to say on this issue as arguments over whether the foetus is a 'person', whether one person has the 'right' to the use of another's body, whether someone has the 'right' to determine what happens in their own body (Judith Jarvis Thompson) and whether having sex amounts to an 'invitation', and the effects of this, are of little interest to the utilitarian.

The hedonistic approach to Utilitarianism is concerned only with the balance of pleasure and pain. Therefore it is concerned with the amounts of pleasure and pain in situations where abortion is allowed as contrasted with the amounts of pleasure or pain where abortion is forbidden.

One approach to this issue might be to consider the parties involved. If you believe the main consideration to be the interests of the *foetus*, you need to estimate its future happiness and so the conditions of its family and so on. Any suffering involved in the abortion procedure itself can be avoided by simply aborting the pregnancy sooner, before the foetus has developed the capacity to suffer.

The next party to consider are the *parents* and *other family*. Here again the situation needs to be taken into account when determining present and future happiness – financial situation (e.g. single mother on benefits), absent or unknown father, continuation of genetic abnormalities and so on. According to some studies, having a baby appears to decrease the happiness in a relationship, even in those cases where the baby is wanted (see Eysenck on happiness).

Utilitarianism also considers the *community* at large – here there may be no consideration of rights or of emotional or religious arguments, but a consideration of maintaining a population level which is felicifically optimal. Thus Utilitarianism is generally against abortion only when it is generally in favour of raising the population and vice versa.

In utilitarian terms, a general prescription either for or against abortion is hard to justify as each case would be unique – you could argue that if a utilitarian finds herself unexpectedly pregnant she should seek an abortion; if Utilitarianism was in favour of her having a child she should have been trying for a baby and so the pregnancy would be expected. This is of course assuming that the decision is not influenced by her personal desires. (Followers of Hare might wonder if abortion is contrary to prima facie principles and whether these should be changed in the face of the happiness of the whole community.)

Utilitarians faced with the dilemma of abortion have to consider more than the questions of rights and personhood; nor can they decide the rightness or wrongness of abortion simply by considering the consequences and the effects on those involved.

REVIEW QUESTIONS

Look back over the chapter and check that you can answer the following questions:

1　Explain the main principle of Utilitarianism.
2　Explain the Utilitarianism of Bentham.
3　Explain the Utilitarianism of Mill.
4　Explain the differences between Act and Rule Utilitarianism.
5　Complete the following diagram:

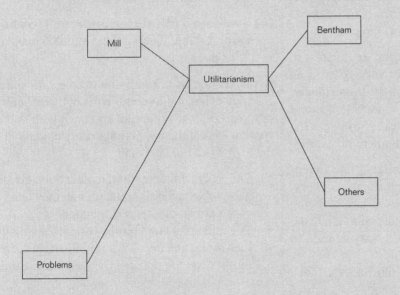

Terminology

Do you know your terminology?

Try to explain the following key ideas without looking at your books and notes:

• 　Consequentialist
• 　Teleological ethics
• 　Act Utilitarianism
• 　Rule Utilitarianism
• 　Preference Utilitarianism

Examination Questions Practice

When writing answers to questions on Utilitarianism, make sure you can explain clearly the different types, as Utilitarianism is more a family of theories than one simple theory.

PAST PAPER QUESTIONS

(a) Explain how Bentham's version of Utilitarianism may be used to decide on the right course of action. (OCR AS Level 2762 June 2003 question 1, 33 marks)

You will need to begin by giving an explanation of Utilitarianism – the rightness or wrongness of an action is determined by its 'utility' or usefulness, which is the amount of pleasure or happiness caused by the action. An action is right if it produces the greatest good for the greatest number.

- You should explain the hedonic calculus (intensity, duration, certainty or uncertainty, closeness or remoteness, the chance it has of being followed by sensations of the same kind, the purity and extent) and how it may be used to measure pleasure and pain.
- You could give examples to illustrate this.
- You may explain that Bentham's version of Utilitarianism is often called Act Utilitarianism, where the principle of utility must be applied for each individual situation.

(b) Evaluate a utilitarian approach to abortion. (OCR AS Level 2762 June 2003 question 1, 17 marks)

Here the question is asking you to assess the different approaches of the various types of Utilitarianism or to contrast the utilitarian approach with that of another ethical theory, perhaps one that considers the foetus as a human being.

- You may consider that most abortions are acceptable to a utilitarian, though they need to consider the long-term consequences.
- The utilitarian view may be contrasted with the idea of the sanctity of life, and the rights of the mother and the rights of the foetus discussed.

SAMPLE AS EXAMINATION QUESTIONS

(a) Explain the main differences between Act and Rule Utilitarianism.
(b) To what extent is Utilitarianism a useful method of making decisions about euthanasia?
(OCR AS Level 2762 specimen question 1)

(a) Describe the main strengths of a utilitarian ethical system.

(b) To what extent is Utilitarianism a useful method of making decisions about abortion?
(OCR AS Level 2762 January 2001 question 1)

(a) Describe the main strengths and weaknesses of Utilitarianism.
(b) Evaluate a utilitarian approach to genetic engineering.
(OCR AS Level 2762 June 2002 question 1)

FURTHER READING

Bentham, J. *Introduction to the Principles of Morals and Legislation*, Harrison, W. (ed.), Cambridge, Cambridge University Press, 1948.

Gensler, H., Earl, W. and Swindal, J. *Ethics: Contemporary Readings*, New York/London, Routledge, 2004 (contains original writings of many classic and contemporary philosophers).

Mill, J.S. *Utilitarianism*, Indianapolis, Hackett Publishing, [1861, 1863], 2002.

Norman, R. *The Moral Philosophers*, Oxford, Oxford University Press, 1998.

Pojman, L.P. *Ethical Theory*, Toronto, Wadsworth, 1989.

Pojman, L.P. *Ethics: Discovering Right and Wrong*, Toronto, Wadsworth, 2002.

Singer, P. *Practical Ethics*, Cambridge, Cambridge University Press, 1993.

Smart, J.J.C. and Williams, B. *Utilitarianism: For and against*, Cambridge, Cambridge University Press, 1973.

7 Religious Ethics
Christian Ethics

For the purpose of this book only Christian ethics will be studied. This chapter covers the requirements for both AS and A2 religious ethics.

Examination questions may be approached by reference to biblical texts and teachings, or by reference to an ethical theory which is essentially religious, or both.

WHAT YOU WILL LEARN ABOUT IN THIS CHAPTER

*   The origins of Christian ethics in Judaism.
*   Christian ethics from the New Testament.
*   The role of authority, tradition and conscience in Christian ethics.
*   The link between religion and morality.
*   Absolutism and relativism in Christian ethics.
*   Christian ethical theories: Divine Command theory, Natural Law and Situation ethics.
*   The relationship between Christian ethics and Utilitarianism.
*   The relationship between Christian ethics and Kantian ethics.
*   The relationship between Christian ethics and contemporary moral thought.

KEY SCHOLARS

*   Thomas Aquinas (1225–1274)
*   Jeremy Bentham (1748–1832)
*   Joseph Fletcher (1905–1991)
*   Immanuel Kant (1724–1804)
*   Søren Kirkegaard (1813–1855)
*   John Stuart Mill (1806–1873)
*   Plato (428–347 BCE)

THE OCR CHECKLIST

- The main ethical principles of any one religion.
- An understanding of how followers of that religion make moral decisions.
- The nature of the ethics of a chosen religion: the main precepts, and the purpose of ethical behaviour; the extent to which religious ethics may be considered deontological or teleological.
- Critical comparisons between the ethics of religion, Utilitarianism, and Kantian ethics.

From OCR A Level Religious Studies Specification 7877.

WHAT IS CHRISTIAN ETHICS?

There is no easy answer to this question, as there is so much diversity within Christianity. Some Christians will base their ethics solely on the Bible and its teachings, others will base their ethics on the biblical teachings but also on Church tradition and **Natural Law**, others will follow a **Situation ethics** approach and others will look to their conscience as a guide. As a result of this diversity, Christians have different responses to ethical issues, whether it is euthanasia, abortion, genetic engineering, foetal research, sex and relationships, war, peace or justice. It is important to understand not only what Christians think on different ethical issues, but also why they think as they do and the basis of their ideas.

In many ways Christian ethics does not look at right and wrong actions, but at the sort of person we are called to become. The Bible teaches that humans are created by God in his image and called to live free and responsible lives, but sin and ignorance have led us to misuse this freedom. In many ways, therefore, Christian ethics has more in common with Virtue ethics than any other ethical theory.

Natural Law
The theory that an eternal, absolute, moral law can be discovered by reason.

Situation ethics
The morally right thing to do is the most loving in the situation.

The Jewish roots of Christian ethics

The early Church brought into Christianity much that belonged to Judaism, and many today would still claim that we can obtain absolute moral rules from the Bible: the Ten Commandments are rules that must be followed without exception, and in the Bible we can find many acts such as homosexuality and divorce that are utterly condemned. However, it is clear that

Christianity left behind the Jewish ethic of law as a divine command made known in a comprehensive legal code and interpreted by lawyers into many ritual requirements and practices. Christians attempted to drop the legalism and keep the law, especially the Ten Commandments, which were seen as an important part of God's revelation and good guidelines for human existence and human flourishing, in accordance with the human nature which God gave us. Jewish ethical teaching, at its core, is based on relationships: our relationship with God and all our many and varied relationships with other people.

Moses and the Ten Commandments. *Moses receives the Tablets of the Law from God on Mount Sinai* (colour litho) by French School (nineteenth century)

© Private Collection/Archives Charmet/The Bridgeman Art Library

The basis of Christian ethics in the Bible

The use of the Bible, both the Old and New Testaments, in Christian ethics is not as straightforward as some would believe; some passages need careful exegesis which is beyond the scope of this book. The Bible is a collection of writings put together over a long period of time and reflecting many different cultural contexts. It is important that this fact is borne in mind and that its diversity is recognised. There is no biblical morality or even New Testament teaching that can be followed in every detail, as it all needs to be understood in its cultural context. Christian denominations have always chosen the Bible teachings that back up their particular take on Christianity, such as the Catholic use of Mark's teaching on divorce and total disregard for Matthew's exception clause, or the Lutheran misuse of Romans (7:1–20):

> For we know that the law is spiritual; but I am of the flesh, sold into slavery under sin. I do not understand my own actions. For I do not do what I want, but I do the very thing I hate. Now if I do what I do not want, I agree that the law is good. But in fact it is no longer I that do it, but sin that dwells within me. For I know that nothing good dwells within me, that is, in my flesh. I can will what is right, but I cannot do it. For I do not do the good I want, but the evil I do not want is what I do. Now if I do what I do not want, it is no longer I that do it, but sin that dwells within me.

The following section will necessarily take a broad-brush approach and follow general themes.

The ethics of Jesus

Although Christian ethics carries with it the Ten Commandments, it is of a totally different mindset from a law-based ethic. It was, from the beginning, attempting to reply to the philosophical questions of *happiness* and *salvation*. Therefore the most concentrated body of ethical teaching in the Gospels, the Sermon on the Mount, begins with the Beatitudes: 'Blessed are the poor . . .'.

The Sermon on the Mount may seem to be a set of impossible commands, but although its teaching is challenging, underlying it all is the commandment of love. However, it is not always easy to see what is meant by 'love': for Jesus in the Synoptics it is love of God and love of neighbour; for Paul it is mostly love of neighbour, especially Christians; John's Gospel seems to speak of love in an even narrower sense. It may be summed up as follows:

'You shall love the Lord your God with all your heart, and with all your soul, and with all your mind.' This is the greatest and first commandment. And a second is like it: 'You shall love your neighbour as yourself.' (Matthew 25:37b–39)

Or:

'In everything do to others as you would have them do to you.' (Matthew 7:12a)

The ultimate Christian ethical teaching seems to centre on love:

Love is the fulfilling of the law. (Romans 13:10b)

This New Testament ethical teaching is part of the relationship with God – what makes Christian ethics different is the 'faith' element; Christian ethics comes from a need to interpret, understand and respond to ethical issues from the point of their particular relationship with God.

Thought Point

Look up some of the following texts to see how Jesus' ethics is based on, yet seems to reinterpret, the Jewish law:

* Matthew 5–7
* Mark 2:23 to 3:6
* Mark 7:1–23

This idea of the special relationship with God is carried on in the idea of the *Kingdom of God*. What the Kingdom of God actually means has been debated endlessly, but it seems to be a state which has arrived, but not yet – a little like a visitor who has arrived at a friend's house and rung the doorbell, but the door has not yet been opened. The problem is how this paradox is to be maintained as far as ethics is concerned. Jesus' ethics can only be connected with the idea of the Kingdom of God by seeing entry into the Kingdom as a result of responding to the appeal to the desire to be children of God; a joyful acceptance of forgiveness and a desire to do God's will. This is no blind obedience, nor is it a morality of law, command, duty and obligation; nor is it motivated by the promise of reward in heaven or punishment in hell, but by a desire to follow God's will – the love commandment.

The ethics of Paul

The other source of biblical Christian ethics is found in the Epistles of Paul. He wrote at a time when the early Christians were attempting to interpret the teachings of Jesus and apply them to a variety of new situations. Paul stresses the importance of Christian freedom, but to be free from the law means to be united with Christ and with one another in love and service. It is *life lived in the Spirit*:

> Live by the Spirit, I say, and do not gratify the desires of the flesh. . . . But if you are led by the Spirit, you are not subject to the law. . . . If we live by the Spirit, let us also be guided by the Spirit. (Galatians 5:16, 18, 25)

For Paul, the whole law may be summed up in *love of neighbour* and this love is limitless, as is shown in the great hymn to love in the Letter to the Corinthians. Paul also calls the Christians to imitate the virtues of Jesus in their daily lives: meekness; gentleness; humility; generosity; mercy and self-giving love. However, the words and life of Jesus could not be made into a blueprint for Christian ethics in the early Church without becoming legalistic, and so it was recognised that following Christ depended on the gift and guidance of the Holy Spirit which was given to the *community* of believers. Paul's list of virtues is called 'the fruit of the Spirit' (Galatians 5:22–23) and love is the greatest sign of the presence and activity of the Holy Spirit (I Corinthians 13).

Christian ethics in this developing Church could be called a *community ethic*: the ethic of a community guided by the Holy Spirit, rather than by law or tradition.

> If then there is any encouragement in Christ, any consolation from love, any sharing in the Spirit, any compassion and sympathy, make my joy complete: be of the same mind, having the same love, being in full accord and of one mind. Do nothing from selfish ambition or conceit, but in humility regard others as better than yourselves. Let each of you look not to your own interests, but to the interests of others. (Philippians 2:1–4)

However, there is no explicit concern with changing society as a whole. The main attitude towards rulers was that of obedience, as their authority was given by God, but if the commands of the state and those of God conflict, then

Aquinas was born in Roccasecca, in Sicily. He died in Fossanova in the Papal States. His feast day is 28 January (originally 7 March).

He studied under the German philosopher Albertus Magnus. He was an Italian Dominican theologian and the foremost medieval scholasticist. He worked on his own ideas from the basis of Aristotle, particularly in the metaphysics of personality, creation and Providence.

Aquinas wished to reconcile faith and intellect. His philosophical works were aimed at a synthesis of the works of

continued opposite

the Christian should obey God. According to Paul the barriers between slaves and free men and women have been broken, both marriage and celibacy are seen as gifts, and wealth is to be shared with those in need. However, there is no evidence of struggling for justice, as it was believed that God would soon intervene in history and establish his kingdom, apart from which Christians were few in number with no political clout. The teaching of love for one's neighbour, however, did eventually lead Christians to exercise greater social responsibility.

Love

This distinctive moral teaching based on love continued to dominate the work of Christian thinkers:

> Love, and do what you will. If you keep silence, keep silence in love; if you speak, speak in love; if you correct, correct in love; if you forbear, forbear in love. let love's root be within you, for from that root nothing but good can spring. (Augustine, *Epistola Joannis* 7.8)

Love, according to **Thomas Aquinas**, is the reason why we were made; it unites us with God and to love is to share his life. Without love no virtue is possible, and love alone leads to happiness and fulfilment.

AUTHORITY AND TRADITION IN CHRISTIAN ETHICS

Although Aquinas followed the early Christian idea of morality as love and grace, not law, it is true that legalism has justifiably been associated with Christian ethics, both in theory and in practice. **Peter Singer** criticises this legalism and accuses Christianity of obscuring the true nature of morality: human fulfilment – happiness. He thinks that the end of the Christian influence on our moral standpoints will open up a 'better way of life for us' and the Judaeo-Christian ethic is 'an empty shell, founded on a set of beliefs that most people have laid aside'. Christian ethics have been seen as deontological and authoritarian, with an emphasis on certain acts as being either right or wrong.

The issue of authority and tradition is treated differently by the different Christian churches. Some *Protestants* see the Bible as the sole authority in every matter and this is more important than the role given to tradition in Catholicism. *Catholics* would argue that scripture does not give guidance on many important matters and so tradition is important, as interpreted by the *magisterium* (the Pope and the bishops). This teaching does not claim to be absolutely accurate or infallible, but is teaching on behalf of the community of the people of God. It can become authoritarian, especially when the issues are new or there is no consensus of views among the episcopacy or the Catholic community – for example, the teaching of *Humanae Vitae* (1968) which banned artificial contraception and has been totally ignored by many Catholics.

This idea of the 'agreement of the faithful' has been further developed by many free churches, which have built their forms of church government on congregational lines – this is going back to Paul's idea of attempting to discern the will of God by the Holy Spirit working in the Christian community. However, many Christian legalists would argue that Christians should keep rules because God has revealed them – is this why Christian ethics has become so irrelevant?

Aristotle and Augustine; of the Islamic scholars Averroës and Avicenna, and of Jewish scholars such as Maimonides and Solomon ben Yehuda ibn Gabirol. His most important theological works are the *Summa Theologiae* and the *Summa Contra Gentiles*. His own system of doctrine, developed by his followers, is known as Thomism.

DIVINE COMMAND THEORY

If God's will is taken as arbitrary, then this does not give any satisfactory explanation for why anyone is morally bound to follow it. If God commands something for good reasons, then it is these reasons which are the source of moral obligations, regardless of God or any religious law.

Does religion give people a reason to be moral? Is there any meaning to life that would make it even possible to talk about morality? In Dostoyevsky's *The Brothers Karamazov*, Ivan says that 'without God everything is permitted' – so does God give a reason to be moral? In Albert Camus' *The Stranger*, the issue of meaning is a central theme – Mersault does not condemn any action as wrong and, when he ends up shooting a complete stranger, he is only sorry that he got caught – killing someone has no more meaning than any other action. However, we do make judgements about what is right and wrong, and many people do so without seeing any involvement from God.

The whole problem of doing something because God commands it was examined by **Plato** in what has become known as the **Euthyphro Dilemma**. Plato asks: 'Is X good because God wills it or does God will it because it is good?'

The first option says that certain actions are good because God commands them – it is the command of God that makes something good or bad. This means that if God commanded 'Make a fat profit', then it would be right – this makes God's commands arbitrary. **Leibniz** in his *Discourse on Metaphysics* sums this up:

So in saying that things are not good by any rule of goodness, but sheerly by the will of God, it seems to me that one destroys, without realising it,

Euthyphro Dilemma
The dilemma first identified by Plato – is something good because God commands it or does God command it because it is good?

all the love of God and all his glory. For why praise him for what he has done if he would be equally praiseworthy in doing the contrary.

The idea that moral rules are true because God commands them is called the **Divine Command theory**. In many ways the laws of the Old Testament may be seen as a good example of this theory (e.g. 'Thou shalt not commit murder'). This view of Christian ethics goes completely against the morality of love and grace, but it was held by many Christian thinkers such as **Duns Scotus**, **William of Ockham** and **Descartes** as well as many conservative Protestants today. If we do good acts simply out of obedience to God, are we being good for the right reasons?

The second option says that God commands things because they are right or wrong in themselves. Murder is wrong in itself and that is why God forbids it. God can see that it destroys life and makes people unhappy, and so it is unlikely that he would ever command it. However, this option seems to be arguing that there is a standard of right and wrong which is independent of God and which influences his commands. **James Rachels** argued that it is unacceptable for religious belief to involve unqualified obedience to God's commands as it means abandoning personal autonomy – the rightness of an action must come from the fact that the action is right in itself.

Divine Command theory
Actions are right or wrong depending on whether they follow God's commands or not.

Thought Point

1 Do we need God to give meaning to life?
2 Do you agree that 'without God everything is permitted'?
3 Explain the difference between 'X is good because God wills it' and 'God wills X because it is good'.
4 Read the Euthyphro Dilemma and work out the key criticisms of the argument.
5 Can morality ever be founded on authority?
6 How do you decide what is good or bad? Justify your view.

SITUATION ETHICS

Situation ethics presumes that it is not necessary to abandon moral autonomy, nor is it necessary to allow everything (antinomianism) or to be totally legalistic. In any situation people need to avoid subjectivism and individualism, and to use in each situation the moral rules of the community, but they should also be prepared to set these aside if love is better served by doing so. Reason, then, is to be used, but based on the Christian principle of *agape*. This centralisation of love is explained most clearly by **Joseph Fletcher** in his book *Situation Ethics* (1963) – nothing is intrinsically good except love. Rules can help us, but they cannot tell us what to do – they are subservient to love. Love wills the good of neighbour, whether we like him or not; love is to be the only motive for action, and consequences need to be taken into account and only the end justifies the means.

Situation ethics has been criticised for being utilitarian and simply substituting love for pleasure, and Fletcher is thought to be rather vague; values and situations are so variable that we cannot easily see all the ramifications, past, present and future. Can Situation ethics be considered Christian? It certainly puts love at the centre, but there are many differences among Christians about what exactly love is and how it is shown. Fletcher's examples are all exceptional cases: Mrs Bergmeier; the last blood plasma to be given to a skid-row drunk or a mother of three; the resistance fighter priest who refused to surrender in spite of the death of hostages. Fletcher's idea of love is not exactly the same as that of Jesus, who individualised love; take, for example, the woman with the haemorrhage, or the healing of the centurion's servant – not a very popular act of love. Fletcher either reinterprets Jesus' actions or dismisses them, so it is hardly surprising that in later life religion played no part in his life and he ceased to describe himself as a Christian Situationist.

Relativism
Nothing may be said to be objectively right or wrong; it depends on the situation, culture and so on.

Teleological ethics
The morally right or wrong thing to do is determined by the consequences.

Thought Point

1   Do you think Fletcher's ethics are Christian?
2   Analyse Fletcher's view that 'the end of love justifies the means'.
3   Is Situation ethics a useful guide for everyday ethical decisions?
4   Are moral rules totally useless in moral decision-making or can you see a role for them?
5   Is the choice for Christian ethics just between legalism and situationism?

NATURAL LAW

A full treatment of Natural Law may be found in Chapter 3.

Natural Law is often seen as centred on law, and so on obligation, and Aquinas himself speaks of the Natural Law. However, by this he meant that our nature is objectively knowable and our reason will help us to understand what is meant by it. Ethics is a matter of our common humanity, not a set of principles from which we make moral decisions, and its purpose is to enable us to become complete and whole humans and to achieve our desires. Morality is rooted in the desire for happiness, but, for Aquinas, Natural Law is not enough if we are to attain final happiness – for this God's grace is needed.

Deontological ethics
Ethical systems which consider that the moral act itself has moral value (e.g. telling the truth is always right, even when it may cause pain or harm).

Natural Law has come to be seen as **deontological** and authoritarian with its application of the primary precepts, but Aquinas said that the primary precepts were always true, as they point us in the right direction; however, different situations require secondary precepts and if our reasoning is faulty these may be wrong – we need to discern what is good and what will help us to become complete and whole human beings. Intention is important, but in Natural Law it is not possible to say that the end justifies the means, although there is certainly flexibility in the Natural Law approach. Aquinas wrote: 'the more you descend into the details the more it appears how the general rule admits of exceptions, so that you have to hedge it with cautions and qualifications'.

However, Aquinas is certain that there is an absolute Natural Law and this has led the Catholic Church, following Aquinas, to emphasise reason as a tool for showing that certain acts are intrinsically right or wrong, as they go against our true purpose; certain **absolutes**, such as the sanctity of life, cannot be changed by the circumstances.

Absolutism
An objective moral rule or value that is always true in all situations and for everyone without exception.

CONSCIENCE

Conscience
Our sense of right and wrong.

Catholics consider that **conscience** plays an important part in Christian ethical decision-making. Here conscience is not seen as some inner voice or oracle which will point us in the right direction – conscience is not about feelings but about reason and judgement. Aquinas saw conscience as reason making moral decisions. But conscience as the 'voice of God' can easily become what we mean by 'right' and 'wrong' – so men persecute 'heretics', slaughter enemies and become suicide bombers in the name of God.

However, conscience does not make the law; it recognises law and uses it to assess conduct. So, for religious ethics, conscience is not so much the voice of God as a response to God's voice. Conscience can be mistaken; doing a bad action when following the guidance of conscience does not make that action good. Conscience is just a way of using reason to come to a decision, but it needs to be informed, and in following conscience we need to be prepared to accept the costs, not just do what we want.

VIRTUE ETHICS

Virtue ethics is also an important source for Christian ethics. Virtue ethics refers to the character of being a good person. This again links back to love as being the highest of all virtues and also the rationale for all the virtues, which simply spell out the form love takes in different circumstances. The virtues, for Christian ethics, point to the goal for which we aim, even if we do not achieve it in this life. This approach to ethics cultivates the inner person and so leads to good actions.

CHRISTIAN ETHICS AND UTILITARIANISM

Is there any link between the deontological commands of the Ten Commandments and the teleological approach of **Utilitarianism**? Natural Law is very different from Utilitarianism, as it maintains that by using our reason we can arrive at moral knowledge and does not believe that the ends justify the means.

Jeremy Bentham reacted against the rule-based morality of his time, with certain actions being intrinsically right or wrong. He was therefore dismissive of any reference to the Bible, conscience or Natural Law as a means of knowing right and wrong. As an empiricist he believed that knowledge had to come from the senses and he tried to make a scientific basis for morality. People should measure the rightness or wrongness of any action in terms of how many units of pain or pleasure it produced – these could be measured quantitatively using the hedonic calculus.

John Stuart Mill calculated pleasures in a qualitative way, regarding intellectual pleasures as superior to merely physical ones. He also thought that most ordinary people should normally stick to some traditional rules, based on utilitarian principles, rather than calculate what they should do in each situation. He likened the principle of utility to Jesus' Golden Rule:

'Love your neighbour as yourself.'
'Do unto others as you would have them do unto you.'

He saw Utilitarianism as universal benevolence, doing good to others and denying self-love. Bentham, in fact, thought that Christianity would support Utilitarianism, as God is supposed to be benevolent.

Situation ethics is accused of being utilitarian and Fletcher recognised the similarity between the two theories. Both are relativist in approach and Fletcher saw love as 'justice distributed' – justice means working out the most loving thing to do for all – which simply replaces the 'good' of Utilitarianism with 'agape'.

Utilitarianism
Only pleasure and the absence of pain have utility or intrinsic value.

John Stuart Mill (1806–1873)

John Stuart Mill (engraving) (b/w photo) by English School (nineteenth century)

© The Illustrated London News Picture Library, London, UK/The Bridgeman Art Library

John Stuart Mill was born on 20 May 1806, the son of James Mill, who had a significant influence on nineteenth-century British thought in philosophy, economics, politics and ethics. From 1822 he worked for his father in India House and stayed there until 1858, when the company closed and he retired. Mill then lived in St Véran, France, until 1865, when he became a Member of Parliament. In 1868 he went to live in France until his death on 8 May 1873. He is most famous for his essay *On Liberty* (1859).

Natural Law is very different from Utilitarianism, as it sees certain actions as intrinsically wrong, regardless of the consequences. Both Utilitarianism and Situation ethics fail to see that love is not always about the collective good, but also about the individual. Love that cares about the individual will not sacrifice the few for the sake of the majority without any attention being given to their particular needs and welfare. Utilitarianism ignores the idea that some actions are intrinsically wrong (e.g. murder).

The empiricism of Utilitarianism results in a very particular under-standing of human nature as only motivated by pleasure/pain. The value of a person, and humanity as a whole, is measured only in terms of experiences with no room for the idea of a human made in the 'image of God' with intrinsic value and rights. The teachings and life of Jesus do not fit with Utilitarianism, except for the manner of his death: 'it is expedient for you that one man should die' (John 11:15a). According to the New Testament Christian ethics, others should always be placed first; we should turn the other cheek, forgive unto seventy times seven and real happiness comes in serving others – how can this be measured using the hedonic calculus?

In Utilitarian ethics motives and character are unimportant compared to the consequences. Unlike Virtue ethics, the act is more important than the agent. In Christian ethics, moral decision-making is about habitual actions, not one-off acts – the virtuous person becomes virtuous by practice. In Galatians 5:22–23 the fruits of the Spirit are shown by the characteristics of Christian living: love, joy, peace, patience, kindness, goodness, faithfulness, gentleness, self-control. Living a Christian ethical life involves modelling one's character on that of Christ.

CHRISTIAN ETHICS AND KANTIAN ETHICS

Kantian ethics would seem, at first glance, to fit in nicely with Christian ethics, especially the second formulation of the categorical imperative which gives humans intrinsic value and says that they should not be treated as 'means to an end but as ends in themselves'. This intrinsic value is clearly seen in biblical ethics: 'So God created man in his own image' (Genesis 1:27a).

For Kant, as for Christian ethics, the end can never justify the means. Kant's idea of universalisability is if you can will your action to be univer-salised, then it would be an action that would be considered good in all situations, including your own. Again this is the same as Jesus' Golden Rule.

However, Jesus teaches that rules are not paramount and that law is given to humans to help them live a good life. Jesus cured people on the Sabbath and, when questioned about this, replies that the Sabbath was made for man, not man for the Sabbath (i.e. man is not subordinate to the law), but Kant enforces rigid rules with no exceptions under his principle of universalisability.

Kant also argues that right moral action can be deduced using reason alone, leaving no room for authority, tradition or even biblical revelation. Kantian ethics are a priori (morality is innate and knowable through reason), unlike Natural Law which is a posteriori and discovers what is right through experience.

APPLICATION OF CHRISTIAN ETHICS TO PRACTICAL ETHICS – THE ENVIRONMENT

The media are full of stories concerning environmental disasters of one kind or another, from global warming to endangered species to destruction of the rain forest. However, there is not a lot of emphasis on this among Christians: some see it as just a liberal or New Age issue; some see it as just plain unimportant, as God will soon destroy everything. However, others do look to Christian ethics to find an answer to the question of our responsibility to the Earth and the creatures on it.

Some people blame Judaeo-Christian teaching for the environmental crisis we now face – they point to Genesis (1:26–28) where humans are given dominion over the Earth. This, they say, has given humanity a licence to exploit the Earth.

Christian ethics, however, points to the creation story – God as creator and man as his steward. All of nature, including man, is equal in its origin, and nature has intrinsic value because God created it and he alone is the owner. In the second creation story God told Adam and Eve to cultivate the garden (Genesis 2:15), and we may certainly use nature for our benefit, but only as God intends. Having dominion means holding in trust.

However, all too often, people evaluate projects in a utilitarian way, by looking at their impact upon humans. The Bible contains many examples of how we are to care for the land and animals (e.g. Leviticus 25:1–12; Deuteronomy 15:4; Isaiah 5:8–10).

Ultimately, Christian ethics is rooted in the relationship with God, and a Christian's relationship with God depends on how he uses creation and contributes to bringing about the Kingdom of God (I Corinthians 15:21–22; Romans 5:12–21). Christians must also observe environmental justice, which means considering how their lifestyles impact on the world. Love of God and love of one's neighbour are fundamental in Christian ethics and apply to the environment also.

REVIEW QUESTIONS

Look back over the chapter and check that you can answer the following questions (Q.5 is more suitable for A2 candidates):

1   Explain the Euthyphro dilemma and how it can be used to criticise Divine Command theory.
2   Is Christian ethics absolute, relative or both? Give your reasons.
3   Is Christian ethics communitarian or individualistic? Give clear explanations.
4   Explain the different approaches of Natural Law and Situation ethics.
5   Can Christian ethics be considered utilitarian?

Examination Questions Practice

As you can see from this chapter, the subject of religious (Christian) ethics is vast and varied. Make sure you know the biblical background and the different approaches.

PAST PAPER QUESTIONS

(a) Explain the ethical teachings of the religion you have studied. (33 marks)

- You may start with biblical ethics and explain ethics as a result of religious belief, and describe the rules, duties and commands from revelation.
- You could also explain that religious ethical behaviour comes from a sense of obedience to God and a desire to live life in the way God wishes it to be lived.
- When explaining Christian ethics you can refer to and explain Natural Law, Situation ethics and Virtue ethics.

- If you have studied a different world religion for your AS examination, such as Islam, Judaism, Buddhism or Hinduism, you can explain the main principles of that religion.

(b) 'Religious ethics are too rigid for moral decision-making.' Discuss. (17 marks)

Here you need to evaluate the deontological and teleological approaches to ethics in the context of religious ethics.

- Some may argue that an absolute approach is right and others may reject this.
- If you are answering from the viewpoint of

Christian ethics, you may consider that Christian ethics is mainly deontological and contrast this with a situationist approach or that of Virtue ethics.

SAMPLE AS EXAMINATION QUESTIONS

(a) Give an account of any one religious method of ethical decision-making.

(b) How far can a religious theory of ethics be justified?
(OCR AS Level 2762 January 2002 question 3)

(a) Explain the main ethical principles of the religion you have studied.

(b) '"Treat others the way you would like to be treated yourself" is the most important ethical principle.' How fair is this claim in relation to the religion you have studied?
(OCR AS Level 2762 second specimen question 3)

(a) Explain the main ethical principles of the religion you have studied.

(b) 'A right ethical act is one approved by God.' Discuss.
(OCR AS Level 2762 June 2003 question 3)

(a) Explain one ethical theory that has its basis in religion.

(b) 'It is indefensible to base ethics on religion.' Discuss.
(OCR AS Level 2762 June 2005 question 5)

SAMPLE A2 EXAMINATION QUESTIONS

• Discuss the view that religious ethics need not be deontological, illustrating your answer from the perspective of the religion you have studied.
(OCR A2 Level 2772 June 2002)

• From the religion you have studied, discuss the view that religious ethics must be either deontological or teleological, but cannot be both.
(OCR A2 Level 2772 June 2003 question 2)

• Discuss the view that only a religious ethic can provide an acceptable basis for medical ethics.
(OCR A2 Level 2772 June 2003 question 3)

• Compare and contrast Utilitarianism with the ethics of the religion you have studied.
(OCR A2 Level 2772 June 2005 question 2)

• 'Only religious ethics can provide answers to the problems raised by euthanasia.' Discuss.
(OCR A2 Level 2772 June 2006 question 4)

FURTHER READING

Cook, D. *The Moral Maze*, London, SPCK, 1983.

Hoose, B. (ed.) *Christian Ethics: An Introduction*, London, Cassell, 1998 – contains an excellent chapter on the Bible and Christian ethics by Tom Deidum.

Macquarrie, J. and Childress, J. *A New Dictionary of Christian Ethics*, London, SCM, 1986.

Plato, 'Euthyphro', in *The Last Days of Socrates*, Tredennick, H. (trans.), London, Penguin, 1969.

Rachels, J. and Rachels, S. *The Elements of Moral Philosophy*, New York, McGraw-Hill, 2007.

8 Medical Ethics 1

Abortion and the Right to a Child

Essential terminology

Abortion
AI (artificial
  insemination)
Consciousness
Doctrine of double
  effect
Embryo
Ensoulment
Foetus
Hippocratic Oath
IVF (in-vitro fertilisation)
Ordinary and
  extraordinary means
Personhood
Quality of life
Sanctity of life
Viability

WHAT YOU WILL LEARN ABOUT IN THIS CHAPTER

* The idea of the sanctity of life and how it applies to abortion.
* Ideas of personhood and the status of the foetus.
* The rights of all those involved.
* The approaches of different ethical theories to abortion.
* The question of infertility and the right to a child.
* What IVF involves.
* The approaches of different ethical theories to the question of the right to a child.

Study hint

Many of the issues of medical ethics are shifting all the time as science and technology moves forward.
    To keep up with these issues it is a good idea to keep a folder of relevant newspaper cuttings and to annotate them with how you think the different ethical theories would react to the issue.

KEY SCHOLARS

* Thomas Aquinas (1225–1274)
* Immanuel Kant (1724–1804)
* Jeremy Bentham (1748–1832)
* John Stuart Mill (1806–1873)
* Pope Pius XI (1857–1939)
* Pope Paul VI (1897–1978)
* Judith Jarvis Thompson (1929–)
* Jonathan Glover (1941–)
* Rosalind Hursthouse (1943–)
* Peter Singer (1946–)
* Helga Kuhse
* Mary Anne Warren

THE OCR CHECKLIST

Medical ethics: abortion, the right to a child.

- An understanding of the ways in which the ethical systems of Natural Law, Virtue ethics, Kant, Bentham and Mill may be applied to issues raised by these areas, and religious responses to these issues.
- The ethical issues that arise in the specified areas of medical ethics.
- Basic knowledge of the law and of medical procedures.
- The concepts of the sanctity of life, personhood, rights and consent, in relation to these issues.

From OCR A Level Religious Studies Specification 7877.

WHAT IS ABORTION?

Abortion is the induced termination of a pregnancy to destroy the foetus. In the UK, abortion is legal up to the twenty-fourth week of the pregnancy. After that time an abortion can be carried out if there is a serious threat to the life of the mother or the **foetus** is severely disabled. According to the law, at present a woman must have the agreement of two doctors for the termination. The twenty-four-week rule was introduced in 1991, as it was established then that babies born at twenty-four weeks are viable and with intensive care can survive. The principle behind this ruling is that, whatever the reasons for an abortion, a foetus should be given legal protection if it is possible for it to survive outside the womb. Medical science has now moved on, and there is some pressure to lower the time to twenty weeks, but as yet this has not happened.

Abortion raises some important moral questions:

- What is a person?
- Is all human life intrinsically valuable/sacred?
- Is all intentional killing of people always wrong?
- Is it always a duty to preserve innocent life?
- When does life begin?

Abortion
The termination of a pregnancy by artificial means.

Foetus
An organism in the womb from nine weeks until birth.

Hippocratic Oath
Written in the fifth century BCE, it became the basis for doctors' ethics. Other promises now replace it, but it is specifically against abortion.

When does life begin? *Personhood*

This question is central to the abortion debate and throws up a number of different answers: at conception; some time after conception; at birth. The answer is vital, as once you have decided this is a human being, you need to give that individual rights and protection under the law.

At conception

Pope Pius XI (1857–1939)

Pius XI was born Ambrogio Damiano Achille Ratti on 31 May 1857, at Desio, Lombardy. He was Pope from 1922 to 1939. His motto was 'The peace of Christ in the Kingdom of Christ'. He died on 10 February 1939.

According to the teaching of the Catholic Church, life begins at conception and at this moment the genetic material of both parents mix and form a biologically distinct entity. This is an attractive view as it is so clear-cut, and marks a definite moment when the foetus becomes a human being. In 1869 **Pope Pius XI** in his encyclical *Casti Connubi* stated that the foetus is a human person from the moment of conception and the life of an unborn child is as sacred as that of its mother; this was reinforced by **Pope Paul VI** in his encyclical *Humanae Vitae* in 1968 and again stated in the *Catechism of the Catholic Church* (1994):

> Human life must be respected and protected absolutely from the moment of conception. From the first moment of his existence a human being must be recognised as having the rights of a person – among which is the inviolable right of every innocent being to life.

Pope Paul VI (1897–1978)

Paul VI was born Giovanni Battista Montini on 26 September 1897 at Concesio, Italy. He became Pope in 1963 during the Second Vatican Council. He died on 6 August 1978 at Castel Gandolfo.

There are several biblical quotations which suggest that life begins before birth:

> Before I formed you in the womb I knew you. (Jeremiah 1:5b)

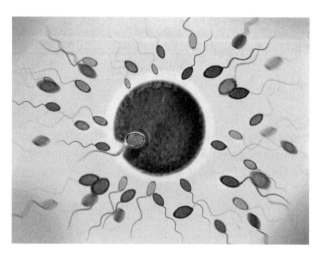

Sperm fertilising egg (digital composite)

Taxi Sarah Jones (Debut Art) Getty Images

For it was you who formed my inward parts; you knit me together in my mother's womb. (Psalm 139:13)

For as soon as I heard the sound of your greeting, the child in my womb leaped for joy. (Luke 1:44)

After conception

As we have seen, according to the Human Fertilisation and Embryology Act of 1991, the foetus is given legal protection from twenty-four weeks if it is possible for it to survive outside the womb. Supporters of the argument that life begins at some point after conception say there is a difference between *potential* and *actual* life. Some would also add that life begins at the moment of implantation in the womb (about six or seven days after conception), others when the heart starts beating or there are signs of brain activity.

Ultrasound image of human foetus (digital enhancement)

The Image Bank (SMC Images) Getty Images

> **Jonathan Glover (1941–)**
>
> Jonathan Glover teaches ethics at King's College, London. He argued that to call a foetus a human person was to stretch the term beyond its natural boundaries. He is quoted as saying: 'Our entanglements with people close to us erode simple self-interest. Husbands, wives, lovers, parents, children and friends all blur the boundaries of selfish concern. Francis Bacon rightly said that people with children have given hostages to fortune. Inescapably, other forms of friendship and love hold us hostage too. . . . Narrow self-interest is destabilized.'

At birth

Thus far there are two clearly defined views of when human life begins – at conception or some time after conception. However, for centuries it was established that birth was the point at which life began and the deliberate killing of a baby after birth was regarded as murder. Some still follow this line; for example, **Mary Anne Warren** argues that birth is the time when the baby no longer relies totally on the mother for his survival. **Jonathan Glover** rejects this, as there are no major differences between a late foetus

Newborn baby

Aurora (Jose Azel) Getty
Images

and a new born or premature baby. He therefore argues for a more flexible
time as the beginning of life.

THE SANCTITY OF LIFE

Sanctity of life
The belief that human life is
valuable in itself.

The teaching on the **sanctity of life** holds that all life is sacred, worthy of
respect and reverence, and intrinsically worthwhile. People therefore have
a duty to preserve life and yet we have very mixed reactions to this idea.

Do we actually see some lives as being more valuable than others? Within
the Christian tradition the views may be roughly divided into strong sanctity
of life arguments and weak sanctity of life arguments.

Thought Point

1   What would your reaction be to the following:

  • A suicide bomber who kills many people in a crowded marketplace.
  • A man who shoots an intruder in his house.
  • A soldier who kills in war.
  • A compulsive serial killer.

2   Do we think some lives are more valuable than others?

  (E.g. how do we justify spending money on fertilisation treatment for a
  couple when the money could be used to improve the quality of life of the
  sick and elderly? Or allowing thousands to die of starvation in Africa? Or
  think it more tragic if a young person dies than if an old person dies?)

Those who hold a strong sanctity of life stance are often called *pro-life* and appeal to the biblical basis of their ideas: God is the giver and creator of life and people have no right to destroy what he has given. People are seen as created in the 'image of God' – *imago dei* – so humans are set apart from other animals and have a 'spark' of divinity within them – the breath of life was breathed by God into Adam. The incarnation, according to Christian teaching, reaffirms the sanctity of human life as God himself became human:

> So God created humankind in his image. (Genesis 1:27a)

> God blessed them, and God said to them, 'Be fruitful and multiply, and fill the earth and subdue it; and have dominion over the fish of the sea and over the birds of the air and over every living thing that moves upon the earth.' (Genesis 1:28)

> And the Word became flesh and lived among us, and we have seen his glory, the glory as of a father's only son, full of grace and truth. (John 1:14)

And if God is the creator of life it is down to him to say when it should start and end. A person does not have the freedom to decide to end his own or anyone else's life.

> He said, 'Naked I came from my mother's womb, and naked shall I return there; the Lord gave, and the Lord has taken away; blessed be the name of the Lord.' (Job 1:21)

Throughout the Bible there is also the command not to take life, and the biblical writers saw this as part of the covenant with God and his people: 'You shall not murder' (Exodus 20:13).

This idea of the sanctity of life is also part of the teaching of *Natural Law* which underlies the ethical teaching of the Catholic Church. Taking life is seen as intrinsically evil and unborn life must be protected. Natural Law states that preserving the innocent is a primary precept and there are no exceptions which make it right.

However, abortion may be justified using the **doctrine of double effect**; for example, in the event of an ectopic pregnancy (where the **embryo** has not implanted in the womb but is developing in the fallopian tubes) it is considered all right to remove the embryo, as the intention is to save the life of the mother rather than to kill the foetus.

This principle is also held by those who hold a weak sanctity of life stance. They realise that the advances of medical science have meant that the

---

Ensoulment

The moment when the soul enters the body – in traditional Christian thought this was at forty days for boys and ninety days for girls. The Church now believes that life begins at conception.

Doctrine of double effect

An action where the main intention is to do good, but which may have a bad side-effect. The good intention makes the action right.

Embryo

The developing bundle of cells in the womb up to eight weeks' gestation.

Ordinary and
extraordinary means
According to Natural Law
moral duties apply in ordinary
situations. A patient may
refuse certain treatments on
the grounds that they are
'extraordinary' (i.e. over and
above the essential).

boundaries between life and death are far more flexible than previously thought and so would allow exceptions to the general sanctity of life position. They would appeal to **extraordinary means** as a justification for killing, and would apply the Christian principle of love and compassion. However, a major criticism of this view is that, like the doctrine of double effect, it is difficult to assess or know true intentions.

Weak sanctity of life is also the basis for other Christian responses to abortion; for example, the Church of England's report of 1965, *Abortion: An Ethical Discussion*, expresses overriding compassion for the needs of the mother, especially where there is a threat to her mental or physical health. This view was reinforced in a more recent document, *Abortion and the Church*, in 1993:

> We do not believe that the right to life, as a right pertaining to persons, admits of no exceptions whatever; but the right of the innocent to life admits surely of few exceptions indeed. Circumstances exist where the character or location of the pregnancy renders the foetus a serious threat to the life and health of the mother, in such circumstances the foetus could be regarded as an 'aggressor' on the mother. The mother would be entitled to seek protection against the threat to her life and health which the foetal life represented.

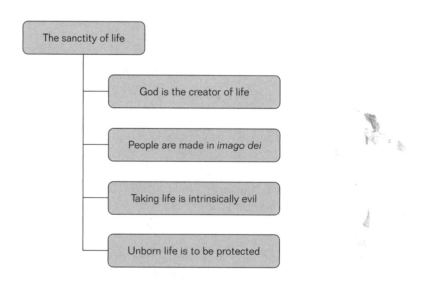

Strengths of the sanctity of life

- It values *all* human life equally, regardless of status or gender.
- It states clearly that killing is always wrong and respects the individual's future.
- It gives everyone equal dignity.
- It avoids too much group pressure and power (e.g. to abort a disabled foetus).

Weaknesses of the sanctity of life

- **Charles Darwin** challenged the biblical view of *imago dei* with his theory of natural selection.
- **Kant** saw no reason to link vital signs to valuing life – but he did link the possession of reason to valuing life.
- **Peter Singer** stated that to treat human life as having a special priority over animal life is 'specieism'.
- So we ought to value all life and not just human foetuses.
- The sanctity of life cannot cope with conflicts of duty – which life is more sacred: that of the mother or that of the foetus?

THE QUALITY OF LIFE

Some scholars think that those who hold a sanctity of life position as regards abortion only make it work by including **quality of life** arguments. The quality of life view allows the value of life to vary with its quality and may factor in the immanence of death, constancy of pain, an ability to think, an ability to enjoy life and make rational choices. However, when considering the foetus there is always the question of who benefits and whose quality of life is being judged: that of the foetus, the parents or society as a whole? There is a danger here of 'playing God' and the quality of life approach may be seen as paternalistic, as it allows others to make decisions. Above all there is the fear that it fails to treat the foetus with dignity and will inevitably lead down a 'slippery slope' to the Holocaust.

However, **Peter Singer** and **Helga Kuhse** both say that there is confusion, and that it would be better to drop the sanctity of life teaching and work out a quality of life ethic instead. This idea is based on what it means to be a person.

Quality of life
The belief that human life is not valuable in itself; it depends on what kind of life it is.

The quality of life

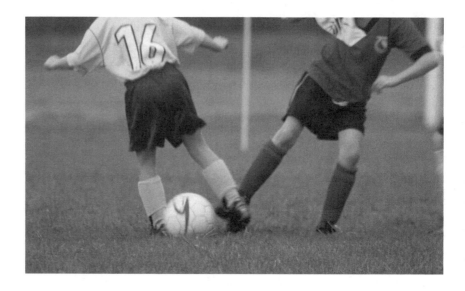

Is the foetus a person? Does the foetus have a right to life?

Thought Point

What do you think makes a human life a person?

This question is vital as the answer depends on whether or not it is right to end the life of the foetus and the answer is crucial for evaluating the following argument:

- The foetus is an innocent person.
- It is wrong to end the life of an innocent person.
- Therefore, it is wrong to end the life of a foetus.

So is a foetus a person, at which stage does it become a person and what are the necessary criteria for personhood?

Consciousness
Awareness of self as an independent being, the ability to feel pain and pleasure.

Personhood
Definition of a human being as a person – having consciousness, self-awareness, ability to reason and self-sufficiency.

It has been argued that a person has to possess a concept of self – a person is self-aware; however, young babies are not self-aware and most people would agree that killing babies is killing human beings.

Other possible criteria also need to be considered:

- A person has to be conceived by humans.
- A person has to have a human genetic structure.
- A person has to look like a human.

- A person has a soul.
- A person is viable – it can survive birth.
- A person has a future like ours.

Mary Anne Warren suggests the following criteria:

- **Sentience** – the ability to have conscious experiences.
- **Emotionality** – the ability to feel happy, sad, loving.
- **Reason** – the ability to solve new and complex problems.
- **The capacity to communicate**.
- **Self-awareness** – awareness of oneself as an individual and as a member of a social group.
- **Moral agency** – the ability to regulate one's actions through moral principles.

She goes on to say that it is not necessary to have all these attributes – many people do not meet all the criteria for personhood and are still considered persons. A foetus, however, does not have any of these attributes and is not a person, though some do develop in later foetuses (e.g. the ability to feel pain). One solution she considers is to regard the foetus as a *potential person*; she rejects this as a basis for giving the foetus a right to life.

Others think this is a significant idea, as if you kill a person the most important thing you take away from them is their future, and the same could be said for a foetus – they and others will never be able to enjoy and benefit from their potential talents. Looking at the foetus as a potential person also removes the difficult speculations about when the foetus has a soul or develops consciousness. But at what point does a foetus become a potential person? In addition, is it right to judge a foetus by what it might be?

It is also possible to argue that even though the foetus is a person, abortion may be morally justified. This is the view of **Judith Jarvis Thompson**, who disputes the idea that 'It is wrong to end the life of an innocent person'. She says that even if a foetus has the same right to life as any other human being, women are not morally obliged to complete every unwanted pregnancy. She bases her argument on the following analogy:

> But now let me ask you to imagine this. You wake up in the morning and find yourself in bed with an unconscious violinist. He has been found to have a fatal kidney ailment, and the Society of Music Lovers has canvassed all available medical records and found that you alone have the right blood type to help. They have therefore kidnapped you, and last night the violinist's circulatory system was plugged into yours, so that your kidneys can be used to extract poisons from his blood as well as your own. The director of the hospital now tells you 'Look we're sorry,

Viability
Where a foetus is considered capable of sustaining its own life, given the necessary care.

the Society of Music Lovers did this to you – we would never have permitted it if we had known. But still, they did it, and the violinist now is plugged into you. To unplug him would be to kill him. But never mind, it's only for nine months. By then he will have recovered from his ailment, and can safely be unplugged from you.' Is it morally incumbent on you to accede to the situation? (Judith Jarvis Thompson, *A Defence of Abortion*)

This story raises a number of moral issues about rights and duties, but Judith Jarvis Thompson concludes that unwilling persons should not be required to be extremely Good Samaritans, whether towards violinists or towards foetuses, and suggests that there is a great gap between the claim that a human being has a right to life and the claim that other human beings are morally obliged to do whatever is necessary to keep him alive.

Thought Point

1   Do we become an individual with rights only at birth?
2   Is the foetus a separate individual like the violinist or is it part of the woman's body?
3   Would unplugging the violinist be the same as actively killing him?
4   The violinist was forced on the woman against her will; does this mean that this argument only supports abortion in cases of rape?
5   Is there a point at which a foetus is not a human being?
6   Does a person's right to life outweigh your right to decide what happens in and to your body?

As we have seen, a potential life cannot have rights and obligations – sperm has the potential to become a human being, yet nobody would claim that a sperm is a human being and should be treated as such. However, when a couple voluntarily cause an egg to be fertilised by a sperm with the intent of creating another life, there is a right to be born. What if the fertilisation was involuntary (rape) or accidental? This is what Judith Jarvis Thompson is examining – even if it is agreed that the embryo has the right to be kept alive, the mother cannot be obliged to carry this unwanted embryo. In addition, does the embryo have the right to use the mother's body and resources in order to sustain its own life?

A further problem about when a foetus becomes a person is the question of twins and the stage at which an embryo might divide into two or more individuals. Conception is not a single act but a process, and until about the fourteenth day it is not possible to say whether there will be a single or a multiple birth. Is it, then, possible to say that the single genetic identity established at conception is the basis for personhood? The Warnock Committee, whose recommendations were the basis for the 1990 Human Fertilisation and Embryology Act, chose the fourteenth day to distinguish the individual human embryo from a collection of cells and allowed them to be used for experimentation up to this stage. **Jonathan Glover** also argues that to call a foetus a person from conception stretches the term beyond normal boundaries.

APPLYING ETHICAL THEORIES TO ABORTION

Utilitarianism

Basic principle – the greatest good for the greatest number.

Utilitarianism does not accept the principle that human life has absolute value and that this should be upheld whatever the consequences, but attempts to assess each individual situation on its own merits to promote the greatest happiness for those concerned.

However, Utilitarianism only works if it is actually possible to assess the results of an abortion and decide whether they favour all concerned. In practice this is difficult as we cannot predict all consequences – the mother may react badly to the operation, which may go wrong, leaving her unable to have further children and so on.

Preference Utilitarianism might be a better approach to abortion, as it considers the preferences of the mother, the harm to other family members and so on.

Utilitarianism does not have one blanket answer to the question of abortion, but looks at the merits of each individual situation – it is easy here to make a judgement that depends primarily on an emotional response to a difficult situation.

Situation ethics

Basic principle – agape which wills the good of others.

Joseph Fletcher said that legalism should not deny compassionate treatment of a woman wanting an abortion. Each case is unique. He argued this using the example of the case in 1962 of an unmarried schizophrenic girl who was raped by another patient in a mental hospital – he stated: 'No unwanted and unintended baby should ever be born.'

However, Fletcher does not see all the consequences and he is not clear as to whether the foetus should be considered. He sees abortion as a form of self-defence, even though the foetus is innocent in the case cited above. Abortion, according to Situation ethics, has to be the most loving thing to do in the situation and so it is not possible to say whether abortion is always right or always wrong.

Natural Law

Basic principle – everything is created for a purpose and when this is examined by human reason, a person should be able to judge how to act in order to find ultimate happiness.

Natural Law does not look at the people involved in a decision about abortion, or the consequences of the action; instead, Natural Law considers the act of abortion itself. Reproduction is a primary precept and abortion goes against this, as it stops the purpose and outcome of procreation. In addition, if you consider the foetus to be a human person from conception, then abortion also goes against the primary principle to preserve innocent life.

Kantian ethics

Basic principle – the categorical imperative: universal maxims; treating others as ends in themselves and living in a Kingdom of Ends.

Immanuel Kant argued that reason enabled people to impose such laws upon themselves and when the categorical imperative is applied to abortion there are immediate difficulties. Abortion would be hard to universalise, as there are so many different situations and motivations for obtaining an abortion – all consideration of emotions is to be disregarded and yet abortion is an emotional decision, especially in situations where the mother has been raped, is very young or is carrying a severely disabled foetus. Kant would also take no account of the stage of pregnancy at which the abortion is to take place.

There is also the emphasis on treating people as ends in themselves and not as a means to an end – abortion would go against this if the foetus is considered to be a person.

Kant's stress on acting out of duty alone, with no account taken of compassion or love, means that all consequences are ignored whatever they may be. However, one could say that Kant does consider the human rights of the foetus.

Virtue ethics

Basic principle – person-centred rather than act-centred or result-centred.

It is difficult to apply Virtue ethics directly to the question of abortion – would a virtuous person ever have an abortion? If so, when? In what circumstances? In some situations the outcome of having an abortion may indeed be virtuous and may help human flourishing. However, there are many points to consider relating to human life, death, parenthood and family relationships. **Rosalind Hursthouse** says that Virtue ethics would need to consider the virtues of all the parties involved and whether the outcomes would lead to a virtuous life or whether some outcomes should be avoided.

THE RIGHT TO A CHILD

The first ever 'test-tube baby', Louise Brown, was born in the UK in 1978, and since then this issue has become more important in ethics as reproductive techniques have developed. This chapter needs to be read alongside Chapter 10, which considers the issue of embryo research.

Discussions about the right to a child cover issues such as whether a child is a gift or a right, whether it is right to obtain sperm samples by masturbation, whether it is right to pay someone to carry a baby and what the moral status of the foetus is on its journey from zygote to newborn baby. The process of **IVF** itself also raises ethical questions, as many more embryos are made than are needed.

There is also the problem of the fact that some of these techniques involve a third party in the sexual relationship – possibly posing physical risks to the resulting baby and replacing normal sexual activity as a method of reproduction.

IVF has the intention of overcoming the common problem of infertility, and may be seen as a practical solution to a medical problem. However, does this mean that the rights of the infertile to reproduce are of prime importance? This is clearly different from the right to have children, as the latter may simply lead the infertile to demand more liberal adoption laws, which this does not seem to be the case. One of the questions to consider in this chapter is whether there is a *right* to reproduce.

AI (artificial insemination)
The injection of sperm into a woman.

IVF (in-vitro fertilisation)
The procedure by which sperm and eggs from a couple are fertilised in a laboratory dish (in vitro = in glass; test-tube babies)

What is IVF?

There are different forms of reproductive technologies – called IVF for the purpose of this chapter.

- AIH = artificial insemination by the husband, where the husband's sperm is injected into the wife's reproductive tract.
- AID = where donor sperm is used.
- IVF = in-vitro fertilisation – outside the human body using the sperm of a husband or donor, and the egg of the wife or a donor egg.

Ethical questions raised by IVF

- When does human life begin and what is the status of the embryo? This involves considering whether human life only starts at implantation in the uterus, and if, as is most likely in the future, artificial wombs are developed, will the resulting human beings be human?
- IVF is supposed to be for treating infertility, but what about the spare embryos that may be kept for up to fourteen days for experimentation?
- The screening of embryos before implantation means that any imperfections can be weeded out. Will this lead parents to choose to remove undesirable traits and who is to decide what is undesirable?
- Custom-made or 'designer' babies. In India already all IVF clinics allow sex selection and nearly all discarded embryos are female. In the future even the genetic make-up of a child could be chosen.
- Older women, past child-bearing age, will be able to have children. This is already the case and a 60-year-old Italian woman has had a child in this way. Women who want to follow a career will possibly be able to store eggs when young and fertile and use them later, achieving pregnancy through IVF.
- IVF means that a quick, if not easy, fix has been found to the problem of infertility and miscarriages, so there is less research into the causes of infertility with a view to prevention.
- Embryos are treated as properties.
- IVF is not very successful. It is expensive and the hormone drugs used to increase fertility are potentially dangerous.

Does an individual have a right to a child?

In 1948 the UN Declaration of Human Rights stated that there is 'a right to marry and found a family free from constraint', but this does not clearly state that there is a right to reproduce. The right to reproduce seems to have followed the technological advances in assisted reproduction. It could, however, be argued that reproduction is fundamental to our freedom to act – but society already places restrictions on this; for example, incestuous reproduction. It could be argued that the right to reproduce is simply a basic need or desire – or do we just have a basic sexual drive rather than a need to continue the human race with our own genes? Reproduction may be seen as contributing to an individual's quality of life and may give her life meaning. Reproduction is seen as a fundamental choice that individuals must be allowed to make, and the lengthy, often unsuccessful and costly treatments reinforce the view that women are 'desperate' to reproduce and so have the right to do so.

Another factor that requires ethical consideration is the increase in foetal screening. This is aimed not only at genetically selecting embryos to aid sick siblings but also at making sure that technology is used to produce only 'perfect' children and to screen out any disabilities.

Who has the right to a child?

Married couples and possibly unmarried couples would head the list. However, what if the couple divorced or separated or, as in the case of Diane Blood, one partner died? Does the right then no longer exist?

The question is made even more complex when surrogate motherhood is considered. This was shown in the case of baby M in the USA – in the court case which followed, the ruling was that the Stern couple had a right to reproduce by whatever means. Mary Beth Whitehead was referred to as the surrogate mother as if Elizabeth Stern was the 'real' mother, despite the fact that the child was not carried by her and nor was it in any way genetically related to her. The court was actually defending the right of William Stern to reproduce – by whatever means. IVF would not have helped William Stern, so do men have as much right to reproduce as women?

IVF uses considerable medical resources that could otherwise be used to treat those with more serious illnesses, and so one solution might be to limit the use of IVF to those whose reproductive ability has been damaged by medical treatments or by exposure to dangerous working conditions.

Thought Point

1   Should IVF be available to all?
2   How should it be paid for? Is IVF a waste of money?
3   What restrictions would you place on it?
4   Who should be allowed to have IVF – married couples? unmarried couples? homosexual couples? single people?
5   Should surrogate mothers be allowed?

continued

6   Why should a child created by sperm or egg donation be allowed to trace
    their biological parent?
7   What should be done with spare embryos?
8   Is IVF demeaning to women?
9   Is IVF 'playing God' or 'co-operating with God'?

APPROACHES TO IVF AND THE RIGHT TO A CHILD

Religious ethics

Nine years after the birth of the first 'test-tube' baby, Louise Brown, the
Catholic Church published the document *Donum Vitae*. The Church welcomed Louise Brown as a gift and as a unique person, but expressed doubts
about the process of IVF and the resulting science of human embryology.
The creation of a surplus of human embryos in a laboratory made it possible
to experiment on them – many embryos would never be transferred to a
womb as Louise was.

The Catholic Church sees human life as sacred, with the parents as co-
creators of new life – the baby is the result of the love the couple have for
each other. IVF takes the new baby away from that expression of love and
becomes simply part of a process:

> IVF and ET [embryo transfer] is brought about outside the bodies of the
> couple through actions of third parties whose competence and technical
> activity determines the success of the procedure.

The Church sees the life of the embryo as entrusted to doctors, and technology as dominant in creating new life. The Catholic Church also sees every
human life from the first moment of conception and at every stage of development, however early, as worthy of protection.

The Catholic Church does not approve of IVF, nor of the destruction of
human embryos, nor of the freezing of embryos, nor of surrogacy; however,
the Church does not disapprove of experiments on human embryos that are
therapeutic and will assist the embryo to overcome the effects of disease.

Protestant ethics see the question of IVF differently. Paul Ramsay has a
Christocentric approach and opposes AID, as it 'means a refusal of the image
of God's creation in our own'. Reproduction should only be within marriage,
as that is the only way to remain faithful to God, since the love between
husband and wife should reflect the love of Christ for the Church.

Joseph Fletcher, on the other hand, was not negative towards IVF or even AID. His Situation ethics was person-centred and saw that there were higher values in a couple's relationship than their biological relationship to their children. Fletcher did not see a third person as personally involved in the sexual relationship – what mattered was the outcome: pregnancy. Using IVF means that humans are using their technologies and creative skills for compassionate reasons.

Natural Moral Law

Natural Law would have many problems with IVF. First of all, there would be the problem of masturbation in order to obtain the necessary sperm – this would be a misuse of the genitalia and would not be following the natural function. IVF also results in the destruction of embryos and the first primary precept demands the protection of innocent life.

Natural Law is an absolute theory and does not take into account any consideration of the outcomes of an action, whether these be the creation of new life or the health benefits from research on spare embryos.

Utilitarianism

The utilitarian approach to this issue would consider the pleasure/pain principle and measure the pain of the unused embryos against the pleasure of the parents and the baby which was created. A utilitarian would also consider the low success rate and the effect this may have on the happiness of the couple, their family and friends. Utilitarianism does not protect the rights of the embryo, nor does it see it as sacred in any way.

Finally, there is the problem of the cost to the health service and whether the money could be better spent saving more lives and so increasing the happiness of the majority. In addition, in considering the population problems the world is facing and the resulting poverty, a utilitarian would ask whether it is ethical to spend money on assisting reproduction for a few and so adding to the population of the world and the pain of the many.

Kantian ethics

Kantian ethics, following the categorical imperative, would require that people are treated as ends in themselves. If the embryo is considered a person, a follower of Kantian ethics would need to ask whether the destruction of so many embryos in order to create one life is justified. There is also a danger of treating the creation of human life as just another consumer good. Selecting an embryo as a genetic match to cure another sibling could also be seen as using the embryo as a means to an end, as would using a surrogate mother. It would also consider the question of universalisation and whether IVF is to be offered to every infertile couple.

REVIEW QUESTIONS

Look back over the chapter and check that you can answer the following questions:

1   Explain the importance of the question 'When does life begin?'.
2   What is meant by the idea of the sanctity of life and what Bible teachings would you use to explain the sanctity of life?
3   Is the sanctity of life a convincing argument against abortion or the right to a child? Explain your reasons.
4   Make a chart applying ethical theories to abortion.
5   Explain whether you think a child is a right or a gift. Give reasons.
6   List the main ethical problems raised by IVF.
7   Make a chart applying ethical theories to the right to a child.

Terminology

Do you know your terminology?

Try to explain the following ideas without looking at your books and notes:

1   Consciousness
2   The doctrine of double effect
3   Ensoulment
4   Personhood

Examination Questions Practice

Be careful not to be side-tracked by the question and just write everything you know about abortion.

PAST PAPER QUESTIONS

(a) Explain how a follower of Natural Law might approach the issue of abortion. (OCR AS Level 2762 second specimen question 2, 33 marks)

You would need to explain the theory of Natural Law as associated with Aquinas, influenced by Aristotle. Key points to include would be:

- Natural Law is absolutist and deontological, depending on the idea that God created things to fulfil a purpose.
- Human reason should be used to work out how to act morally.
- This should then be applied to the question of abortion by explaining how in Natural Law the preservation of the innocent is a primary precept and that the foetus deserves the same status as a born human.
- The concept of primary and secondary principles.

- The doctrine of double effect could also be applied to abortion, explaining how Natural Law would allow this.

(b) 'A woman has the right to choose an abortion.' Discuss. (OCR AS Level 2762 second specimen question 2, 17 marks)

- You could consider the rights of the foetus as against those of the mother, any other children and the rights of the father.
- Potential life may be considered as against actual life.
- On the other hand, you might include sanctity of life arguments and the question of person-hood and the concept of soul.
- This could be contrasted with the woman's rights over her body, her choice to have sexual intercourse and whether her life is threatened.

SAMPLE AS EXAMINATION QUESTIONS

(a) Explain how the principles of Natural Law might be applied to decisions about fertility treatment.
(b) 'Every adult has the right to become a parent.' Discuss.
  (OCR AS Level 2762 specimen question 4)

(a) Explain the argument that all women have the right to a child.
(b) 'The right to a child should not be an absolute right.' Discuss.
  (OCR AS Level 2762 June 2005 question 6)

(a) Explain the arguments against moral absolutism.
(b) How useful is absolute morality in dealing with the issues surrounding the right to a child?

(a) Explain how the principles of Natural Law might be applied to the argument that every woman has the right to a child.
(b) To what extent could a believer in the Natural Law theory accept foetal research?
  (OCR AS Level 2762 June 2001 question 3(b)(i) and (ii))

(a) Describe the main strengths of a utilitarian ethical system.
(b) To what extent is Utilitarianism a useful method for making decisions about abortion?

(a) Describe the main features of moral absolutism.
(b) Discuss the claim that an absolutist morality is the best way of preserving the sanctity of life.
(OCR AS Level 2762 June 2002 question 3)

(a) What is Virtue ethics?
(b) Discuss the view that it is never virtuous to obtain an abortion.
(OCR AS Level 2762 June 2002 question 4)

(a) Explain how a follower of Natural Law might respond to issues raised by abortion.
(b) 'A Natural Law approach is the best approach to abortion.' Discuss.
(OCR AS Level 2762 second specimen question 2)

FURTHER READING

Glover, J. *Causing Death and Saving Lives*, London, Penguin, 1990.

Hinman, L. 'Ethics Updates', available at http://ethics.acusd.edu/.

Kuhse, H. 'Why Killing Is Not Always Worse – and Sometimes Better – than Letting Die', in *Bioethics – An Anthology*, Kuhse, H. and Singer, P. (eds), Oxford, Blackwell, 1999.

Lafollette, H. (ed.) *Ethics in Practice – An Anthology*, Oxford, Blackwell, 2002 (contains articles by Judith Jarvis Thompson, Mary Anne Warren and Rosalind Hursthouse on abortion).

Macquarrie, J. and Childress, J. *A New Dictionary of Christian Ethics*, London, SCM, 1986.

Singer, P. *Rethinking Life and Death*, Oxford, Oxford University Press, 1994.

9 Medical Ethics 2

Euthanasia and the Right to Life

Essential terminology

Active euthanasia
Assisted dying/suicide
Autonomy
Involuntary euthanasia
Passive euthanasia
PVS (permanent
 vegetative state)
Slippery slope
Voluntary euthanasia

WHAT YOU WILL LEARN ABOUT IN THIS CHAPTER

*   Definitions of the different types of euthanasia.
*   The idea of the sanctity of life and how it applies to euthanasia.
*   Ideas of autonomy.
*   The difference between killing and letting die/acts and omissions.
*   The approaches of different ethical theories to euthanasia.

KEY SCHOLARS

*   Thomas Aquinas (1225–1274)
*   Immanuel Kant (1724–1804)
*   Jeremy Bentham (1748–1832)
*   John Stuart Mill (1806–1873)
*   Germain Gabriel Grisez (1929–)
*   Jonathan Glover (1941–)
*   James Rachels (1941–2003)
*   Peter Singer (1946–)
*   Helga Kuhse
*   Joseph Boyle
*   Daniel Maguire (1931–)

THE OCR CHECKLIST

Medical ethics: euthanasia, the right to a life.

*   An understanding of the ways in which the ethical systems of Natural Law, Virtue ethics, Kant, Bentham and Mill might be applied to issues raised by these areas, and religious responses to these issues.
*   The ethical issues that arise in the specified areas of medical ethics.
*   Basic knowledge of the law and of medical procedures.
*   The concepts of the sanctity of life, personhood, rights and consent, in relation to these issues.

From OCR A Level Religious Studies Specification 7877.

Study hint

Many of the issues of medical ethics are progressing all the time as science and technology move forward.

To stay abreast of these issues it is a good idea to keep a folder of relevant newspaper cuttings and annotate them with how you think the different ethical theories would react to the issue.

WHAT IS EUTHANASIA?

'Euthanasia' comes from the Greek *eu* meaning 'well' and 'easy', and *thanatos* meaning 'death'. Euthanasia is the intentional premature ending of another person's life either by direct means (**active euthanasia**) or by withholding medical treatment, food and hydration (**passive euthanasia**), because the patient asks for it (**voluntary euthanasia**) or without their express request (**involuntary euthanasia**).

The ending of a life by euthanasia may thus be either through acts of omission or through intentional acts.

The debate about euthanasia includes the following issues:

- The sanctity of life and the idea that it is God-given.
- The maintenance of life as an absolute.
- Is the act in itself wrong or do the consequences make it wrong?
- The question of personal autonomy.
- The motives that lead to euthanasia.
- The difference between killing and letting die.

EUTHANASIA, PERSONHOOD AND THE SANCTITY OF LIFE

There is an explanation of the sanctity of life and personhood in Chapter 8 on abortion, but we also need to consider its particular application to the question of euthanasia. Human life is recognised by most people as 'something sacred', and believers also see it as a 'gift from God'. There are, however, different views on what it is that makes us human: many believers would say that we are human from conception or at the latest from birth, whereas others might say that we can only be considered human when we think and act as conscious human beings. According to the first viewpoint, we are fully human whether we are embryos or comatose patients – immature or damaged we are still persons, whereas others may argue that a patient who is in a **persistent vegetative state (PVS)** may be a human but is not really a person because he or she is unable to be so; thus in all important aspects they are already dead. If this view of personhood is taken to its logical conclusion, all sorts of people, including the mentally disabled and the paralysed, could also be considered as incomplete persons and so already dead.

The sanctity of life is central to the Catholic position, set out in the *Declaration on Euthanasia* (1980), which defines euthanasia as 'an act or an omission which of itself or by intention causes death, in order that all suffering may in this way be eliminated'. To do this to another or to ask it for oneself is not allowed – in accordance with Natural Law; the first primary

---

Active euthanasia

The intentional premature termination of another person's life.

Passive euthanasia

Treatment is either withdrawn or not given to the patient in order to hasten death. This could include turning off a life-support machine.

Voluntary euthanasia

The intentional premature termination of another person's life at their request.

Involuntary euthanasia

This term is used when someone's life is ended to prevent their suffering, without their consent, even though they are capable of consenting.

PVS (permanent vegetative state)

When a patient is in this condition, doctors may seek to end their life. The relatives have to agree and usually the patient must be brain-stem dead.

A syringe

precept is self-preservation and so death should not be hastened by euthanasia. The document does, however, recognise that while a time to prepare for death is useful, suffering can be so great both physically and psychologically that it can make a person wish to remove it whatever the cost. It accepts that very few can follow the path of Mother Teresa of Calcutta and limit the dose of painkillers so as to unite themselves with the sufferings of Christ, but it also says that 'suffering has a special place in God's plan of salvation'.

The doctrine of double effect plays an important part in Catholic thinking about euthanasia according to the teaching of Pope Pius XII, which distinguishes between painkillers that have a secondary effect of shortening life and drugs used to hasten death with a secondary effect of killing pain. It is the intention which is all important. The document says that it is 'important to protect, at the moment of death, both the dignity of the human person and the Christian concept of life against a technological attitude that threatens to become an abuse'. The document refers to 'ordinary' and 'extraordinary' means – ways of attempting to save life which are disproportionate to the pain suffered. A major problem here is how 'extraordinary' means are to be measured – there is a lack of clarity here, as fifty years ago a patient kept alive today on a life-support machine would have died. Issues of quality of life are now being seen as important, and when death is imminent a patient may refuse unnecessary treatment so long as 'the normal care due the sick person is not interrupted'. The introduction of proportionalism is significant but not all Catholic scholars would agree with this.

Germain Grisez and **Joseph Boyle** stress the importance of personhood and reject the view that one can cease to be a person and yet be bodily alive – they do not accept that a patient in a persistent vegetative state has lost that which makes them distinctively human: a human being is one, and bodily life is seen as a good in itself. Grisez and Boyle say that there are certain basic goods necessary for human well-being, including play and recreation, knowledge of the truth, appreciation of beauty, life and health, friendship and integration. They do not require this list to be in any particular order but they would absolutely reject euthanasia, as it attempts to achieve one good, such as freedom and dignity, by putting it in direct conflict with another: life and health. These basic goods cannot be compared or balanced off each other, and the key issue for them where euthanasia is concerned is that it is against the basic good of life.

The question of personhood, however, lies at the heart of the proportionalist position held by **Daniel Maguire**. This view states that life is a basic but not an absolute good and, while it is important to respect and value life, nobody should always be obliged to prolong it in every situation. Maguire rejects the idea that God alone has the power over life and death and that God alone should decide the time of death for each person; this seems to imply that we belong to God and are his property. He points out that we do, in fact, intervene to save life and to preserve it, and that there is no real difference between ending life and preserving it so long as the principle of achieving a good death is adhered to. Maguire uses the ideas of weighing up the proportional values of living in any condition and choosing a good death in certain specific circumstances. He recognises that this is a departure from the traditional Christian ethic of 'not destroying innocent life', and that making judgements between conflicting values is difficult and can lead to mistakes, but ethical reflection can lead to euthanasia being on some occasions a legitimate moral choice.

Euthanasia may also be seen as legitimate once the dying process has begun – this view still maintains the sanctity of life and respects life, but the dying process shows that life has reached its limit. The use of euthanasia to shorten the time taken to die by not prolonging life is considered legitimate, as humans can still have power over this without denying the sanctity of life.

Peter Singer believes that the traditional sanctity of life ethic must collapse and we need to develop a new ethic, as people now believe that the low quality of a person's life, as judged by the person, can justify them taking their life or justify someone else doing it for them. In cases where a person cannot make a judgement or express a view about the quality of their own life, someone else should do it for them. However, there is so much more that contributes to the quality of a person's life than that which can be measured medically, and Singer also fails to consider that a person's life has a value to the wider community as well as to the individual.

Consideration of the quality of life looks at whether the use of extraordinary means would usefully improve the quality of life of the patient. This idea is basically utilitarian, as doctors consider the possible length of life of the patient, their state of mind, how the procedure would enhance their life, the resources needed and even the resources available – essentially the QUALYS (quality adjusted life year schedules) used in the USA. This is very different from the Catholic view which allows the patient to refuse treatment if there is 'an acceptance of the human condition, or a wish to avoid the application of a medical procedure disproportionate to the results that can be expected, or a desire not to impose excessive expense on the family or the community'. No one is obliged to have a medical procedure which is risky or burdensome.

EUTHANASIA AND THE RIGHT TO LIFE

A person's right to life corresponds to the duty of others not to kill that person. The idea of a duty not to kill seems to rule out any form of euthanasia – but we do not see the duty not to kill as absolute, as we think some wars can be justified, or killing in self-defence or in the defence of others as justified; even capital punishment is justified by some people. It is, in fact, easier to justify killing in voluntary euthanasia, where the person chooses death, than in these other cases, where the person who dies does not choose to do so. Life is a person's most valued and precious possession; can this then be just overturned if the person no longer wishes to live? Can the right to life, like any other right, be overturned or renounced? If that happens, can others say that they have a duty to kill him? If the person asks for voluntary euthanasia, is he then actually asserting his right to be killed in a particular way? However, who then has the duty to kill him? Many doctors who are happy to let people die, withdraw treatment or even assist suicide may not be so happy about having a positive duty to kill at a patient's request.

Thought Point

1   Is the sanctity of life ethic out of date? What could replace it?
2   What problems do you see in the doctrine of double effect?
3   Is there any point to suffering and can it help a person to become nearer to God?
4   What problems do you foresee in stressing the quality of life?
5   Is it wrong to help humans to die when they are actually dying? How do we decide when the dying process has begun?

EUTHANASIA AND SUICIDE

Suicide is the deliberate terminatation of one's own life, and many people, not only those who are religious, are appalled that people could even think of choosing death over life. They feel it demeans life and denies its meaning. All sorts of things give our life meaning – it may be 'God's plan' or it may be

Assisted dying/suicide
When a person takes their own life with the assistance of another person. When the other person is a doctor, it is called physician-assisted suicide.

family or career – and suicide makes all this meaningless and trivial, as the act is not natural and breaks the timeless cycle of birth and death.

Henry Sidgwick said that only conscious beings can appreciate values and meanings, and so they see life as significant and part of some eternal plan, process or design. Suicide, therefore, is a statement by an intelligent, conscious being about the meaninglessness of life, but it is a statement which society rejects and in the past suicide was seen as a criminal act.

Suicide, then, breaks the social contract, but it also breaks the bond between God and man – Thomas Aquinas also saw suicide as an unnatural act and a rejection of God's gift of an immortal soul. This view lay at the heart of the old legislation about suicide, which the state had a right to prevent and punish.

Today suicide is no longer illegal but the state still attempts to treat people as possessions and not allow them full autonomy and freedom – so the 'nanny state' protects drug addicts, alcoholics, smokers and the obese from themselves.

However, suicide is subject to a double moral standard: self-sacrifice in the form of martyrdom either for religious or political beliefs is admired, and for a believer such a death is seen as part of a journey leading to life with God; to die on the battlefield is courageous, and many people are involved in life-threatening occupations such as the fire and rescue service, the armed forces and the police; certain industries such as the manufacture of cigarettes, alcohol and armaments increase the mortality rate. Death here is controlled by religion, the state and political parties, whereas suicide is a free act and does not serve any social ends or uphold group values and structures.

- Is it morally justified to commit suicide to avoid forthcoming pain, loss of self-control or coma?
- Is it morally justified to ask others to help you commit suicide if you are incapable of doing it yourself?

EUTHANASIA AND PERSONAL AUTONOMY

John Stuart Mill (*On Liberty*, 1859) writes that in matters that do not concern others individuals should have full autonomy. Those who support voluntary euthanasia believe that personal autonomy and self-determination are paramount and any competent adult should be able to decide on the time and manner of their death.

The right to have one's life ended by euthanasia is the subject of ethical, social and legal limitations. In some countries such as the Netherlands and Belgium it is allowed and socially acceptable to have a doctor end one's life if death is imminent and the quality of life is very poor. However, the patient has to be of sound mind and to request death repeatedly.

However, what if the patient's wishes are based on faulty information about their illness or depression clouds their judgement? What if a cure is found just after the patient's death? What if the request for euthanasia is easier to respond to than providing good palliative care?

Personal **autonomy** is an important value but it is often in conflict with other equally important ones – how do we work out which value overrides another and which are the true basic goods?

Autonomy

In ethics this means freely taken moral decisions by an individual.

KILLING AND LETTING DIE

Many doctors will argue that euthanasia goes on already, as they will give patients painkillers in such doses that death will be hastened, and in the case of the brain dead or those in persistent vegetative states they will withdraw or withhold treatment to bring about death.

However, we do see a difference between killing (taking life) and letting die (not saving life). There is a right not to be killed, but no right to have one's life saved.

James Rachels saw no distinction between active euthanasia (killing) and passive euthanasia (letting die). If anything he believes that passive euthanasia is worse, as it is cruel and inconsistent and the process of dying may be long and drawn out, bringing about more suffering than is necessary. The result is the same – the patient is dead.

Many arguments concerning euthanasia, whether active or passive, are influenced by the fear that allowing one kind of euthanasia will be the first step on a **slippery slope**, and the value of human life will be depreciated and made subordinate to economics and personal convenience. **Helga Kuhse** challenges this 'slippery slope' view and concludes that the situation in the Netherlands is not following the example of Nazi Germany in making some lives valueless for reasons other than mercy or respect for autonomy.

James Rachels (1941–2003)

James Rachels taught at the University of Richmond, New York University, the University of Miami, Duke University, and the University of Alabama at Birmingham. Rachels argued for moral vegetarianism and animal rights, preferential quotas, and the humanitarian use of euthanasia.

Slippery slope

This means that when one moral law is broken others will also be gradually broken and there will be no moral absolutes.

APPLYING ETHICAL THEORIES TO EUTHANASIA

Utilitarianism

Basic principle – the greatest good for the greatest number.

One of the first questions we need to ask when considering Utilitarianism and euthanasia is: what counts as a good consequence? One answer is that given by **John Stuart Mill**: good consequences are simply happiness, and happiness is pleasure and freedom from pain – not only physical but also mental and psychological pain. In his *Essay on Liberty*, Mill states that good consequences depend not only on the quantity of the pleasure but on the quality as well – this higher happiness stresses self-development and develops people's rational nature. Mill's notion of victimless crime may also be applied to voluntary euthanasia: as there is no victim of crime since the patient wishes to die. However, even though the patient has their wish and the doctor is merely carrying it out, there are still the effects on society and on the doctor–patient relationship, making society itself the victim as human life loses its value.

Both **Jeremy Bentham**'s hedonistic Utilitarianism and Mill's view argue that euthanasia is right. Bentham would say that if a person's continued existence brings more pain than suffering, both to them and to their family, then their life could be ended. Utilitarianism would also consider the resources that are being spent in keeping them alive and argue that more happiness could be produced if these resources were used in other ways. The idea of 'death with dignity' through voluntary euthanasia also fits Mill's Utilitarianism, as it is possible to claim that the good they seek is not just the absence of pain but the preservation of dignity and the exercise of personal autonomy.

However, there is a problem with the way Utilitarianism can be used to justify euthanasia, as it seems to justify too much – if enough people gain happiness and quality of life from the death of one person, then such an action is justified. There is no protection for the individual against the majority and no safeguarding of the individual's rights.

Situation ethics

Basic principle – agape which wills the good of others.

Situation ethics looks at the consequences of an action and makes a decision according to the most loving thing to do in the circumstances. Fletcher would maintain that there is more to being human than just being alive and in certain circumstances humans can rationally make the choice to die.

Natural Law

Basic principle – everything is created for a purpose and when this is examined by human reason, a person should be able to judge how to act in order to find ultimate happiness.

Natural Law does not look at the people involved in a decision about euthanasia, or the consequences of the action – instead Natural Law considers the act of euthanasia itself. Protection of life is a primary precept and euthanasia goes against this.

Natural Law does allow a patient to refuse treatment if it is over and above what is needed for existence – extraordinary means. Proportion is important in Natural Law and actually enables each situation to be looked at individually so that the action which is proportionate to the needs of the patient is chosen. The weak sanctity of life argument says that where death is inevitable the doctor treats the patient with care and compassion: 'Thou shalt not kill; but need not strive officiously to keep alive.' Arthur Clough's poem *The New Decalogue* sums up this view.

Virtue ethics

Basic principle – agent-centred not act-centred. Practising virtuous behaviour will lead to becoming a virtuous person and contribute to a virtuous society.

Virtue ethics needs to be applied to the persons involved in euthanasia: the doctors whose commitment to healing could be seen to be at odds with euthanasia. Virtue ethics would also consider the values of compassion which would lead to a desire to relieve suffering – this means not only pain, which can usually be relieved with modern pain relief, but also the suffering caused by the indignities of dying and the meaninglessness of the person's situation and life. The virtues of the terminally ill patient also have a part to play – the development through life of virtues such as humility, humour and courage will allow the person to live well while dying and to cope with the feelings of hopelessness and meaninglessness.

Virtue ethics also considers the role of developing virtues within the community – the virtues of caring that will give the sick and dying the support they need. The practice of Virtue ethics may be seen in the Hospice Movement, which tries to improve the lives of the dying without euthanasia.

Thought Point

In pairs or groups research one of the following and apply ethical theories to it:

1   Tony Bland and his doctor, Jim Howe.
2   Diane Pretty.

continued

3   Annie Lindsell.

4   Baby Charlotte Wyatt.

5   Mary Ormerod.

6   Terri Schiavo.

7   Dr Anne Turner and *dignitas*.

Further research

Dr Andrew Fergusson – chairman of Healthcare Opposed to Euthanasia (HOPE)
Dame Cecily Saunders – founder of the modern Hospice Movement
Baroness Warnock
Euthanasia in the news

REVIEW QUESTIONS

Look back over the chapter and check that you can answer the following questions:

1   (a)   Explain the link between euthanasia and the sanctity of life.

      (b)   Explain the link between euthanasia and the quality of life.

2   What is the difference between killing and letting die? Does it matter?

3   What are QUALYS?

4   Make a chart applying the different ethical theories to euthanasia.

Terminology

Do you know your terminology?

Try to explain the following ideas without looking at your books and notes:

- Autonomy
- Active euthanasia
- Involuntary euthanasia
- Voluntary euthanasia
- Passive euthanasia
- Slippery slope

Examination Questions Practice

Read the question carefully – if it asks you to write about voluntary euthanasia, do not write about other sorts just because you know about them. Do not just reproduce 'My euthanasia essay'.

PAST PAPER QUESTIONS

(a) Explain what is meant by the sanctity of life. (33 marks)

You will need to include some of the following concepts:

- This teaching means that life is special and sacred, ordained by God.
- Life begins at conception and continues until natural death.

To write a good answer you need to include biblical teaching and/or link the sanctity of life to the precept to preserve innocent life in Natural Moral Law.

You could also explain that this view rejects autonomous or secular ethics and contrast the idea of the sanctity of life with teleological and quality-of-life arguments.

(b) 'The concept of the sanctity of life is not helpful in understanding the issues surrounding euthanasia.' Discuss. (17 marks)

- A common argument is to contrast the sanctity of life with the argument for autonomy and quality of life.
- You could also argue that the sanctity of life argument leaves no room for compassion and consider a relative theory of ethics such as Situation ethics as an alternative.
- You may put the alternative point of view and argue in support of the sanctity of life, possibly linking it to the precept to preserve innocent life in Natural Moral Law.
- It is a good idea to use biblical teaching to back up your argument.

SAMPLE AS EXAMINATION QUESTIONS

(a) Give an account of Kant's theory of ethics.
(b) How helpful would this theory be when faced with the problem of dying without dignity?
 (OCR AS Level 2762 January 2001 question 2)

(a) Describe the main differences between the Utilitarianism of Bentham and Mill.
(b) Evaluate the claim that Utilitarianism is a useful method in judging issues of voluntary euthanasia.
 (OCR AS Level 2762 June 2001 question 1)

(a) Explain the main features of moral relativism.
(b) Discuss moral relativism in relation to voluntary euthanasia.
 (OCR AS Level 2762 January 2002 question 1)

(a) Explain how a relative morality might be applied to euthanasia.
(b) 'One set of moral principles should apply to all societies.' Discuss.
 (OCR AS Level 2762 June 2003 question 2)

(a) Explain how a follower of Natural Law might respond to issues raised by voluntary euthanasia.

(b) 'A Natural Law approach is the best approach to voluntary euthanasia.' Discuss.
(OCR AS Level 2762 June 2004 question 3)

(a) Explain religious objections to euthanasia.

(b) 'Religious objections to euthanasia ignore human dignity.' Discuss.
(OCR AS Level 2762 January 2005 question 6)

FURTHER READING

Cook, D. *The Moral Maze*, London, SPCK, 1983.

Glover, J. *Causing Death and Saving Lives*, London, Penguin, 1990.

Hinman, L. 'Ethics Updates', available at http://ethics.acusd.edu/.

Kuhse, H. and Singer, P. (eds) *Bioethics – An Anthology*, Oxford, Blackwell, 1999 (contains articles by Jonathan Glover, Grisez and Boyle, James Rachels and Helga Kuhse).

Lafollette, H. (ed.) *Ethics in Practice – An Anthology*, Oxford, Blackwell, 2002.

Macquarrie, J. and Childress, J. *A New Dictionary of Christian Ethics*, London, SCM, 1986.

Singer, P. *Practical Ethics*, Cambridge, Cambridge University Press, 1993.

Singer, P. *Rethinking Life and Death*, Oxford, Oxford University Press, 1994.

Warnock, M. *An Intelligent Person's Guide to Ethics*, London, Duckworth, 1999.

Wilcockson, M. *Issues of Life and Death*, London, Hodder & Stoughton, 1999.

10 Medical Ethics 3

Genetic Engineering and Embryo Research

WHAT YOU WILL LEARN ABOUT IN THIS CHAPTER

- An understanding of genetic engineering and embryo research, and the issues involved.
- The idea of the sanctity of life and how it applies to embryo research.
- Religious approaches to genetic engineering and embryo research.
- The ethical implications of our knowledge of the human genome.
- The approaches of different ethical theories to genetic engineering and embryo research.

KEY SCHOLARS

- Thomas Aquinas (1225–1274)
- Immanuel Kant (1724–1804)
- Jeremy Bentham (1748–1832)
- John Stuart Mill (1806–1873)
- Peter Singer (1946–)
- Celia Deane-Drummond
- Joseph Fletcher (1905–1991)
- Jonathan Glover (1941–)
- Paul Ramsay
- Robert Song (1962–)

THE OCR CHECKLIST

Medical ethics: genetic engineering and embryo research.

* An understanding of the ways in which the ethical systems of Natural Law, Virtue ethics, Kant, Bentham and Mill might be applied to issues raised by these areas, and religious responses to these issues.
* The ethical issues that arise in the specified areas of medical ethics.
* Basic knowledge of the law and of medical procedures.
* The concepts of the sanctity of life, personhood, rights and consent, in relation to these issues.

From OCR A Level Religious Studies Specification 7877.

WHAT IS GENETIC ENGINEERING?

Genetics is about our genes, which are made of DNA and are the basic building blocks of life. Every cell has a full set of genes, carried in strands of DNA which are chromosomes. When new cells are replicated, each new cell has characteristics passed on by the DNA – genes are like a blueprint of life. In humans the genes decide the characteristics inherited from each parent.

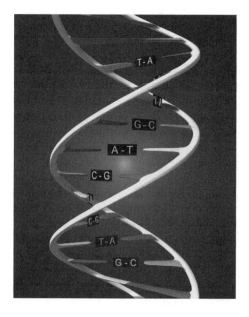

DNA helix – blue glow 2

(microscopic) Getty Images

It was in the mid-1970s that scientists first discovered how to move pieces of genetic material from one species to another – this came to be called **genetic engineering**. Some said that this was simply an extension of what breeders of plants and animals had been doing for hundreds of years and what nature did through evolution and natural selection, but others claimed that it was 'playing God' and was unnatural. Genetic engineering, however, continued to develop, and the technology was extended from plants to animals and finally to human cells. Today genetically altered crops, such as soybean and maize, are grown extensively, especially in the USA, and marketed all over the world. Scientists working for pharmaceutical companies use altered genes to produce 'designer' drugs, and research is gathering pace to treat certain inherited diseases by gene therapy.

The ethical questions first aired in the 1970s continue to be raised, both about the process itself and about the results. Others will say that humans have always altered their environment to benefit themselves, and this new biotechnology could help fight hunger and disease.

Genetic engineering
The technology involved in cloning, gene therapy and gene manipulation.

WHAT IS EMBRYO RESEARCH?

Embryo research has as its aim to find cures for serious illnesses using tissue or cells from **embryos**. Most of this research concentrates on **stem cells** and the field of regenerative medicine – the repair of damaged organs and body parts. Stem cells can change into other types of cells such as heart cells, muscle cells, nerve cells or skin cells. The ultimate stem cells are the system cells in the early embryo because they can develop into every single cell type. There is very little debate over the use of adult stem cells which can be taken from body tissue without harming the patient; so far these are the only ones which have successfully helped patients. Embryonic stem cells are removed from early embryos in a process which destroys the embryo – this makes it inherently problematic as far as ethics is concerned. These embryonic stem cells may be taken from embryos left over from IVF treatment or created in a laboratory from donated sperm and eggs. At the present state of the science no cure has been achieved using embryonic stem cells and they will always cause problems, as they do not have the same genetic make-up as the patients and will be rejected unless anti-rejection drugs are used. So the best option, at present, is to make new embryos by **therapeutic cloning** – the same method as used to create Dolly the sheep. This of course gives rise to another problem – the potential of this development is limited by the supply of human eggs and possible exploitation if poor women are to be paid for eggs.

Reproductive cloning has been tried in animals and there have been some successes after many, many failures. The only dividing line between therapeutic cloning and reproductive cloning is the intention of the scientists.

Embryo
The developing bundle of cells in the womb up to eight weeks' gestation.

Stem cell
A 'master' cell that can become any kind of material.

Therapeutic cloning
A method of producing stem cells to treat diseases such as Alzheimer's.

Cloning
A form of genetic engineering by which a plant, an animal or a human is created with the same genetic identity as another.

In the UK the law is clear: embryos may not be experimented on past fourteen days; a human embryo cannot be placed in an animal; human cloning is not allowed; the genetic structure of any cell cannot be altered while it is part of an embryo.

The Human Fertilisation and Embryology Authority allows embryo research for the following purposes only:

- to promote advances in the treatment of infertility
- to increase knowledge about the causes of congenital disease
- to increase knowledge about the causes of miscarriage
- to develop more effective techniques of contraception
- to develop methods for detecting the presence of gene or chromosome abnormalities.

For the purpose of this book we will look at genetically engineered crops, genetic selection, genetic testing and screening, the alteration of human genes, stem cell research, and whether the Human Genome Project understands humans primarily in terms of their genetic inheritance.

GENETICALLY ENGINEERED CROPS – 'FRANKENFOOD'?

The production of genetically modified (GM) crops has led to very strong reactions. In the UK press they were called 'Frankenfoods' after Mary Shelley's scientist and his manufactured monster.

These GM crops have certain obvious advantages: the food has better taste and quality and a greater resistance to pests and diseases; it is environmentally friendly in that it does not require chemical pesticides and will conserve soil, water and energy. The most talked-about advantage is that these GM crops offer the world's best chance to end or at least greatly reduce hunger and malnutrition through greater yields and sturdier crops.

However, critics say that these GM crops threaten the environment and may cause havoc through cross-pollination. Genetically engineered crops could have as yet unknown effects on human health by causing unexpected allergic reactions and eventually reducing resistance to disease and transferring antibiotic resistance markers. A potentially more serious criticism does not concern the effects on the developed world, which can protect itself, but on the developing world: many poor farmers are encouraged to grow GM crops. Giant multinationals such as Monsanto and Novatis own patents on these altered crops and demand that farmers buy new seeds each year at great expense instead of reusing seeds from the previous year's crop. One country that has stood out against this is Zambia, which does not have enough food of its own but refuses to import from the USA and rejects any seeds or foods that have been genetically modified. This decision is partly to protect its export of vegetables to Europe and partly a response to health warnings and damage to the environment; it is also concerned that this new biotechnology is part of a globalized system of agriculture which favours large producers and argues that it is more important to retrain small farmers to farm organically as they did in the past.

Finally, GM food cannot be seen as the sole solution to world hunger – that problem is far more complex, and questions of injustice in the social situations of today's world need to be examined.

SELECTING HUMAN GENES – 'DESIGNER BABIES'?

The ethical debate surrounding the selection of human genes is even more complex than that over GM foods. There are a number of reasons why embryos are selected: to screen for genetically inherited diseases such as Huntington's disease, Tay-Sachs and cystic fibrosis or for genetic conditions such as Down's syndrome; to create a healthy baby to treat a sick sibling; or to select the sex of the child (this is illegal in the UK).

In order to do this, embryos are created by in-vitro fertilisation and a single cell is removed from each for genetic testing; one embryo is selected for implantation and the rest discarded.

Case studies

In 2002 a British couple, Michelle and Jayson Whittaker, asked the Human Fertilisation and Embryology Authority if they could genetically select an embryo which would be a match for their son Charlie, who had a life-threatening blood disorder. They were refused permission and went to the USA for IVF treatment.

In 2003, however, the Hashmis, who also had a son with a rare blood disorder urgently needing a bone marrow transplant, were granted permission to select an embryo after many months of wrangling in the courts.

- Is this just a brilliant way of saving a child's life?
- Are scientists 'playing God'?
- What about the motivations of the parent?
- How could different ethical theories approach these situations?

Sex selection

The Mastersons have sons, but their only daughter died, and they want to use sex selection to have another daughter.

- If they want a daughter so badly will they just want her to be like the daughter they had? Will this damage her?
- Can we even begin to know their motives?
- Would we feel differently if the sex selection was for medical reasons (e.g. to select a female to have a baby free from the haemophilia gene)?

Genetic screening, and the idea of 'designer babies', involves destroying unwanted and unsuitable embryos. If the embryos are seen as persons from the moment of conception and, therefore, as having an intrinsic dignity and value that cannot be compromised in the name of other values, then any destruction of embryos would be opposed. However, fertilisation is a process that takes about twenty-four hours to complete and so there is no specific moment when personhood may be said to be conferred. **Peter Singer** points out that up to fourteen days after conception the fertilised egg has the capacity to divide into two and become identical twins. In some cases it has been observed that such divided eggs blend back together into one **blastocyst**. If the egg is fertilised in vitro, one cell can be removed to have its genetic structure tested and the developmental process is unharmed. In fact, all the cells of the blastocyst can be separated and each has the capacity to become a whole human being – this is important as the blastocyst does not have true individuality. Without individuality it is difficult, according to Singer's argument, to see how the organism can be a person. However, even if the early embryo is not a person with full human rights, we do not yet have enough knowledge of early brain activity to know whether an early embryo feels pain.

Some people are concerned that the newborn baby will be subject to painful medical procedures to help a sibling, but, in fact, the necessary cells are taken from the umbilical cord. There are also concerns that, in an increasingly materialistic society, the baby is being treated as a commodity – just made to be a donor or to fulfil parental desires. As it is so difficult to assess the motives of others, some may say that embryo selection is the beginning of a 'slippery slope', with babies ultimately being chosen for eye colour or intelligence. However, we have been doing the same to animals for hundreds of years – would the selection or enhancement of humans be any different?

Blastocyst
A fertilised egg at about four to five days of development.

Zygote
A 'proto-embryo' of the first two weeks after conception – a small collection of identical cells.

TESTING AND GENETIC SCREENING

Genetic testing

Scientists have created tests for various genetic diseases – for example, whether a patient is carrying the gene which produces breast cancer or sickle cell anaemia. Patients have to agree to the tests and understand the implications of the test should they prove positive. One of the main ethical questions is whether the tests should remain private or whether the results should be divulged to employers or insurance companies. If the government goes ahead with plans for an identity card which carries genetic information, it would be difficult to keep such information private and could lead to discrimination. Genetic problems could also affect other family members – should they be informed if they have not given consent? Gene testing usually gives only a probability of developing the disorder and a limitation of all medical testing is the possibility of laboratory error.

Genetic screening

Genetic testing is done on sections of the population who are known to be at risk – this may be done on an adult, a child or a foetus. There are some advantages in knowing, in that the person can be encouraged to change their lifestyle to reduce the danger of developing the disease. However, it may lead to discrimination against certain groups, such as the wish of a Jewish committee in New York to prevent Ashkenazi Jews who carry the Tay-Sachs gene from marrying each other. It may also lead to aborting a foetus which has a genetic flaw, which may prevent the child from pain and suffering but which also raises questions about how we as a society define 'normal' and 'abnormal'. If, for example, scientists were to discover a gene for being born violent, should we test everyone to see if they are carrying the gene and then eliminate them to make society a safer place?

Gene therapy

A further problem involves the use of gene therapy to correct, alter or replace genes. This has proved successful in some areas but also causes problems, as in the case of sickle cell anaemia which is prevalent among Afro-Caribbeans – this gene affects a few in a terrible way but it is the same gene which gives natural immunity from malaria.

There is also the issue of the allocation of health resources and how they are used. Can genetic screening be justified for a few individuals? Can it be justified if there is no cure available, e.g. Huntington's disease? How do we even know what to test for as more and more diseases are discovered to have genetic links?

THE ALTERATION OF HUMAN GENES

Human genome
A map of the human genes.

Germ line engineering
Changes in the parent's sperm or egg cells with the aim of passing on the changes to their offspring.

Somatic cell engineering
Changes in somatic (body) cells to cure an otherwise fatal disease. These changes are not passed on to a person's offspring.

Gene therapy aims to cure or ultimately prevent disease by changing genes. The science is only in its infancy and primarily experimental. Gene alteration can be targeted to somatic (body) cells, in which the patient's **genome** is changed, or to germ (egg and sperm) cells, in which the parent's egg and sperm cells are changed with the aim of passing on the changes to future generations. **Germ line** therapy is often confused with genetic selection, but it is not, in fact, being actively investigated in larger animals or humans. Ethically this therapy is questionable, as it could ultimately change the whole of humanity and what it means to be human – we take charge of our own evolution.

The alteration of genes in a patient's **somatic cells** was first used successfully in 1990 – this type of genetic therapy raises the fewest ethical questions, especially when it is used to treat a life-threatening disease. However, gene therapy given to a foetus before birth could again mean that we decide which genetic predispositions are to be altered – for example, at present conditions such as obesity, below-average intelligence and poor eyesight are seen as normal inheritable characteristics, but in the future may be considered to be grounds for alteration or even abortion. Some people feel that there is no difference between gene alteration to prevent a minor disability and paying school fees so that children get a first-class education. This may of course create a further ethical issue whereby a division is created between the genetically rich and everyone else.

However, most diseases involve the interaction of many genes and the environment. Many people who develop cancer not only inherit the disease gene, but may not have inherited particular tumour-suppressing genes. Diet, exercise, smoking and other environmental factors may all have contributed to their disease. Studies of identical twins show that individuals with the same genetic make-up do not develop the same diseases – environment plays a part.

STEM CELL RESEARCH

Stem cells are cells that can change into other types of cells – in the very early embryo they are *totipotent*: they can become any kind of body cell; in the adult they are *pluripotent*: they have the capacity to become a variety of cells, but not all. Adult stem cells can be taken from an adult, a child or even from the placenta of a newborn baby without harming the patient, but those

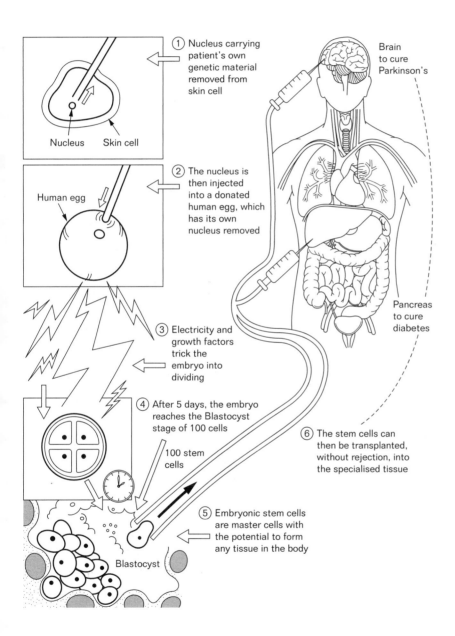

① Nucleus carrying patient's own genetic material removed from skin cell

Nucleus   Skin cell

② The nucleus is then injected into a donated human egg, which has its own nucleus removed

Human egg

③ Electricity and growth factors trick the embryo into dividing

④ After 5 days, the embryo reaches the Blastocyst stage of 100 cells

100 stem cells

Blastocyst

⑤ Embryonic stem cells are master cells with the potential to form any tissue in the body

Brain to cure Parkinson's

Pancreas to cure diabetes

⑥ The stem cells can then be transplanted, without rejection, into the specialised tissue

Two diagrams of stem cell research

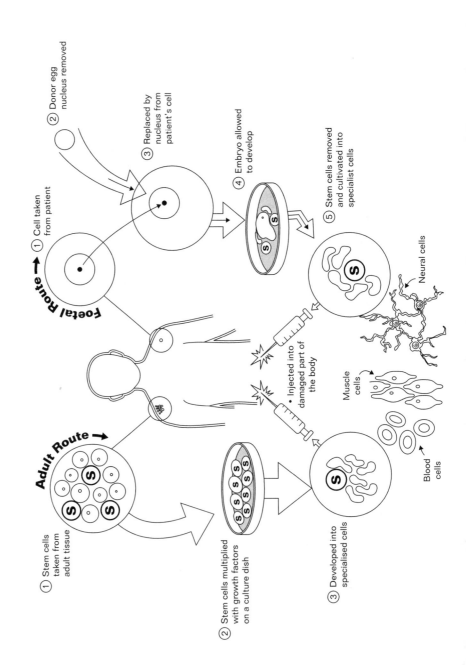

removed from early embryos destroy the embryo. There are also foetal stem cells which are taken from aborted foetuses and are believed to have almost the same potential as embryonic stem cells.

Scientists hope that stem cells can be used to cure many disorders such as Parkinson's disease, diabetes, spinal cord injuries, heart disease and cancer – but all this is a long way off, decades in the future. In 2006 it was reported in the *Lancet* how, five years previously, patients' own cells had been used to grow and replace bladders in seven children who suffered from spina bifida. These were not stem cells, but more specialised cells which can only grow into bladder cells. This has improved the lives of these children beyond measure, and they do not have to take anti-rejection drugs, as the bladders are made from their own cells. A bladder is a much simpler organ than a liver or a kidney, but they are now testing kidneys successfully in cows. This is a very different situation from the use of embryonic stem cells, which necessitates the destruction of embryos for the benefit of others, which goes against the teaching on the sanctity of life.

Embryonic stem cell research is the threshold of cloning – first developed at the Roslin Institute by Ian Wilmot in 1997, when Dolly the sheep was cloned. Human cloning is illegal in the UK, but several rogue scientists have attempted it elsewhere. Scientists simply say that it is unsafe for the cloned child, as, from the experience of cloning other mammals, producing one child might need hundreds of pregnancies and many abnormal late-term foetuses could be produced. Others oppose human cloning on the grounds that it would produce confusion in family relationships and encourage parents to see cloned children as objects rather than independent human beings. However, the problems will eventually be overcome and many will argue that cloning is a possible solution for infertile couples, and that clones would simply be like identical twins, which are natural clones of each other.

Many scientists now say that it is unnecessary to use embryonic stem cells in their search for cures:

- Embryonic stem cells are very 'plastic', which means they can be unstable and become malignant, causing cancer.
- Adult stem cells are found in umbilical cord blood and placenta blood, as well as virtually every major organ of the human body.
- Adult stem cells have already been successfully used in treatments, while embryonic stem cells are still at the theoretical stage.
- The benefits of embryonic stem cells are a long way off.
- Adult stem cells overcome the problem of immune rejection.
- With the rise of animal rights activists and the problems involved in using adults to test drugs, it is likely that embryos will be used less for actual research and more for testing by pharmaceutical companies.

THE HUMAN GENOME PROJECT – A LIMITED VIEW OF HUMANITY?

Robert Song asks whether the human genome project and the resulting advances in biotechnology simply reduce human beings to their genetic inheritance. He does not criticise the science itself, nor does he say that the new genetics is intrinsically reductive in itself. He sees the developments in genetics as shaped by what he calls the 'Baconian Project' – the aim to eliminate suffering and maximise choice. This view may be traced back to the rise of the natural sciences in the seventeenth century (and also follows Francis Bacon's emphasis on the necessary social use of scientific knowledge), the Utilitarianism of the eighteenth century and the Romantic emphasis on individual fulfilment and autonomy. The result of this is that all suffering is seen as pointless (the rise in a desire to legalise euthanasia could follow from this), which has brought about an increase in the number of medical interventions and an understanding of our bodies as things to be changed according to our individual tastes through plastic surgery and so on. The human genome project has given us not just the knowledge of the 'basic building blocks' of the body and how it is constructed, but also the knowledge of how it may be reconstructed.

APPLYING ETHICAL THEORIES TO GENETIC ENGINEERING AND EMBRYO RESEARCH

Religious ethics

The sanctity of life is a key theme with which to approach the questions of genetic engineering and embryo research. The Bible teaches that God created the human in his image and so human life has intrinsic value. Using an embryo for the sake of another human is wrong, as the embryo has intrinsic worth. Any technology that creates spare embryos to be used or discarded is wrong.

However, there are not the same objections to using adult stem cells or to the modification of animals or plants.

Catholic ethics are based on Natural Law and so are positive about advances in science that improve human life, but never at the expense of human life, which is sacred from the moment of conception. The Catholic Church also expresses concern about who is investing in the research and who will benefit from it. However, the Catholic Church recognises the need for humans to use their God-given intelligence to transform and humanise the world. This was the view of Pope Pius XII when he justified the use of painkillers: 'Man preserves, even after the Fall, the right of dominating the forces of Nature, of using them in his service, and of employing the resources so offered to him to avoid or suppress physical suffering.'

Catholics claim that certain actions are intrinsically evil, as they go against what it is to be human. Evil is seen as falling short of what humans are intended to be and is a result of free will. They make a distinction between *doing evil* and *suffering an evil*. Humans that are physically impaired (e.g. are blind or have Down's syndrome) are suffering an evil because they fall short of what it is to be fully human. Correcting these impairments is therefore a good thing – but the use of genetic engineering to achieve this is still ruled out. There is also concern that too much stress is placed on being physically perfect and the spiritual side of what it means to be human is neglected.

The Catholic Church rules out embryo research as being unnatural and destroying life, but it approves of genetic engineering which respects human life and human rights on the basis of its help for the individual and society.

Other Christian churches may take a different view and follow a Situation ethics line based on agape. An action is good if it is based on love and bad if it is based on selfishness. Two influential Protestant writers on bioethics were the Episcopalian **Joseph Fletcher** and the Methodist **Paul Ramsay**. Fletcher saw a human being as 'a maker and a selecter and a designer' who acts morally when in control of genetics. He was not opposed to IVF and therefore it could be concluded that embryo research is the most loving thing to do with spare embryos when the only other option is to destroy them, especially when such research could lead to cures for terrible diseases. However, creating embryos for the direct purpose of stem cell research is difficult to justify as being the most loving action.

Ramsay opposed separating procreation from conjugal love and was pessimistic about our attempts to 'play God', but his arguments were always teleological and looked at the benefits for humanity of genetic engineering. He approved of genetic screening as doing 'more good than harm' and said it was important that 'the benefits from any course of action must be weighed up against any risk'.

Christians in general seem to look favourably at genetic medicine, while acknowledging both the risks and the limits that should be imposed on research in terms of respect for human life.

Natural Law

Basic principle – everything is created for a purpose and when this is examined by human reason, a person should be able to judge how to act in order to find ultimate happiness.

Natural Law has the primary precept of self-preservation and from this may be deduced the secondary precept 'no embryo research', as it destroys life.

However, it could be argued that the research can be justified, as it preserves life by curing diseases.

Utilitarianism

Basic principle – the greatest good for the greatest number.

Utilitarianism does not accept the principle that human life has absolute value and this should be upheld whatever the consequences, but attempts to assess each individual situation on its own merits to promote the greatest happiness for those concerned.

However, Utilitarianism only works if it is actually possible to assess the results of genetic engineering and embryo research and decide whether they favour all concerned. In practice this is difficult, as we cannot predict all consequences. However, it is possible to say, from a utilitarian point of view, that it is better to save many lives in the future by embryo research at the cost of a few embryos now.

Bentham's hedonic calculus can only be applied to those who suffer. Early embryos, it is assumed at the present stage of knowledge, do not have the capacity to feel pain and so cannot be measured according to the hedonic calculus. However, the benefits of genetic engineering and embryo research are justifiable using the hedonic calculus – the pleasures brought about by cures for diseases such as Parkinson's outweigh the cost to the embryos. However, the costs to the Health Service, as mentioned above, also need to be considered and the likelihood of success taken into account.

Kantian ethics

Basic principle – the categorical imperative: universal maxims; treating others as ends in themselves and living in a Kingdom of Ends.

Kant argued that reason enabled people to impose such laws upon themselves and when the categorical imperative is applied to genetic engineering and embryo research there are immediate difficulties: both would be hard to universalise simply. For example, it would be possible to universalise the maxim 'use spare embryos left over from IVF for stem cell research' but not 'create embryos for stem cell research', as there would be no embryos left to reproduce and the human race would die out.

There is also the emphasis on treating people as ends in themselves and not as a means to an end – embryo research would also go against this if the embryo is considered to be a person. Kant was not clear on the moral status of embryos. However, the Kantian idea of respect for persons and the requirement for human rights to be respected, that informed consent should be obtained and so on will mean that genetic medicine, testing, screening and adult stem cell research will be truly humanising. Respect for autonomy and privacy is also essential to Kantian ethics.

Kant's stress on acting out of duty alone, with no account taken of compassion or love, means that all consequences are ignored, whatever they may be.

Virtue ethics

Basic principle – person-centred rather than act-centred or result-centred.

Celia Deane-Drummond attempts to apply the virtues of prudence (practical wisdom), justice, fortitude and temperance in the process of decision-making to the problems of biotechnology. At another level the virtue of compassion could be used to show that embryos required for embryo research are being used for the good of others and compassion is being shown to those suffering from genetic diseases.

Virtue ethics emphasises that moral acts do not take place in a vacuum, but in a relationship which entails responsibilities and care of others. Virtues operate on the private level (e.g. loving and caring), but also on the public level (e.g. justice and beneficence). Alasdair MacIntyre says that people are basically communitarian and community life is held together by tradition and by the virtues that groups encourage in individual members. However, this can be very limiting and even liberal communities may put belonging before being and exclude as much as include. If Virtue ethics is to be of any help in making decisions about genetic engineering or embryo research, it will need to consider the community of humankind – an ethics that expands our vision rather than contracts it.

REVIEW QUESTIONS

Look back over the chapter and check that you can answer the following questions:

1   Explain the differences between therapeutic and reproductive cloning.

continued

2   How could genetic engineering be used to alleviate world hunger? What are the problems with this?

3   Explain the difference between adult and foetal stem cells – why is this important ethically?

4   Take a current newspaper article about any form of genetic engineering or foetal research. Stick it on a piece of A3 paper and write brief notes around it on how different ethical theories would approach the issue.

5   List some of the ethical problems with genetic engineering and foetal research.

Terminology

Do you know your terminology?

Try to explain the following key terms without looking at your books and notes:

- Blastocyst
- Cloning
- Germ line engineering
- Somatic cell engineering

Examination Questions Practice

When writing answers about genetic engineering, make sure you know and understand the terminology and can explain the ethical implications of genetic engineering.

PAST PAPER QUESTIONS

(a) Explain how Utilitarianism might be applied to embryo research. (OCR AS Level 2762 January 2005 question 4, 33 marks)

- You need to begin by explaining Utilitarianism – the amount of pleasure or happiness caused by an action.
- You should explain that Utilitarianism is teleological and focused on consequences – an action is right if it produces the greatest good for the greatest number.
- You should then apply this to embryo research – balancing good over evil and bringing benefit to sufferers of inherited diseases.
- You need to explain that a utilitarian would look at the merits of each situation, but would also need to consider the costs involved.

(b) To what extent can embryo research be justified? (OCR AS Level 2762 January 2005 question 4, 17 marks)

Here you need to contrast and analyse the different approaches:

- You could defend embryo research, as it brings relief to sufferers and improves their quality of life, curing diseases that were once thought incurable.
- On the other hand, you may question the techniques and the misuse of spare embryos.
- You could explain that some people may object to interfering with nature using Natural Law theory.

SAMPLE AS EXAMINATION QUESTIONS

(a) Describe the main strengths and weaknesses of Utilitarianism.
(b) Evaluate a utilitarian approach to genetic engineering.
(OCR AS Level 2762 June 2002 question 1)

(a) Explain the differences between a relative morality and an absolute one.
(b) How useful is a relative morality in dealing with issues surrounding genetic engineering?
(OCR AS Level 2762 January 2001 question 3)

(a) Explain how the religious ethics you have studied might be applied to the issues raised by genetic engineering.
(b) 'Genetic engineering is ethically justified.' Discuss.
(OCR AS Level 2762 January 2004 question 5)

(a) Explain the Natural Law theory of ethics.
(b) How useful, if at all, is the theory of Natural Law in relation to embryo research?
(OCR AS Level 2762 January 2003 question 4)

(a) Explain how Natural Law could be applied to embryo research.
(b) 'A Natural Law approach to embryo research does society more harm than good.' Discuss.
(OCR AS Level 2762 June 2003 question 5)

(a) Explain Kant's theory of the categorical imperative.
(b) How useful is the categorical imperative when considering embryo research?

FURTHER READING

Deane-Drummond, C. (ed.) *Brave New World*, London/New York, T & T Clark, 2003.

Deane-Drummond, C. *Genetics and Christian Ethics*, Cambridge, Cambridge University Press, 2005.

Glover, J. *Causing Death and Saving Lives*, London, Penguin, 1990.

Hinman, L. 'Ethics Updates', available at http://ethics.acusd.edu/.

Kuhse, H. and Singer, P. (ed.) *Bioethics – An Anthology*, Oxford, Blackwell,1999.

Lafollette, H. (ed.) *Ethics in Practice – An Anthology*, Oxford, Blackwell, 2002.

Macquarrie, J. and Childress, J. *A New Dictionary of Christian Ethics*, London, SCM, 1986.

Peters, T. *Playing God? Genetic Determinism and Human Freedom*, London, Routledge, 1997.

Song, R. *Human Genetics: Fabricating the Future*, London, Darton, Longman & Todd, 2002.

A2 ETHICS

PART III

11 Free Will and Determinism

WHAT YOU WILL LEARN ABOUT IN THIS CHAPTER

*   The link between free will and moral responsibility.
*   The ethical theories of hard determinism, libertarianism and soft determinism or compatibilism.
*   The influences of genetics, psychology and social environment on our moral choices.
*   Religious ideas of free will and predestination.
*   The strengths and weaknesses of determinism and free will.
*   The link between free will, determinism and moral responsibility.

KEY SCHOLARS

*   Augustine of Hippo (354–430)
*   John Calvin (1509–1564)
*   John Locke (1632–1704)
*   Baruch Spinoza (1632–1677)
*   Isaac Newton (1642–1727)
*   David Hume (1711–1776)
*   Paul-Henri Thiry (Baron) d'Holbach (1723–1789)
*   Immanuel Kant (1724–1804)
*   Pierre Laplace (1749–1827)
*   Ivan Petrovich Pavlov (1849–1936)
*   Clarence Seward Darrow (1857–1938)
*   John B. Watson (1878–1958)
*   John Hospers (1918–)
*   Richard Dawkins (1941–)
*   Steven Pinker (1954–)
*   Werner Heisenberg (1901–1976)
*   B.F. Skinner (1904–1990)
*   Jean-Paul Sartre (1905–1980)
*   Ted Honderich (1933–)
*   Peter Van Inwagen (1942–)

This chapter contains the views of many scholars and philosophers about which you do not need to know for the OCR examination, but which will add to your understanding of this subject.

THE OCR CHECKLIST

Free will and determinism:

- The views of 'hard' and 'soft' determinists and libertarians.
- The implications of these views for moral responsibility.
- The way in which the religion studied contributes to debates about human free will and moral responsibility.

From OCR A Level Religious Studies Specification 7877.

WHAT IS DETERMINISM?

Most people agree that people are morally responsible *only* for the actions they carry out freely and deliberately – actions that are freely chosen. Determinism, however, states that there are laws of nature which govern everything which happens and that all our actions are the result of these scientific laws and every choice we make was determined by the situation immediately before it, and that situation was determined by the situation before it and so on as far back as you want to go. Freedom of choice is just an illusion and so personal responsibility is a meaningless concept, as are blame and punishment. This makes it difficult to make any sense of the idea that people are to be held morally and legally responsible *only* for actions carried out freely and deliberately. However, we do feel a sense of responsibility for what we have done even if we did not choose that action; for example, a driver who kills a child who ran out in front of his car would blame himself for the death, even if it was not his fault and he could not have prevented it.

Philosophers have traditionally responded to this problem in different ways:

- **hard determinists** accept determinism and reject freedom and moral responsibility;
- **libertarians** reject determinism and accept freedom and moral responsibility;
- **soft determinists** or **compatibilists** reject the two previous views that free will and determinism are incompatible and argue that freedom is not only compatible with determinism, but actually requires it.

Hard determinism
The belief that people do not have any free will and that all moral actions have prior causes. This means that nobody can be held morally responsible.

Libertarianism
The belief that determinism is false and people are free to make moral choices and so are responsible for their actions.

Soft determinism
The belief that determinism is true in many aspects, but we are still morally responsible for our actions.

Compatibilism
The belief that it is possible to be both free and determined, as some aspects of our nature are determined, but not our ability to make moral decisions.

DETERMINISM

Determinism

The view that every event has a cause and so, when applied to moral decisions, we do not have free will.

Determinism states that everything in the universe has a prior cause, including all human actions and choices. This means that all our decisions, viewpoints and opinions can be best understood when translated into the neutral language of natural science.

This view has a long history and may be seen in the *fatalism* of Greek tragedy, in which people are the helpless victims of circumstances, necessity and the Fates.

Predestination

Predestination

The belief that God has decided who will be saved and who will not.

Determinism can also be seen in some versions of Christian **predestination**: the total irrelevance of our actions in this life as God has already decided whether we are saved or not saved. The doctrine of predestination was formulated by such theologians as **Augustine of Hippo** and **John Calvin**, and is based on the idea that God determines whatever happens in history and that man has only a very limited understanding of God's purposes and plans. This idea is not based on words or particular passages in the Bible but on ideas about revelation, and has to sit side by side with teachings about individual freedom and responsibility. According to Augustine, people need the help of God's grace to do good, and this is a free gift from God, regardless of individual merit. Consequently, God alone determines who will receive the grace that assures salvation.

St Augustine of Hippo (354–430)

St Augustine in his cell, 1490 (tempera on panel) by Botticelli, Sandro (1444/5–1510)

Galleria degli Uffizi, Florence, Italy/The Bridgeman Art Library

St Augustine was born on 13 November 354, in Tagaste, Numidia. His father was a pagan but his mother Monica worked for Augustine's conversion.

continued opposite

The fall of dominoes

However, the further idea that while some were predestined to salvation, others were predestined to damnation was rejected. Many Christians, such as Pelagius, rejected any deterministic ideas, but determinism was formulated more precisely by John Calvin during the sixteenth century and is still followed by Presbyterian churches today. This belief says that as man is a complete sinner who is incapable of coming to God, and has a sinful free will that is only capable of rejecting God, then predestination must occur or nobody could be saved. God is in total control and people cannot do anything to achieve salvation. According to Calvin, people are not all created with a similar destiny:

> eternal life is fore-ordained for some, and eternal damnation for others. Every man, therefore, being created for one or the other of these ends, we say, he is predestined to life or death. (Institutes of the Christian Religion Bk3 Ch21 s5)

This idea suggests that people have no free will as far as their ethical decisions are concerned. It states that God makes his choice about who is to be saved independently of any qualities in the individual – God does not look into a person and recognise something good; nor does he look into the future to see who would choose him, but simply decides who will be saved because he can, and all the rest are left to go their natural way: to hell. So people only do good because God made them that way and put them in a certain environment; and the rest are just limited by their naturally sinful nature and can only choose to be sinful. Logically then, if we have no control over our actions, we have no responsibility for them.

HARD DETERMINISM

> In the mind there is no absolute or free will; but the mind is determined to wish this or that by a cause, which has also been determined by another cause, and this last by another cause, and so on to infinity. (Baruch Spinoza)

Hard determinists are called 'hard' because their position is very strict: according to hard determinism all our actions had prior causes – we are neither free nor responsible. Hard determinism is incompatible with free will and moral responsibility, and as all our actions are caused by prior causes we are not free to act in any other way. A person is like a machine, and if a machine is faulty it just needs fixing. The same applies to a person. A person cannot be blamed for their violence; violence either needs 'fixing' or, if this fails, the person needs imprisoning to stop their violence impinging on

From the age of 15 to 30 Augustine lived with a woman from Carthage and in 372 had a son named Adeodatus, 'the gift of God'. Augustine was ordained in 391. He became Bishop of Hippo in 395.

John Calvin (1509–1564)

John Calvin (engraving) (b/w photo) by English school (sixteenth century)

© Private Collection/The Bridgeman Art Library

John Calvin was born in Noyon on 10 July 1509. He studied for the priesthood at the Collège de la Marche and the Collège de Montaigue, in Paris. He then studied law at Orléans and Bourges.

In 1536 the first edition of his *Christianae Religionis Institutio* (Institutes of the Christian Religion) was published and this work led him to the

continued

Baruch Spinoza (1632–1677)

Portrait of Baruch or Benedict Spinoza, Dutch philosopher (engraving)

© Bibliothèque Nationale, Paris, France/The Bridgeman Art Library

Baruch Spinoza was born in 1632 in Amsterdam to a Portuguese-Jewish family.

He was one of the most original and radical thinkers of his time.

continued opposite

others. **John Hospers** was a modern hard determinist who advocated this approach; he says that there is always something which compels us both externally and internally to perform an action that we would think was the result of our own free will. He uses several psychoanalytical examples to make his point and concludes: 'It is all a matter of luck.' This is seen most clearly in the film *Clockwork Orange* (1971).

The same position was taken up by **Clarence Darrow** in 1924, when he defended two young men, Nathan Leopold and Richard Loeb, on a charge of murdering a young boy, Bobby Franks. The perfect crime the two men planned went wrong and in the subsequent court case Darrow, their defence lawyer, pleaded for the death penalty to be commuted to life imprisonment, as the two young murderers were the product of their upbringing, their ancestry and their wealthy environment.

> What has this boy to do with it? He was not his own father; he was not his own mother; he was not his own grandparents. All of this was handed to him. He did not surround himself with governesses and wealth. He did not make himself. And yet he is to be compelled to pay. (Clarence Darrow)

Darrow was successful in his plea and the case makes us question whether criminals are morally responsible for what they do:

> Punishment as punishment is not admissible unless the offender has the free will to select his course. (Clarence Darrow)

More modern versions of hard determinism point to our genetic heritage, social conditioning or subconscious influences as prior causes. The most extreme modern version of hard determinism is **behaviourism**.

Behaviourism

White laboratory rats (*Rattus* sp.) in laboratory, close-up

Stone (Jonathan Selig) Getty Images

Psychological behaviourism was first discussed by **John B. Watson**, who suggested that behaviour can be predicted and controlled, as people live and act in a determined universe so that all human behaviour, including ethical decisions, is controlled by prior causes which are, in principle, knowable. Behaviour is influenced, according to Watson, by heredity and environment – nature and nurture. By manipulating the environment people's behaviour can be altered. This idea is called 'conditioning' and was influenced by the work of **Ivan Pavlov**, who conditioned dogs to salivate (as if they were about to be fed) when they heard the sound of a bell. We are all familiar with this, as in schools we are conditioned to act in certain ways when we hear the school bell ring for a lesson change.

However, we are not always conditioned by our environment but will often use it to get what we want – even dogs will eventually go in search of food if no food appears. This sort of behaviour is known as operant conditioning and is most often linked to the work of **B.F. Skinner**, who investigated behaviour modification through reward and punishment. He claimed that, behavioural science develops and psychologists learn to determine and control human behaviour, it is highly probable that human behaviour is not free but most likely determined. Moral behaviour is about what people ought and ought not to do, but if they could not have done anything else then they had no freedom of choice and cannot be blamed for their actions.

Steven Pinker approached determinism from another angle and looked at the ideas of **Darwin**, developed recently by **Richard Dawkins**, that emotions such as guilt, anger, sympathy and love all have a biological basis. He developed the theory that our moral reasoning is a result of natural selection but he claims that this does not mean the end of moral responsibility. Evolution might, for example, predispose men to violence or to sleeping around, but this does not necessitate or excuse such behaviour – a moral sense is innate in us and so is 'as real for us as if it were decreed by the Almighty or written into the cosmos'.

All theories of determinism are influenced by **Isaac Newton**'s physics, according to which the universe is governed by immutable laws of nature such as motion and gravitation. The world is seen as a mechanism dominated by the law of predictable cause and effect. Followers of Newton, such as **Laplace**, placed such confidence in the all-pervasive power of causality that they thought that the minutest prediction could be made if only we knew the various causal factors involved. This included the actions of people – there is room for neither chance nor choice.

So freedom of choice is just an illusion – we may appear to have moral choices, but we only think we choose freely because we do not know the causes that lie behind our choices. This is illustrated by the philosopher **John Locke**, who describes a sleeping man in a locked room; on awakening he decides to stay where he is, not realising that the door to the room is locked.

Spinoza had great influence on the Enlightenment and also influenced the development of modern philosophical, political and religious thought.

Clarence Seward Darrow (1857–1938)

Darrow was an American lawyer. In 1924 he defended Richard Loeb and Nathan Leopold on the charge of murdering 14-year-old Robert Franks in Chicago. They were imprisoned, but were saved from the death penalty because of Darrow's defence.

In the Scopes Monkey Trial heard in Dayton, Tennessee (10–21 July 1925), Darrow defended a teacher who had broken state law by teaching Darwin's theory of evolution.

In the Sweet case in Detroit (1925–6), he successfully defended a black family that had fought against a mob which was trying to expel the family from their home in a white neighbourhood.

John Broadus Watson (1878–1958)

John B. Watson was born in Greenville, South

continued

Carolina, and studied at the Furman University and the University of Chicago. He is the founder of the school of psychology known as behaviourism.

Ivan Petrovich Pavlov (1849–1936)

Ivan P. Pavlov was born in Ryazan in Russia. He studied theology and then medicine. He was the first Russian winner of the Nobel Prize for Physiology or Medicine (1904). At the presentation ceremony, Pavlov explained his ideas of 'unconditioned reflexes', 'conditioned reflexes' and reaction to an unrelated external stimulus. His research was published in *Conditioned Reflexes* (1926).

Burrhus Frederic Skinner (1904–1990)

B.F. Skinner was born in Susquehanna, Pennsylvania. He studied at Harvard University. Skinner became the leading exponent of the behaviourist school of psychology, explaining human behaviour in terms of physiological responses to external stimuli.

The man thinks that he has made a free decision, but in reality he has no choice. So it is with our moral choices – we think we make free decisions simply because we do not know the causes. This view was also taken by **Paul-Henri Thiry (Baron) d'Holbach**, who said that humans and human society and actions can all be understood in terms of cause and effects – freedom is again an illusion:

> You will say that I feel free. This is an illusion, which may be compared to that of the fly in the fable, who, upon the pole of a heavy carriage, applauded himself for directing its course. Man, who thinks himself free, is a fly who imagines he has power to move the universe, while is himself unknowingly carried along by it.

Ted Honderich also drew the conclusion that, since everything is physically determined, there is no choice and so no personal responsibility; there is not even any 'self' within us that is the origin of our actions. According to Honderich, there is no room for moral blame and no point in punishment for the sake of punishment.

Evaluating hard determinism

- Hard determinism means we cannot blame or praise people for their actions.
- If hard determinism were true then people would not be morally responsible, and so would not deserve blame for even the most cold-blooded and calmly performed evil actions.
- All choices we make are just illusions – they are determined.
- Hard determinism, therefore, rejects the idea of punishment as retri-

bution, but it does not reject any other views about the justification of punishment; for example, deterrence, self-defence or moral education.

- Classical physics is indeed deterministic, but modern quantum physics is not deterministic and so it makes no sense to worry about determinism in the twenty-first century. Modern physics maintains that the most basic laws of nature are not deterministic but probabilistic.

- If determinism is true then all the horrible things that happen in the world had to happen – this is a very pessimistic view of the world.

LIBERTARIANISM OR INCOMPATIBILISM

The view of those who reject determinism and say we have complete moral responsibility is called libertarianism, or **incompatibilism**, as they believe determinism is false and we have free will. Libertarians say that the ideas of cause and effect cannot be applied to human behaviour and choices; we do have freedom to act and we are morally responsible for our actions. Libertarians do not believe that we are compelled to act by outside forces but that moral actions are the result of the values and character of the individual.

This view means that we have free choice and can choose different ways to act, whereas determinism means that we do the only thing we can do and so never really have a choice about anything. The most common argument for libertarianism is that it appeals to our *intuitions* – we see ourselves as free agents, able to make moral choices, not as puppets on a string or robots. Unlike puppets or robots we have a mind, and it seems reasonable to conclude that having a mind is necessary in order to have free will. **Peter van Inwagen** uses the analogy of choosing which branch to go down when travelling along a road, whereas determinism is like travelling along a road with no branches – we cannot choose a different way, or reach a different destination.

Libertarians also argue that, unlike **Darrow**'s argument that we do not 'make ourselves', we do 'make our actions' and we could have chosen to do something else. This, they argue, is clear because when asked to defend our actions we blame ourselves, or wonder if we did the right thing – we evaluate our action by asking ourselves whether, at that time, we could have acted differently. We would only blame, criticise or regret, if we believed we had alternative ways of acting. This is a common-sense view of ourselves as choosers and agents with the future open to us in the way the past is not. We know that unforeseen events can alter events in the future – for example, a student may always achieve A grades in practice examination papers, but this does not mean that on the day of the final examination he will do so. His experience may predict that he will do so, but on the day of the examination he may have a bad cold, his dog may have died or he may misread a question

John Locke (1632–1704)

Portrait of John Locke by Sir Godfrey Kneller (1646–1723) (after)

© Private Collection/© Philip Mould, Historical Portraits Ltd, London, UK/The Bridgeman Art Library

John Locke was born in Somerset on 29 August 1632. He studied at Oxford and lectured in Greek and moral philosophy there from 1661 to 1664. In 1675 Locke moved to France, returning to England in 1679. From 1683 to 1688 he lived in Holland. He returned to England in 1688 after the Glorious Revolution put William III, a Protestant, on the throne. Locke founded the school of empiricism and supported the idea of a social contract. He died in Oates on 28 October 1704.

Paul-Henri Thiry (Baron) d'Holbach (1723–1789)

Baron d'Holbach was born in December 1723 at

continued

Edesheim in the Rhenish Palatinate.

He was a French encyclopaedist and philosopher, a celebrated exponent of atheism and materialism. His most famous book was *Système de la nature* (1770), which he wrote under the pseudonym of J.B. Mirabaud. He denounced religion and put forward an atheistic materialism. He died on 21 June 1789 in Paris.

Ted Honderich (1933–)

Honderich is a Canadian from a Mennonite family. He was Grote Professor at the University of London from 1988 until 1998. His book *After the Terror* (2002) caused controversy over the questions he raised about the events of 11 September 2001.

Incompatibilism

The belief that determinism is logically incompatible with free will. Thus some incompatibilists will say that determinism is a fact and so we are not free, but most take the opposite view that free will is a fact and so determinism is false.

– from our observation of the world around us we know that things can always go wrong.

Another answer to the claim of determinism is that it is not the case that all events have a cause: some events are uncaused, and human decisions and choices are an example of such uncaused events. Modern physics is often used to defend this view and especially **Werner Heisenberg**'s uncertainty principle, which says that we cannot know both the location and the momentum of subatomic particles at the same time. He therefore thought it was better to refer to the statistical probabilities rather than formulate general laws. Using this principle as a basis, it seems that determinism is false.

Many scientists now agree that since the idea of cause does not apply to subatomic particles, not every event in the universe is caused – some are, in principle, unpredictable. **Honderich** rejects the claims of quantum physics, saying that they only apply at the subatomic level; it is certainly not true to think that quantum physics refutes Newtonian mechanics – it is more accurate to say that it qualifies Newton's view and puts his theories in a broader context.

However, using this argument to support libertarianism misses the point. The principle of causality is actually presupposed when considering freedom, as the opposite of causality is *randomness*. A universe in which there are random events is not one in which we have free will. Behaviour caused by a random event is no more freely chosen than behaviour completely determined by the laws of Newtonian physics. Nobody could be held morally responsible for an act that was caused by a random event occurring in his brain. Modern physics seems to maintain that the most basic laws of nature are not deterministic but probabilistic. Einstein said, 'God does not play dice' – but apparently Einstein was wrong.

For free choices to be real, a person must be able to cause the events he chooses. If all human actions take place independently of any cause at all, including the will of the individual, then there is no genuine freedom. I am only *not* free to act if I am forced or compelled.

This idea of freedom is also seen as a goal of moral action – even if our freedom is limited, we show our freedom in our aim to be free and act freely. This is one of the great themes of *existentialism*. For **Jean-Paul Sartre**, freedom is both the goal and the measure of our lives – from nothing man makes himself what he chooses. Freedom here is an end in itself, as it does not matter *what* a person chooses as long as he chooses freely. A person must fill his nothingness with freedom – everything depends on the individual and the meaning he gives to his life. A person may try to avoid this freedom; then he is guilty of *mauvaise foi* and just conforms to what is decided by others. He sees life as ultimately *absurd*, meaningless, and without any reason why an individual exists or chooses to do one thing rather than another. 'To be free is to be condemned to be free.' So freedom is both the underpinning of any morality and it is a goal – to be free is to have a humanly fulfilling life.

```
┌─────────────────┐
│ Libertarianism  │
└─────────────────┘
     ├──── All human actions are free
     ├──── We make free moral choices
     └──── We are morally responsible for our actions
```

Evaluating libertarianism

- Libertarianism recognises that people have a sense of decision-making, a sense of freedom, a sense of deliberating over their choices in life.
- Personal responsibility underpins our whole system of ethics and law.
- David Hume pointed out that, even if in nature event B consistently follows event A on every observed occasion, to say that event A causes event B is to go beyond observation. It is our way of interpreting the events, not a feature of the events in themselves.
- Libertarians insist that free will is the uncoerced power to choose – but how does a person decide what to do? What criteria does he use to make a decision? What about his past experiences, emotions, beliefs and values?

SOFT DETERMINISM OR COMPATIBILISM

Soft determinism or compatibilism says that some of our actions are determined but that we are morally responsible for our actions. Soft determinists argue that there is confusion between determinism and fatalism about what we mean by freedom of choice. Freedom of choice is not compatible with fatalism, 'what ever will be will be', which says that nobody can change the course of events, but it is compatible with determinism, a theory of universal causation, if we include our own values, choices and desires among the choices that determine our actions. Soft determinists agree that all human actions are caused, since if they were not they would be unpredictable and

Werner Heisenberg (1901–1976)

Werner Heisenberg was born on 5 December 1901 in Würzburg and studied at the University of Munich. As a physicist and Nobel Laureate he developed a system of quantum mechanics. His uncertainty principle had a profound influence on physics and philosophy.

Jean-Paul Sartre (1905–1980)

Jean-Paul Sartre was born in Paris on 21 June 1905. He studied at the École Normale Supérieure, the University of Fribourg, Switzerland, and the French Institute in Berlin. Sartre was a leading existentialist. In his writings he related his philosophical theory to literature, psychology and political action.

random. They mean that when an individual's actions are free, they are not forced or compelled by any external pressure.

Soft determinism may be seen as the view that determinism is compatible with whatever sort of freedom is necessary for moral responsibility. Linking this to the developments in physics, perhaps we live in an indeterministic universe that is not completely described by modern physics because there are some events (e.g. some human behaviours) which are not determined and not random either. After all, who knows what physics will be like in twenty-five or fifty years' time?

A clue to solving this argument is given by **Immanuel Kant**, who believed that determinism applied to everything which was the object of knowledge, but not to acts of the will. He said that people work from two different and seemingly incompatible standpoints: the theoretical (pure reason) and the practical (practical reason). Pure reason concerns knowledge, the mind and the way we see the scientifically explicable world; practical reason concerns actions, the will and the way we see ourselves. We cannot look rationally for causes of our actions beyond a genuine act of our will. When we act we always think of ourselves as free. Kant says freedom is a postulate of practical reason. Kant's argument is that our own self-awareness, without which the world would not make sense to us, forces on us the idea that we are free, so we cannot get rid of the idea that we are free without ceasing to see ourselves as the originator of our actions.

Soft determinism, then, is not a position that combines the determinist and libertarian positions; it is not a compromise, it does not limit free will, but is a position taken due to the need to have some accountability and responsibility for human behaviour. Soft determinists clarify what they mean by free: we are not free to fly just using our own bodies to propel us through the air – this is to misuse the word 'free' and change it from meaning 'being able to choose' to 'being physically able to do'. According to soft determinists,

'Ought implies can'
The idea that someone cannot be blamed for what he could not do, but only for what he was capable of doing but did not do.

we are morally responsible for, and can reasonably be punished and praised for, those actions which are caused by our own desires and decisions.

Evaluating soft determinism

- Soft determinism agrees that moral responsibility is important in our society, but that it is not reasonable to hold a person responsible for actions caused by his emotions, beliefs, desires and decisions if he has no choice about having them.
- It is, however, hard for the soft determinist to decide what exactly is determined and what can be freely chosen. The complex nature of people and the roles of physics, genetics and psychology make deciding what exactly is, or is not, a determining factor very hard.
- Soft determinism also allows for creativity in our choices – so not all our choices are the result of existing desires and habits.

Thought Point

- Do we, as Einstein said, 'dance to a mysterious tune, intoned in the distance by an invisible piper'?
- From your own life and experiences list examples that show we are all determined. Can you think of other explanations for these events?
- Does hard determinism mean there is no point in the moral education of children?
- Does soft determinism overcome the problems of both hard determinism and libertarianism?
- If the future is determined, is God irrelevant?

Activities

Here are some situations in which there is, in principle, freedom of action. Yet how free are we to choose? Consider the problems faced when the influences of the society in which we live are considered:

- The influence of *upbringing* – you need to lie to save a friend's reputation. You know it is the kindest thing to do but you also know that your face will give the game away. What do you do?

continued

- The influence of *common politeness*. You find a lesson really boring and covering material you already know; there are still thirty minutes to go. You are free to walk out but. . . .
- The influence of *convention* – you are going to your sixth-year ball. Everyone is dressing up in their ball gowns and dinner suits. You are free to turn up dressed in jeans – or are you?
- The influence of *social pressures* – you visit your boyfriend's/girlfriend's parents and they serve you your least favourite meal and then ask if you enjoyed it. What do you do?

Can you add to this list any situations in which in one sense you are free to act as you like, but in another sense your hands are tied?

REVIEW QUESTIONS

Look back over the chapter and check that you can answer the following questions:

1 Explain the roles of science, society and psychology in determinism.
2 Copy and complete the following revision chart on A3 paper: their

Theory	Key scholars	Key ideas	Strengths	Weaknesses	Possible quotations
Hard determinism					
Predestination					
Soft determinism					
Libertarianism					

Essay question

'We do not possess any genuine freedom to act ethically.' Discuss.
(OCR A2 Level 2772 June 2004 question 2)

Remember that in A2 questions both the AO1 and the AO2 assessment objectives are assessed together – you need to evaluate and criticise different views as you write your answer. An examination essay must show that you know what the question is about and that you are answering it – it is basically an argument showing your knowledge and that you can use it to justify a point of view. You also need to show that you understand the different viewpoints and all their strengths and weaknesses. Above all you must answer the question set – not the one you would like to have been set.

In your answer to this question you will need to include the arguments of hard determinists, libertarians and soft determinists, and relate these to what it means to act freely in an ethical way. Be careful not to talk just about acting freely.

You could explore the implications of being free to act ethically with reference to libertarianism and possibly Kant. You might explain how having no genuine freedom to act ethically implies that it is impossible to blame or praise someone for their ethical decisions and actions. You need to discuss the views of soft determinists that determinism does not rule out free will and so we are free to act ethically.

FURTHER READING

Honderich, T. *How Free Are You?*, Oxford, Oxford University Press, 1993.

Macquarrie, J. and Childress, J. *A New Dictionary of Christian Ethics*, London, SCM, 1986.

Palmer, M. *Moral Problems*, Cambridge, Lutterworth Press, 1991.

Van Inwagen, P. *An Essay on Free Will*, Cambridge, Clarendon Press, 1983.

12 Conscience

WHAT YOU WILL LEARN ABOUT IN THIS CHAPTER

- Different ideas of what conscience is.
- An understanding that conscience requires freedom and knowledge of the good to operate.
- Whether it is right to always follow one's conscience – arguments for and against relying on conscience for making ethical decisions.
- The origins of conscience: society, God or inner feelings?

KEY SCHOLARS

- Augustine of Hippo (354–430)
- Thomas Aquinas (1225–1274)
- Joseph Butler (1692–1752)
- John Henry Newman (1801–1890)
- Sigmund Freud (1856–1939)
- Jean Piaget (1896–1980)
- Erich Fromm (1900–1980)

- Lawrence Kohlberg (1927–)
- Richard Gula (1947–)
- Enda McDonagh (1930–)
- Daniel Maguire (1931–)
- Vincent MacNamara
- Jack Mahoney
- Timothy O'Connell
- Vernon Ruland

THE OCR CHECKLIST

The nature and role of the conscience:

- The views of Aquinas, Butler and Freud.
- Other understandings of the conscience as innate, God-given or acquired (e.g. the views of Newman or Piaget).

   From OCR A Level Religious Studies Specification 7877.

WHAT IS CONSCIENCE?

Most people probably understand **conscience** as something which tells us right from wrong, but when the issues are considered in more depth the actual nature and function of conscience are harder to establish.

When considering the nature and function of conscience there are four questions to keep in mind:

- What is conscience?
- Where does conscience come from?
- Is conscience innate or acquired?
- What is its function in ethical decision-making?

Conscience is generally seen as a moral faculty, sense or feeling which compels individuals to believe that particular activities are morally right or wrong. Conscience may also be seen to prompt different people in quite different directions – one person may feel a moral duty to go to war, while another may feel a moral duty to avoid war in all circumstances.

Most of us could make lists of behaviours we could not indulge in and actions we could not perform due to the dictates of our consciences. We consider conscience to be a reliable guide. We could perhaps even agree with Mark Twain who wrote: 'I have noticed my conscience for many years, and I know it is more trouble and bother to me than anything else I started with.' The last phrase is important, as it implies that conscience is something we inherit at birth and remains a fellow traveller with us throughout our lives. Experience seems to tell us, however, that this cannot be so – conscience lacks consistency, whether between people in general or in any particular person. Just think what appalling acts are performed with a clear conscience (just obeying commands) or even in the name of conscience. Even individuals are inconsistent and matters about which we once had conscientious feelings no longer affect us. If conscience is so changeable, how can it be a reliable guide? Does it only represent our views on moral issues as we see them at any given moment?

Views about conscience vary, and different writers will see it in different ways and have different opinions about its role in ethical decision-making.

There are two main types of view that influence which stance is taken:

1 *Religious views*, including biblical teaching, Divine Command theory, the works of Augustine, Aquinas, Butler, Newman, Bonhoeffer and so on.
2 *Secular views,* including psychological, sociological, humanitarian and authoritarian.

Conscience
Our sense of moral right and wrong.

BIBLICAL TEACHING

It is assumed by some biblical writers and early Christian teachers that our conscience is God-given. This view is put clearly in Paul's letter to the Romans:

> When Gentiles, who do not possess the law, do instinctively what the law requires, these, though not having the law, are a law to themselves. They show that what the law requires is written on their hearts. (Romans 2:1415a)

Traditional Christian teaching is based on this – everyone knows what is right and wrong, as God has given us this ability. It is also implied that by following their conscience, everyone can follow the divine law.

AQUINAS' APPROACH – REASON SEEKING UNDERSTANDING

Thomas Aquinas (1225–1274) saw conscience as the natural ability of people to understand the difference between right and wrong. He believed that all people aim for what is good and try to avoid the bad, and he called this the **synderesis rule** (*synderesis* is Greek for conscience) and reckoned it was innate to seek the good – sin is a falling short of God's ideals, seeking what people think is good and is actually bad because they are not using their powers of reason properly. Aquinas understood that different societies have different views on what is right and what is wrong and, though he says people should always follow their conscience, he does see that people will sometimes get things wrong and make the wrong choices. He argued that conscience 'was the mind of man making moral judgments' and described it as containing two essential parts – *synderesis* and **conscientia**.

Synderesis means the repeated use of what Aquinas termed 'right' reason, by which a person acquires knowledge of basic moral principles and understands that it is important to do good and avoid evil. *Conscientia* is the actual ethical judgement or decision a person makes which leads to a particular course of action based upon these principles. Conscience, therefore, for Aquinas, is being able both to distinguish right from wrong and to make decisions when a person is confronted with difficult moral situations.

When Aquinas says it is always right to follow your conscience, he means that it is always right to apply your moral principles to each situation as best you can. He does not mean that if you follow your conscience you are always right – as if your principles are wrong, your conscience will be wrong too.

Synderesis

Aquinas' idea of what he termed 'right' reason by which a person acquires knowledge of basic moral principles and understands that it is important to do good and avoid evil.

Conscientia

Aquinas called this the actual ethical judgement or decision a person made.

Aquinas says conscience is reasoning used correctly to find out what God sees is good. It is not just a voice inside us. Do we always use reason in this way? Is reason, always guided by conscience, going to determine what we do, or do we rather use our emotions when making moral choices?

Some Christians would say that Aquinas' rationalistic approach does not consider revelation that comes directly from God.

BUTLER'S APPROACH – CONSCIENCE COMES FROM GOD

The eighteenth-century Anglican priest and philosopher **Joseph Butler** wrote that the most crucial thing which distinguished women and men from the animal world was the possession of the faculty of reflection or conscience. So being human involves being moral. He stated in one of his Sermons: 'There is a principle of reflection in men by which they distinguish between approval and disapproval of their own actions . . . this principle in man . . . is conscience.'

Like Aquinas, Butler believed conscience could determine and judge the rightness or wrongness of different actions and thoughts. Conscience, for Butler, also held a powerful position within human decision-making because, as he wrote, it 'magisterially exerts itself' spontaneously 'without being consulted'.

Therefore, there is something authoritative and automatic for Butler about the way conscience works when moral decisions have to be made. He gave to conscience the final say in moral decision-making. Conscience, he said, governed and ordered such aspects and was the final moral authority: 'Had it strength, as it has right; had it power as it has manifest authority, it would absolutely govern the world.'

> **Joseph Butler (1692–1752)**
>
> Joseph Butler became Dean of St Paul's Cathedral, London, in 1740 and Bishop of Durham in 1750. He is best known for his work *Analogy of Religion* (1736). He argued that belief in natural religion was no more rational than belief in revealed religion. He saw the two as complementary.

Butler saw human nature as hierarchical and at the top is conscience. At its base are drives such as the drive for food which influence us without any thought for the consequences, and above these drives are two general impulses: **self-love** (wanting the well-being of self or enlightened self-interest, not selfishness) and **benevolence** (wanting the well-being of others). Higher than these and linked closely to the conscience is the 'principle of reflection' which makes us approve or disapprove of our actions. This is given to us by God and we have to use it to lead a proper, happy life. Conscience has supreme authority, and all moral decisions are decided under the guidance and authority of conscience.

An important point made by Butler was that conscience came from God. He believed conscience was a person's God-given guide to right conduct and its demands must therefore always be followed. He does not try to analyse whether conscience is based on reason or feeling or both: he just says that it obviously exists; it comes from God and must be obeyed if a person is to be truly happy.

Butler did not see mistakes made by conscience as a serious problem, as he believed that in any moral dilemma most people will see intuitively what is the right thing to do. However, he considers it wicked to 'blind' one's conscience to clear the way for a wrong action. People can easily convince themselves that all sorts of wrong actions are right and, for Butler, this corruption of conscience by self-deception is worse than the evil action which results from it.

Butler thinks that your conscience will tell you to watch out for the interests of others as far as possible.

Butler has some important ideas which may be applied further:

- The consequence of an action is not what makes it right or wrong, as that has already happened.
- The purpose of conscience is to guide a person into a way of life that will make him happy.
- Conscience will harmonise self-love and benevolence – this may take some sorting out, and so in moral dilemmas we may be uncertain what to do.
- Conscience controls human nature.

NEWMAN'S APPROACH – CONSCIENCE AS THE VOICE OF GOD

The nineteenth-century theologian **Cardinal John Henry Newman** also adopted an intuitionist approach to conscience. For example, in his *Letter to the Duke of Norfolk* in 1874, he wrote that when a person follows conscience

Self-love

Butler thought of this as wanting the well-being of self or enlightened self-interest, not selfishness.

Benevolence

Butler saw this as wanting the well-being of others.

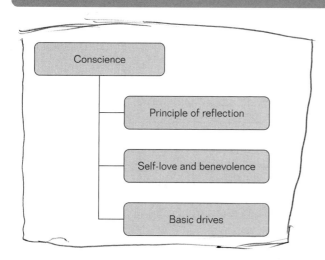

he is simultaneously, in some mysterious way, following a divine law. Conscience is 'a messenger' of God and it is God speaking to us when we feel this intuitive moral knowledge and make decisions. He argued that, for Christians, conscience is more than simply 'a law of the mind', since it comes from God. Conscience does not invent the truth, but at its best it detects the truth. Elsewhere in his writings (*The Grammar of Assent*, chapter 5) Newman says: 'If, as is the case, we feel responsibility, are ashamed, are frightened, at transgressing the voice of conscience, this implies there is One to whom we are responsible, before whom we are ashamed, whose claims upon us we fear.'

The fourth-century theologian **Augustine of Hippo** (354–430) had said the same thing, and he also believed that conscience was to be identified with the voice of God speaking to us. When we listen to it, we are really hearing the word of God whispering to us about what is right and what is wrong. Augustine urged all Christians to be concerned about conscience and to consider it most seriously. 'Return to your conscience, question it. . . . Turn inward, brethren, and in everything you do, see God as your witness', he wrote.

Butler's, Newman's and Augustine's ideas on conscience are much less rationalist than Aquinas' and rely on a more *intuitionist approach*, whereby people are able to sense or intuit what is right and wrong, because God reveals this to them personally.

SECULAR

FREUD'S APPROACH – CONSCIENCE IS GUILT

Sigmund Freud was a psychiatrist who formed a very influential theory of personality. He studied the human mind, and its effects on and reactions with the body. Freud believed there was no such thing as a soul and his view of the mind was essentially mechanistic. From his work, Freud concluded that the human personality consisted of three areas:

1 The **super-ego** – the set of moral controls given to us by outside influences. It is our moral code or conscience and is often in conflict with the id.
2 *The ego* – the conscious self, the part seen by the outside world.
3 *The id* – the unconscious self, the part of the mind containing basic drives and repressed memories. It is amoral, has no concerns about right and wrong and is only concerned with itself.

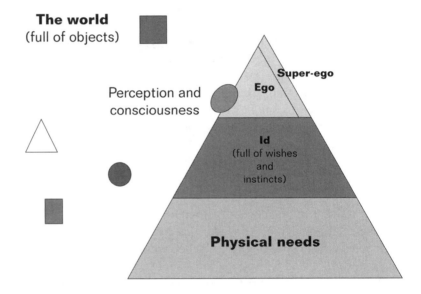

Super-ego

Freud's idea is that the super-ego reinforces ideas of correct behaviour implanted in us when we are young.

Sigmund Freud (1856–1939)

Portrait of Sigmund Freud c.1900 (b/w photo) by Austrian photographer (twentieth century)

Oesterreichische Nationalbibliothek, Vienna, Austria/Archives Charmet/The Bridgeman Art Library

Sigmund Freud was born in Freiberg, Moravia, on 6 May 1856. His family were driven out by anti-Semitic riots and moved, via Leipzig, to Vienna.

He was inspired by the scientific work of Johann Wolfgang von Goethe and began his medical education in 1873. He studied the central nervous system under Ernst Wilhelm von Brücke.

continued opposite

For Freud, the conscience is most clearly connected with the sense of guilt we feel when we go against our conscience. Conscience then is simply a construct of the mind – in religious people this would be in response to perceptions of God and in non-religious people it would be their responses to externally imposed authority. Freud did not believe in any absolute moral law and held that all our moral codes, and thus the content of our consciences, are shaped by our experiences – it is culturally dependent and this explains the varieties of moral codes that are to be found in different societies.

So if children learn their moral behaviour from their parents, teachers and other authority figures, is any moral choice they may make free? If the super-ego internalises the disapproval of others and creates the guilty conscience which grows into an internal force regardless of any individual rational thought or reflection, is it not just a form of moral control which traps us in its grasp?

PIAGET AND KOHLBERG – THE DEVELOPMENTAL CONSCIENCE

Psychologists since Freud have expanded his ideas to include that of immature and mature consciences which develop as we grow up. This will not necessarily be a continuous development and some people will never reach the stage of having a mature conscience. According to **Jean Piaget** a child's moral development grows and the ability to reason morally depends on cognitive development.

Piaget suggested two stages of moral development:

1   *Heteronomous morality* (between the ages of approximately 5 and 10 years) when the conscience is still immature, rules are not to be broken and punishment is expected if a rule is broken. The consequences of an action will show if it is right or wrong.

2   *Autonomous morality* (approximately ages 10+) when children develop their own rules and understand how rules operate in and help society. The move towards autonomous morality occurs when the child is less dependent on others for moral authority.

Child development

Lawrence Kohlberg followed Piaget's ideas and identified six stages of moral development which he believed individuals had to follow in sequence. People move from behaving in socially acceptable ways because they are told to do so by authority figures and want to gain approval, to keeping the law, to caring for others and finally to respect for universal principles and the demands of an individual conscience. Kohlberg felt that most adults never got beyond keeping the law.

Both Piaget and Kohlberg believed that most moral development and the development of a conscience occur through social interaction.

FROMM'S APPROACH (1) – THE AUTHORITARIAN CONSCIENCE

Erich Fromm believed that all humans are influenced by external authorities – parents, teachers, Church leaders – who apply rules and punishments for breaking them, and that these rules are then internalised by the individual. A guilty conscience is a result of displeasing authority and if that authority is God then the fear of being rejected will have a powerful influence on an individual. Disobedience produces guilt, which in turn weakens our power and makes us more submissive to authority. The way that the Nazi government in Germany in the 1930s manipulated the consciences of its people to feel guilty about helping or not harming Jews is a classic

Poland, Lesser Poland region, Auschwitz entrance gate

Photographer's Choice (Ulf Sjostedt) Getty Images

example of the **authoritarian conscience**. Fromm himself escaped Nazi Germany in 1934.

FROMM'S APPROACH (2) – THE HUMANISTIC CONSCIENCE

Fromm's views changed over time and he obviously saw the humanistic conscience as being much healthier, since it assesses and evaluates our behaviour. We use it to judge how successful we are as people. It is our real self and leads us to realise our potential as far as possible. We use our own discoveries in life, and the teachings and examples of others, to give us personal integrity and moral honesty – quite the opposite of the slavish obedience and conformity of the authoritarian conscience.

These psychological accounts of conscience may seem to conflict with the religious views of Aquinas, Butler and Newman – but they do not necessarily undermine the possibility of God having some role in our conscience.

MODERN UNDERSTANDINGS OF CONSCIENCE

The Roman Catholic Church at its Second Vatican Council (1962–5) discussed the issue of conscience and agreed that there was a law inside each person which speaks to the individual heart. The emphasis given here was on an understanding of conscience as a personal and inner sense of right and wrong, but which worked like any law, and which held the person to obedience. One Council document, *The Pastoral Constitution of the Church in the Modern World*, stated that this law of the heart is, in fact, 'a law written by God. To obey it is the very dignity of man; according to it he will be judged.'

Modern scholars have attempted to define what conscience is in different ways from earlier thinkers. **Vincent MacNamara**, for example, argues that it is misleading to describe conscience as 'a voice', since this makes it sound like a special faculty or a piece of equipment which human beings possess, a separate thing inside the individual. He says it is much better to see conscience in terms of *an attitude* or *an awareness* people have that there is a moral path to be followed through life and that true human living does not revolve around profit and pleasure. MacNamara argues that the fact that people see that goodness and truth are important is another way of describing conscience; he puts it like this: 'it is not so much that I have a conscience – a special piece of equipment – as that I am a conscience. That is how I am, that is how I find myself. That is a basic truth about life.' This way of

Authoritarian conscience
Our sense of moral right and wrong formed in us by authority figures whom we want to obey.

> **Erich Fromm (1900–1980)**
>
> Erich Fromm was born in Frankfurt am Main in Germany, studied at the universities of Heidelberg and Munich, and later at the Psychoanalytic Institute in Berlin. In 1934 he emigrated to America, soon after the Nazis came to power. As a psychoanalyst, Fromm is best known for his application of the theory of psychoanalysis to social and cultural problems.

describing conscience is based in ideas about the kind of people we are and how we 'see' the world. You could say in a sense that it is linked to Virtue ethics.

There are similarities in the work of **Richard Gula**, who argues that to consider conscience in terms of a series of laws, even a series of internal laws, is also misleading. He highlights two key terms in respect of the conscience: *vision* and *choice*. This is the ability to act, within a learned framework, through the needs of a Christian community and developed within a Christian understanding. The various communities which form our way of 'seeing' the world also determine the way our conscience works. Therefore, conscience is a way of 'seeing' and then responding, through the choices we make, to the world in which we live. Both MacNamara and Gula focus on a *holistic approach* to conscience.

Vernon Ruland tries to find a *via media* between rationalism and uncritical Divine Command theory and sees a moral decision as reflecting an 'ethics of loyal scrutiny' enriched by many sources of moral and religious wisdom. He explains that the God invoked in our conscience is not the exclusive property of Christians and points out that there are many interlinked sources of what he calls the ways of religious wisdom. Conscience seems to be less the 'voice of God' than our interpretation of that 'voice'.

Timothy O'Connell sees conscience as having three aspects or levels: first, it is our general sense of personal responsibility for who we are and what we become; second, it is our sense of obligation to search out the good, using all the resources of moral reasoning available to us, including the assistance of a moral community such as the Church; and finally it is the concrete judgement a person makes so that good as he sees it must be done. On this final level conscience is infallible and must be followed, but on the second level people can disagree in their conscientious judgements and wrong judgements can be made. Moral values are discovered by moral reasoning and are imposed by neither external nor internal laws but are discovered by historical human experience of the consequences of action for human fulfilment. **Daniel Maguire** agrees with O'Connell, but adds that in discerning what is the correct moral choice we also need to consider the place of creative imagination, humour and the tragic experiences of life, especially great loss, as these open us up to new perceptions of value. Both O'Connell and Maguire see conscience as based on more than human reason; it is also based on the shared experience of the past, the shared experience of a culture and personal experience and affectivity.

CONSCIENCE AS A MORAL GUIDE

Crucial questions we need to address when considering conscience are: how important is it as a moral guide, and can it be relied upon? This brings us into discussion of two important areas. First, what authority or status should be given to individual conscience in moral decision-making, and, second, how is a person's conscience formed so that it might be a good basis for making moral choices?

Within the Christian tradition, conscience is given overriding importance in moral decision-making. Conscience must always be followed; a person is obliged to act in accordance with the dictates of conscience.

Aquinas gave considerable weight to the role of conscience. He believed that not following the dictates of conscience was always wrong, because by not following it a person was ignoring what he believed to be true. He believed conscience was a deep sense of right and wrong which came from God. Following one's conscience was like following the law of God and, even when conscience was mistaken, Aquinas believed that a person had a duty to follow it.

However, following one's conscience is no guarantee that one is always doing the right thing. It is sometimes possible to be mistaken about what is the right thing to do. This brings us to the second question about the reliability of conscience. For example, many people believe a particular course of action to be right at one time in their lives and then change their minds about that action at a later stage. Aquinas is again helpful in addressing this problem. He argued that it is the duty of everyone to inform and educate one's conscience. However, acting according to conscience, for Aquinas, is not a guarantee that a person is doing what is right; it ensures only that he will be morally blameless.

THE FORMATION OF CONSCIENCE

There are many external guides and pointers which help the individual conscience to make the right decision. To acquire an informed conscience is the responsibility of every person. Most of the approaches to conscience we have considered here think that conscience needs educating and forming.

In using conscience to make moral choices, individuals must ultimately make their own individual decision. No matter how influential external agencies are, following one's conscience always involves a personal evaluation. This is what separates the role of conscience in decision-making from other methods. Following the dictates of conscience demands following what springs from the unique perception and grasp of the situation as perceived by the individual. No one can really be said to be following his conscience if he does not possess the courage to work things out and decide for himself.

PROBLEMS WITH CONSCIENCE

We have stated that for Christians conscience is often regarded as the voice of God. However, this raises some serious questions. If we were always certain that what our conscience told us to do in any moral situation was in fact God's command, it could be argued that we would never err or make mistakes, as God would not tell us things which are wrong. Clearly people do make errors of moral judgement which they regret later. In answer to this, some might reply that God does speak to us, but that we have not built up a sufficiently sensitive conscience to hear God's voice clearly – it is our fault, not God's.

If conscience is defined as being God's voice speaking to us, this implies that we know for certain what God commands of us. In addition, people often have doubts about what is the right thing to do and have difficulty deciding. Besides, even Christian denominations disagree on moral matters such as abortion – deciding what is the right thing to do is not always as clear-cut as 'the voice of God' definition suggests.

Furthermore, many atheists claim that conscience is important to them. Such claims do not rely upon God who, in some sense, regulates the moral order of the universe. For atheists, agnostics and humanists, conscience is part of being human and there is no need to involve God when moral decisions have to be made. Conscience appears to be a universal part of human moral living.

Most people also seem to agree that both reason and the emotions are involved in the workings of conscience and that it is a most natural part of our human make-up, whether we are religious or not. When reason or the heart or both decide what ought to be done, we often feel emotionally drawn towards it, or even emotionally divided, if we partly shrink from doing it. Following one's conscience, therefore, often implies that the whole being, body, mind and heart, is involved, in some way, when making the decision. We may often feel 'pangs of conscience' after doing what we consider to be the wrong thing or experience feelings of approval if we believe we have done the right thing. Enda McDonagh says: 'Conscience enables us to judge good and evil, reproaches us when we have done wrong, gives us peace when we have done well.' In this sense, conscience, although a deep part of us, appears to exist simultaneously as a separate entity, often standing over and against us as a judge or a supporter. Finally, conscience implies personal responsiblity, as Jack Mahoney wrote:

And perhaps a little demythologising may be in order, for conscience is not a still small voice, not bells, nor a blind stab in the dark; it is simply me coming to a decision. When I say 'my conscience tells me' all I am really saying is 'I think'. (*Seeking the Spirit*, p. 18)

IS CONSCIENCE INNATE OR ACQUIRED?

Conscience needs two things if it is to work successfully – freedom and knowledge of the good. Unless you are free to do something, there is no point in your conscience telling you to do it. Conscience also implies an innate knowledge of what 'good' is. If it is innate we would expect everyone to have a conscience and for it to work more or less the same for everyone. As we have seen, people have different ideas of what is right when faced with a moral situation and they hold different moral principles. Are these principles acquired from parents, teachers, society or religion?

Freud and other psychologists challenge the traditional idea of conscience, but is it the moral principles that are acquired rather than conscience itself? Is conscience more of a skill? As with other skills, does listening to conscience need to be developed? The skill may be innate but the moral principles that guide it are acquired.

Thought Point

- What philosophical problems occur when someone suggests 'Conscience is the voice of God'?
- Is conscience learnt or innate?
- 'It is not so much that I have a conscience – a special piece of equipment – as that I am a conscience.' What do you think MacNamara means by this?
- What is the relationship between conscience and external authority in moral decision-making?

Activities

Form groups of two or three and agree on your own group definition of conscience, giving reasons for your choice.

Choose one recent event in the media which in your opinion demonstrates a courageous decision of conscience. Give reasons for your choice.

Essay question

Assess the view that conscience is not the voice of God, but is learned. (OCR A2 Level 2772 June 2005 question 4)

In your answer to this question you will need to include the arguments of Aquinas, Butler and Newman, and you may connect these views with the concept of innateness. You will need to discuss the opinion that 'the voice of God' can easily become what we mean by 'right' and 'wrong' and can even lead people to indefensible acts, such as the events of 9/11. You need to ask whether 'God's voice' would be the same for all, and whether it is the source of values and answerable only to itself – does conscience make the law or does it rather recognise the law and use it to assess the right course of action? The influence of sociologists and psychoanalysts may be introduced to defend the proposition (e.g. Freud and Fromm).

This question could be argued either way. You could claim that it is God-given but not infallible and requires training. You could relate the idea of conscience as the 'voice of God' to revelation. The idea of *synderesis* may be introduced to defend the case that it is the divine voice. Or alternatively, you may prefer a Freudian or a sociological explanation.

FURTHER READING

Baelz, P. *Ethics and Belief*, New York, Seabury Press, 1977.

Bolt, R. *A Man for All Seasons*, London, Methuen, [1960] 1996.

Gill, R. *A Textbook of Christian Ethics*, London/New York, T & T Clark, 1995.

Gula, R. *Reason Informed by Faith*, New Jersey, Paulist Press, 1989.

Hodge, R. *What's Conscience for?*, London, Daughters of St Paul, 1995.

Macquarrie, J. and Childress, J. *A New Dictionary of Christian Ethics*, London, SCM, 1986.

Maguire, D. *The Moral Choice*, New York, HarperCollins, 1979.

Mahoney, J. *Seeking the Spirit: Essays in Moral and Pastoral Theology*, London, Sheen & Ward, 1981.

O'Connell, T. *Principles for a Catholic Morality* (revised edn), New York, HarperCollins, 1990.

Preston, R. 'Conscience', in *A Dictionary of Christian Ethics*, Macquarrie, J. (ed.), London, SCM, 1967.

Rulan, V. *An Ethics of Global Rights and Religious Pluralism*, San Francisco, CA, University of San Francisco Press, 2003.

Singer, P. (ed.) *A Companion to Ethics*, Oxford, Blackwell, 1994.

13 Environmental Ethics

WHAT YOU WILL LEARN ABOUT IN THIS CHAPTER

*   Different ethical approaches to the environment, both religious and secular.
*   An understanding of the underlying principles and implications of these different approaches for making decisions about the environment.
*   How to assess the different approaches and to evaluate their strengths and weaknesses.
*   The approaches of different ethical theories to the environment.

KEY SCHOLARS

*   St Francis of Assisi (1182–1226)
*   Aldo Leopold (1887–1948)
*   Alan Marshall (1902–1984)
*   Rachel Carson (1907–1964)
*   Arne Naess (1912–)

*   James Lovelock (1919–)
*   Richard Sylvan (Routley) (1935–1996)
*   J. Baird Callicott (1941–)
*   Peter Singer (1946–)

THE OCR CHECKLIST

Ethical theory (Natural Law, Virtue ethics, relativist views, Kant, various forms of Utilitarianism) and religious ethics as applied to:

*   Environmental ethics.

From OCR A Level Religious Studies Specification 7877.

WHAT IS ENVIRONMENTAL ETHICS?

Environmental ethics considers the ethical relationship between people and the natural world and the kind of decisions people have to make about the environment:

- Should we continue to cut down the rain forests for the sake of human consumption?
- Should we continue to manufacture petrol-driven cars when we have the technology to make cars which do not pollute the environment?
- Should we knowingly cause the extinction of other species?
- What are our environmental obligations to future generations?
- Should humans be forced to live a simpler lifestyle in order to protect and preserve the environment?

Most people recognise that our planet is in a bad way and we all seem to have an opinion on environmental issues, such as climate change or the use of four-wheel drive cars in cities. The importance of environmental ethics is brought home daily by the news of global warming and its effect on our lives, both now and in the future.

There has been a rapid growth in knowledge and technology, so that humans now face choices we have never had to face before that affect the continuation of humanity and the world within which we live.

Environmental ethics has grown in importance in our times because to make no decisions about environmental issues is to decide in favour of the status quo, and that, we are told, is no longer an option.

However, there is no agreed ethics for environmental issues, and no international environmental code. Environmental ethics simply tries to answer the questions of how humans should relate to their environment, how we should use the Earth's resources and how we should treat other species, both plant and animal, but there are also those who are of the opinion that constant change is simply a fact of this planet and the planet will readjust to new conditions as it did in the past. There are differences among scientists as to the exact cause and nature of environmental problems and how to solve them, and so there are differences in the approaches to environmental ethics; some think the traditional forms of ethical thought are good guides and some that these traditional forms (at least in the West) are too human-centred.

There are also the views of Christians and other religious believers who have a particular take on their role and responsibility towards the natural world.

THE RELIGIOUS APPROACH TO ENVIRONMENTAL ETHICS

For the purpose of this book a Christian approach will be followed.

Dominion

The foundation for a Christian approach to the environment is seen by many believers to be the Bible, but as with many ethical issues biblical teaching is not always clear, and the idea that we humans have 'dominion' over the natural world is seen by many as **anthropocentric**. **Peter Singer** criticises this tradition in his book *Practical Ethics*:

> According to the Dominant Western tradition, the natural world exists for the benefit of human beings. God does not care how we treat it. Human beings are the only morally important members of this world. Nature itself is of no intrinsic value. . . . Harsh as this tradition is, it does not rule out concern for the preservation of nature, as long as that concern can be related to human well-being.

Singer points out that the teachings of **Aristotle** influenced **Aquinas** and continued to view humans as the only morally important beings – there being no intrinsic value in the natural world.

The value of creation

However, the story of creation, upon which so much of this understanding is based, is itself open to interpretation.

God seems to value the natural world, 'God saw that it was good' (Genesis 1:10a), and the blessing to 'Be fruitful and multiply' (Genesis 1:22a) is given to all creation. Creation is called to praise and glorify God (e.g. Psalm 148:3–10; Isaiah 55:12; Micah 6:1–2).

God is shown as having continuing concern about his creation – not even a sparrow falls without God's knowledge and permission:

> Are not two sparrows sold for a penny? Yet not one of them will fall to the ground apart from your Father. And even the hairs of your head are all counted. So do not be afraid; you are of more value than many sparrows. (Matthew 10:29)

If God values creation and creation in return can respond to God, then it seems that the Bible says that all of creation has **intrinsic value**.

Anthropocentric
An approach to the environment that places human interests above those of any other species.

Intrinsic value
Something's value lies in itself.

This contrasts with the view that God has a special concern for humanity – we are made in God's image:

> So God created humankind in his image, in the image of God he created them; male and female he created them. (Genesis 1:27)

We are given **dominion** over all creatures:

> Then God said, 'Let us make humankind in our image, according to our likeness; and let them have dominion over the fish of the sea, and over the birds of the air, and over the cattle, and over all the wild animals of the earth, and over every creeping thing that creeps upon the earth.' (Genesis 1:26)

This surely backs up Singer's view of anthropomorphism and anthropocentrism in the biblical texts. Or are humans, being made in the image of God, also supposed to delight in the intrinsic value of the natural world?

St Francis of Assisi understood that God communicates to us through the natural world – through animals, birds and trees – and that it is a sin to destroy them. In general, his attitude towards the environment was typical of his time: the natural world is inherently good and it is a sign of God's goodness, and so its purpose is to inspire our respect and love. However, he took this a stage further, as he believed that *all* creatures had the ability and the duty to worship God, all are part of the same creation with the same intrinsic value.

Stewardship

Dominion may be understood as considering that the natural world can be treated however we wish and be tamed for our use. According to **Singer** this is the root cause of our environmental problems, and it is true that the command to 'subdue' the Earth (Genesis 1:28) needs looking at.

When the second creation account in Genesis 2 is compared to the first, we are told that man is put in Eden to protect and preserve it: 'The Lord God took the man and put him in the garden of Eden to till it and keep it' (Genesis 2:15).

Humans may be the peak of creation, but only because we have the role of **stewardship** – we are to care for and conserve creation because it belongs to God: humans are merely caretakers of this property. Humans are co-creators with God and need to use and transform the natural world with care. Creation is made by God and is good, and so must be preserved because it has intrinsic value.

Dominion

The Judaeo-Christian idea that humans have a special place in the natural world and have responsibility for it.

St Francis of Assisi (1182–1226)

St Francis of Assisi, c.1490 (tempera on panel) by Francia (Francesco di Marco Raibolini) II (1450–1517)

© Galleria degli Uffizi, Florence, Italy/The Bridgeman Art Library

St Francis of Assisi was born in Assisi as Giovanni Francesco Bernardone. He came from a rich family but, after being held prisoner for a year in Perugia, he suffered a severe illness and then changed his way of life. In 1205 he began working with lepers and

continued

started to restore damaged churches. He was disinherited by his father and spent three years working with lepers in the woods of Mount Subasio. He then founded the First Order with twelve disciples. In 1212 the Order of the Poor Ladies (later the Poor Clares) was established. After several missionary trips to Spain and Egypt, Francis went to the Holy Land until 1220. On his return to Assisi there were disputes among the friars, and he resigned as Superior and formed the Third Order of Franciscans. In 1224 the marks of Jesus' crucifixion (stigmata) appeared on his body after a period of fasting and prayer. In 1225 he wrote *Canticle of the Creatures*. He was made a saint in 1228 and in 1980 he was proclaimed the Patron Saint of Ecologists.

Stewardship

A way of interpreting the use of dominion, which sees humans as caretakers of the natural world.

The effect of man's sin

The Fall (Genesis 3) is seen by some as the reason for our environmental problems because from this point we became poor stewards of creation:

> The earth dries up and withers, the world languishes and withers; the heavens languish together with the earth. The earth lies polluted under its inhabitants; for they have transgressed laws, violated the statutes, broken the everlasting covenant. (Isaiah 14:4–5)

Christians teach that we need to use our increasing knowledge to rectify this and re-establish the bond between God and man, between God and the natural world. Thus for Christians the environment must be protected, and past mistakes must be used as learning tools and rectified where possible – this will ensure that the Western style of life does not impinge unfairly on the lifestyles of those in poorer nations and on the natural world as a whole.

Christians believe that care for the environment and the avoidance of needless exploitation of the natural world for selfish gain will help bring about peace, harmony and justice. Ultimately, Christian ethics is rooted in the relationship with God and a Christian's relationship with God depends on how he uses creation and contributes to bringing about the Kingdom of God (I Corinthians 15:21–22; Romans 5:12–21). Love of God and love of one's neighbour are fundamental in Christian ethics and also apply to the environment.

Rapture and end-time theology

However, there are some Christians, especially an influential group of right-wing fundamentalists in the USA, who would follow Singer's interpretation of biblical teaching. They do believe that humans have 'dominion' and that the Genesis creation story teaches that 'man' is superior to nature and can use its resources unchecked. Those who believe in the 'end-time' feel that concern for the Earth and the natural world is irrelevant because they have no future. Destruction of the environment is to be welcomed, and even helped along, as it is a sign of the coming of the Apocalypse and the Second Coming of Christ:

> When he opened the sixth seal, I looked, and there came a great earth-quake; the sun became black as sackcloth, the full moon became like blood, and the stars of the sky fell to the earth as the fig tree drops its winter fruit when shaken by a gale. The sky vanished like a scroll rolling itself up, and every mountain and island was removed from its place. (Revelation 6:12–14)

Pastor John Hagee from Texas says that the environmental and social crises of today are portents of the Rapture, when born-again Christians living and dead will be taken up into heaven: 'All over the earth, graves will explode as the occupants soar into the heavens', he preaches. Non-believers left behind will have seven years of suffering, culminating in the rise of the Antichrist and the final battle of Armageddon. Once the battle is won, Christ will send the non-believers to hell and re-green the Earth, where he will reign in peace with his followers.

All this may sound totally far-fetched, but this view is powerful in the world and held by many Americans in positions of power – why care about climate change or signing the Kyoto Agreement to limit greenhouse gases if you and those close to you will be rescued in the Rapture?

Thought Point

1 If all life is created by God, show how the teleological argument for the existence of God implies respect for his creative design.
2 Explain how the biblical sources could back up differing approaches to the environment.
3 Explain why it is important that the natural world should have intrinsic value.
4 'Humans should care for their own kind first.' How far do you think religious ethics would agree with this?

Biocentric

An approach to the environment that considers the biological nature and diversity of the Earth to be of supreme importance.

Rachel Louise Carson (1907–1964)

Rachel Carson was born in Springdale, Pennsylvania and studied at the Pennsylvania College for Women and Johns Hopkins University. From 1931 to 1936 she taught zoology at the University of Maryland. She held the post of aquatic biologist at the United States Bureau of Fisheries from 1936 to 1952.

Deep ecology

An approach to environmental ethics that sees all life forms as of value and human life as just one part of the biosphere. It rejects anthropomorphism.

Gaia hypothesis

A theory of James Lovelock.

Shallow ecology

The Earth is cared for to make conditions better for humans.

SECULAR APPROACHES TO ENVIRONMENTAL ETHICS

The modern study of environmental ethics was a response to the work of scientists such as **Rachel Carson** and her influential book *Silent Spring*, which explored the idea of interconnectedness through a study of the use of pesticides and how their effect is felt through the food chain. The fate of one species is linked with that of all other species, including humans.

The Australian writer **Alan Marshall** wrote that over the past twenty years there have been three main ethical approaches to the environment:

1 libertarian extension or **deep ecology**
2 ecologic extension or eco-holism (including the **Gaia hypothesis**)
3 conservation ethics or **shallow ecology**

These divisions within the environmental movement are separated by the terms shallow and deep and, when applied to thought, shallow is bad and deep is good, so today they are often referred to as dark green and light green, including all possible shades in between.

Libertarian extension – deep ecology

This really began in 1949 when Aldo Leopold's book *Sand County Almanac* was published shortly after his death. This inspired a new approach to the environment and an interest in ecology as a science. The book is a mixture of natural history and philosophy, and calls for a new approach to the environment: 'A thing is right when it tends to preserve the integrity, stability, and beauty of the bionic community. It is wrong when it tends otherwise.'

Leopold stated that we need to develop an ethics to deal with man's relationship to land, animals and plants, and to extend our social conscience from people to land, and that it is not right to see the natural world simply in terms of its economic worth to humans.

In 1973 one of the founding fathers of environmental philosophy, **Arne Naess**, published a short paper called 'The Shallow and the Deep, Long-range Ecology Movement'. He basically stated that there are two ecology movements: the first is concerned mostly with pollution, the depletion of natural resources and the usefulness of the Earth for humans (anthropocentrism), and the second is concerned with the richness, diversity and intrinsic value of all the natural world – this is deep ecology.

He argued for the intrinsic value and inherent worth of the environment. According to Naess, every being, whether human, animal or vegetable, has an equal right to live and blossom. He called this **ecosophy**, which he defined as follows: 'By an ecosophy I mean a philosophy of ecological harmony or equilibrium' (*The Deep Ecology Movement*, p. 8).

> **Ecosophy**
> A word formed by contracting the phrase 'ecological philosophy'. It refers to philosophies which have an ecocentric or biocentric perspective such as deep ecology.

Naess rejected any idea that humans were more important because they had a soul, use reason or have consciousness. So nature does not exist to serve humans; humans are simply a part of nature and all species have a right to exist for their own sake, regardless of their usefulness to humans. This view requires a complete change in how humans relate to the natural world, and Naess actually opposes the Christian view of stewardship as arrogant and depending on the idea of superiority which underlies the thought that humans exist to watch over nature like some sort of middleman between God and his creation.

Naess and the American philosopher George Sessions listed an eightfold deep-ecology platform that may be summarised as follows:

1   All life has value in itself, independently of its usefulness to humans.
2   Richness and diversity contribute to life's well-being and have value in themselves.
3   Humans have no right to reduce this richness and diversity except to satisfy vital needs in a responsible way.
4   The impact of humans in the world is excessive, and rapidly getting worse.
5   Human lifestyles and population are key elements of this impact.
6   The diversity of life, including cultures, can flourish only with reduced human impact.
7   Basic ideological, political, economic and technological structures must therefore change.
8   Those who accept the foregoing points have an obligation to participate in implementing the necessary changes and to do so peacefully and democratically.

Naess proposes therefore that humans should:

- radically reduce the Earth's population
- abandon all goals of economic growth
- conserve diversity of species
- live in small, self-reliant communities
- 'touch the Earth lightly'.

However, many consider these ideas are simply not practical or realistic, especially as the human population is increasing rapidly and humans have just as much right to reproduce as any other species.

As a result of these problems, **Richard Sylvan** developed an alternative approach to deep ecology called *deep green theory*, which involves respect but not reverence for the environment.

Ecologic extension – eco-holism

This emphasises not the rights of humans but the interdependence of all ecosystems and sees the environment as a whole entity, valuable in itself. This is often known as *eco-holism* and its most popular form is **James Lovelock's Gaia hypothesis**.

The Gaia hypothesis challenges the view that humans are the most important species and sees humans as part of a living whole – Gaia. Gaia theory was put forward by James Lovelock in a number of books. The word 'Gaia' was first used by William Golding and comes from the name of the

Holistic

An approach to the environment that considers a range of factors, including the importance of balance within the ecosystem.

Gaia – Earth from space

Greek goddess of the Earth. All the life forms of the planet are a part of Gaia – looking at the Earth from space, Lovelock saw not so much a planet of diverse life forms as a planet transformed by a self-regulating living system; it was almost a living being.

In his early work Lovelock argued that Gaia is regulated by the living organisms within it to maintain suitable conditions for growth and development – he later rejected this position and saw the regulation as conducted by the whole of Gaia, not just the living organisms. He examined the fossil evidence which showed that climatic change had, in fact, taken place within a very narrow range so that life was never destroyed. Conditions seem to have favoured life; they are not random but intelligently organised – this he claims was not carried out by God, as religious believers maintain, but by Gaia herself. However, God could be an explanation for the existence of Gaia and for maintaining her in existence. This theory opposes the Darwinian idea of the survival of the fittest, whereby species evolve to suit the conditions available, and says that the conditions on Earth are actually managed by Gaia herself. The world is not a result of chance but of self-engineering.

According to Lovelock, life could not be destroyed. There are many types of algae that are resistant to ultraviolet radiation, so even if the ozone layer were to be destroyed, life would continue and new life would evolve. On the Bikini atoll where nuclear bombs were tested, life has returned; the same may be said for the site of the Chernobyl disaster. Human life may be wiped out, but humans are just a part of Gaia, and Gaia herself would survive without our presence. This theory challenges humans to change their perceptions and see themselves as part of a whole. If we abuse Gaia then we risk our own survival, as Gaia owes us nothing and we owe her our very existence.

The Earth, then, is a unified, holistic living entity with ethical worth, and in the long run the human race has no particular significance, but we are part of it and all the organisms on Earth are interdependent.

Lovelock's latest book, *The Revenge of Gaia*, is more pessimistic about climate change and our reluctance to confront it. He now considers that as the global temperatures rise higher and higher and there are more climatic disasters, the planet may not be able to recover as he previously thought. With a three-degree rise the rain forests will start to die, releasing vast new amounts of carbon dioxide; in the oceans the algae will fail and stop absorbing carbon; there will be floods, crop failures and massive human migrations. Lovelock advocates the rapid expansion of nuclear power to cut fossil fuel emissions. He writes:

> Renewable energy sounds good, but so far it is inefficient and expensive. It has a future, but we have no time now to experiment with visionary energy sources: civilisation is in imminent danger and has to use nuclear energy now, or suffer the pain soon to be inflicted by our outraged planet.

James Ephraim Lovelock (1919–)

James Lovelock was born on 26 July 1919 in Letchworth. He read chemistry at the University of Manchester and then biophysics in London. He held posts at Harvard Medical School and Yale University.

In 1957 he invented the electron capture detector which has since been used to study the global atmosphere. His studies of the differences between the atmospheres of the Earth and other planets led to the development of the Gaia theory.

Conservation ethics – shallow ecology

Instrumental value
Something's value lies in its usefulness for others.

This approach takes a conflicting view to the two previous ones – the only value in animals and plants is their extrinsic, **instrumental value** for humans. They are a means to an end – conservation is important for our welfare and that of future generations.

Conservation ethics
The ethics of the use, allocation, protection and exploitation of the natural world.

Conservation ethics looks at the worth of the environment in terms of its utility or usefulness to humans. Conservation is a means to an end and is purely concerned with humanity – so a person chooses to avoid pollution and to reduce, reuse and recycle because these actions seem beneficial to humans in one way or another.

This is the ethic which formed the underlying arguments for the three agreements reached in Rio in 1992 and for the Kyoto summit in 1997.

Biodiversity
The variety of living things on Earth.

Shallow ecology or light green environmentalism restricts independent moral status to humans – it is anthropocentric. **Biodiversity** should be preserved, as particular species of animals and plants provide us with medicines, food and raw materials. So shallow ecology will accept that environmental damage can continue if humans benefit from it. The clearing of rain forests can be justified if it can be shown to benefit humans – making space for people to live or for farming. The preservation of a rain forest may also be the right thing to do provided it can be shown to benefit humans. Neither animals nor plants have rights, and any respect shown to them depends on how humans benefit.

However, for many people contact with the natural world is a part of the good life – part of having a good quality of life – so swimming with dolphins, hill walking, seeing cherry trees in bloom are experiences that are valued for their own sake, not just as an instrumental good.

Looking at this from another angle, **Michael La Bossiere** argues in the *Philosopher's Magazine* (issue 15) that species should be allowed to die out, as this is just part of the natural process of evolution – humans, he says, are a natural species and so any species that becomes extinct due to human activity is simply becoming naturally extinct. Humans have no obligation to prevent natural extinction, but this does not mean that humans should have a free hand in eradicating species, even when it would benefit humanity.

Humanist theories of the environment – Peter Singer

Sentience
The ability to feel pleasure and pain.

Peter Singer used a set of criteria for moral status based on **sentience**. This means that moral worth includes animals – if not, we are guilty of 'specieism'. Our treatment of all humans and animals should be equal –

Shallow ecology versus deep ecology

Shallow ecology	Deep ecology
Natural diversity is valuable as a resource.	Natural diversity has intrinsic value.
Species should be saved as a resource for humans.	Species should be saved for their intrinsic value.
Pollution should be decreased if it threatens economic growth.	Decrease in pollution has priority over economic growth.
Population growth threatens ecological equilibrium.	Human population is excessive today. Overdeveloped countries.
'Resource' means resource for humans.	'Resource' means resource for living things.
Decrease in standard of living is intolerable.	Decrease in quality of life is intolerable.

Singer is a preference utilitarian, and so believes that animals should receive equal preference. Singer argues that because plants are non-sentient, there is a problem in trying to determine their interests in staying alive. He is not, therefore, convinced by the arguments of deep ecology and admits that, although the argument for the preservation of the environment may be strong, it is difficult to argue for its intrinsic value.

In his book *Practical Ethics*, Singer advocated the preservation of 'world heritage sites', unspoilt parts of the world that acquire 'scarcity value' as they diminish over time. Their preservation ensures their survival for future generations to enjoy. It should be left to future generations to decide whether they prefer unspoilt countryside or urban landscape.

A tropical rain forest would be a good example of a world heritage site, as it is a very specialist ecosystem with vegetation that has taken years to evolve. Clearing the rain forest to develop farmland is often pointless due to the soil conditions, and once destroyed the rain forest cannot be replaced.

Geocentric
An approach to the environment that considers the geological nature and diversity of the Earth to be most important.

APPLYING ETHICAL THEORIES TO THE ENVIRONMENT

Utilitarianism

Utilitarianism is not a single theory, but more of a family of theories with different variations. Some utilitarian approaches are more useful than others when applying them to environmental issues.

As may be seen from the different approaches to the environment examined already in this chapter, many are based to some extent on Utilitarianism. Since it is clear that destroying the environment will bring long-term harm to all species, including humans, utilitarians will weigh up the long-term harm against the short-term gain made from exploiting natural resources.

Quantitative Utilitarianism looks at a situation and weighs up whether the moral course of action is the maximisation of higher pleasures for present and future generations. So, for example, when in the Lake District there was a proposal to impose a 10mph speed limit on Windermere, a lake that lies within the National Park, a designated area of peace and tranquillity, but which is much used by power-boat enthusiasts and water-skiers, whose activities contribute substantially to the local economy, Bentham would weigh up the amount of pleasure and pain of all those involved. However, the assumption that pleasure is a uniform feature of different types of experience, and simply varies according to how much there is, is questionable. Modern utilitarians would use a cost–benefit analysis, and this was the approach of David Pearce's *Blueprint for a Green Economy*. Applying this approach to Windermere, it is easy to assess the economic benefit of some of the elements in the situation: power boating brings money into the area. But how can this be weighed against the loss of tranquillity? Environmental economics would say that tranquillity is also of value and it is simply a case of determining the strength of preferences for it – but is money an appropriate measure of environmental goods? And do people's preferences accurately reflect what is good for them? Should the fate of the environment be dependent on human preferences? In addition, we never know the final result of our actions. What may seem to be to the advantage of the environment now, may in the long term prove to be harmful.

It is worth noting the approach of qualitative Utilitarianism; Mill puts the enjoyment and study of nature at the top of his list of higher pleasures – and therefore environmental preservation is imperative.

Preference Utilitarianism considers that the moral course of action is the maximisation of preference satisfaction for the current generation. Assuming that neglecting the environment has no major effect on the current generation, then the case for preserving the environment is weak.

In *Practical Ethics* **Peter Singer** uses the example of building a hydro-electric dam across a gorge that would create employment, stimulate economic growth and provide a cost-effective energy supply but have associated costs. Such costs would include the loss of a beauty spot favoured by walkers and a good place for white-water rafting and the destruction of the habitat of some endangered species and wildlife.

For the preference utilitarian, the preference satisfaction of a cheap source of electricity would outweigh the preferences of the walkers and the white-water rafters, as well as those of the animals and plants. However, the qualitative utilitarian would consider the long-term interests of future generations.

Kantian ethics

Kant's ethical theory is generally seen as anthropocentric, based on the idea that rational nature alone has absolute and conditional value. It may seem that a theory of this kind would allow the exploitation of the natural world; if only rational nature counts as an end in itself, then everything else may be used as a means to an end. However, Kant denies that domestic animals are only to be treated as tools and insists that there are moral limits on how we should use them. Animals should not be worn out and over-worked, nor should they be cast aside once they are too old. Kant thinks it is all right to kill animals for food, but killing for sport he sees as morally wrong. Kant also thinks that we have moral duties regarding the natural world and must not destroy it. This seems at odds with Kant's statements that we only have duties towards rational beings, but he explains that treating animals or the natural world badly makes us into cruel and callous people who will then treat other people badly. People who torment animals are likely to do the same to humans, according to Kant. So cruelty towards animals would not be condemned in its own right, but due to its consequences for humans it should be considered intrinsically wrong. According to Kant, a person cannot have good will unless he shows concern for the welfare of non-rational beings and values the natural world for its own sake.

As well as this approach we can also consider the first formulation of the categorical imperative – that of making a maxim into a universal law. This would forbid much of the exploitation and pollution of the natural world, as it would be illogical to want everyone to be able to act so. The neo-Kantian Paul Taylor takes the view that respect for nature is a universal law for all rational beings – but he would not go so far as to accord animals and plants moral rights; instead he suggests giving them legal rights so that they are protected.

Virtue ethics

Environmental ethics seeks to examine human relationships within the natural world. As we have seen, in the past the emphasis has been on anthro-pocentric theories based more on duty and consequences, which has led to environmental ethics being somewhat unbalanced. Environmental Virtue ethics is a new approach which attempts to meet the challenge of a non-anthropocentric theory of values which looks at our relationship with the natural world more objectively.

Environmental Virtue ethics does not ask why environmental preservation is important for humanity, but what characterises an environmentally good person. It shifts the emphasis from duty and consequences to who we are and how we are to live in the natural world. Environmental Virtue ethics sees a virtuous life in nature as a necessary condition of human flourishing, *eudaimonia*. Extremes of behaviour are unhelpful both for society and the environment.

Virtue ethics also looks at examples of virtue to follow and might look at the example of people such as Rachel Carson and Aldo Leopold.

Thought Point

- Read the passage below assigned to your group.
- Summarise the main points.
- Identify the key ethical arguments in the passage.
- Choose one environmental problem (e.g. destruction of the rainforest, saving an endangered species, pollution or global warming) and consider the implications of implementing the environmental ethic from the passage you have read. Look at both positives and negatives.
- Give your own views on the environmental ethic put forward in your passage – as a group or as individuals if there is disagreement.

Reading 1 'The Land Ethic' from Aldo Leopold's *A Sand County Almanac* (pp. 201–4)

There is as yet no ethic dealing with man's relation to land and to the animals and plants that grow upon it. Land, like Odysseus' slave girls, is still property. The land relation is still strictly economic, entailing privileges, but not obligations.

The extension of ethics to this element in human environment is, if I read the evidence correctly, an evolutionary possibility and an ecological necessity. . . .

The land ethic simply enlarges the boundaries of the community to include soils, waters, plants, and animals, or collectively: the land.

This sounds simple: do we not already sing our love for obligation to the land of the free and the home of the brave? Yes, but just what and whom do we love? Certainly not the soil, which we are sending helter-skelter downriver. Certainly not the waters, which we assume have no function except to turn turbines, float barges, and carry off sewage.

Certainly not the plants, of which we exterminate whole communities without batting an eye. Certainly not the animals, of which we have already exterminated many of the largest and most beautiful species. A land ethic of course cannot prevent the alteration, management, and use of these 'resources' but it does affirm their right to continued existence, and, at least in spots, their continued existence in a natural state.

In short, a land ethic changes the role of *Homo sapiens* from conqueror of the land-community to plain member and citizen of it. It implies respect for his fellow-members, and also respect for the community as such.

Reading 2 'Utilitarian Environmental Ethics' from Peter Singer's *Practical Ethics* (pp. 56–7)

The argument for extending the principle of equality beyond our own species is simple, so simple that it amounts to no more than a clear understanding of the principle of equal consideration of interests. We have seen that this principle implies that out concern for others ought not to depend on what they are like, or what abilities they possess (although precisely what this concern requires us to do may vary according to the characteristics of those affected by what we do). It is on this basis we are able to say that the fact that some people are not members of our race does not entitle us to exploit them, and similarly the fact that some people are less intelligent than others does not mean their interests may be disregarded. But the principle also implies that the fact that beings are not members of our species does not entitle us to exploit them, and similarly the fact that other animals are less intelligent than we are does not mean that their interests may be disregarded. . . . A stone does not have interests because it cannot suffer. Nothing that we can do can possibly make any difference to its welfare. A mouse, on the other hand, does have an interest in not being tormented, because mice will suffer if treated in this way.

Reading 3 'Instrumental Environmental Ethics' from Pearce *et al.*'s *Blue Print for a Green Economy* (pp. 5–7)

One of the central themes of environmental economics, and central to sustainable development thinking also, is the need to place proper values on the services provided by natural environments. The central problem is that many of these services are provided 'free'. They have a zero price simply because no market place exists in which their true values can be

continued

revealed through the acts of buying and selling. Examples might be a fine view, the water purifications and storm protection functions of coastal wetlands, or the biological diversity within a tropical rainforest. The elementary theory of supply and demand tells us that if something is provided at a zero price, more of it will be demanded than if there was a positive price. Very simply, the cheaper it is the more will be demanded. The danger is that this greater level of demand will be unrelated to the capacity of the relevant natural environments to meet the demand. For example, by treating the ozone layer as a resource with zero price there never was any incentive to protect it. Its value to human populations and to the global environment in general did not show up anywhere in a balance sheet of profit or loss, or of costs and benefits. The important principle is that resources and environments serve economic functions and have positive value. To treat them as if they had zero value is seriously to risk overusing the resource. . . . We have a sound *a priori* argument for supposing that the environment has been used to excess.

Reading 4 'Deep Ecology' from Devall and Sessions' *Deep Ecology* (p. 70)

Basic Principles:

1 The well-being and flourishing of human and non-human life on Earth have value in themselves (synonyms: intrinsic value, inherent value). These values are independent of the usefulness of the non-human world for human purposes.
2 Richness and diversity of life forms contribute to the realisation of these values and are also values in themselves.
3 Humans have no right to reduce this richness and diversity except to satisfy *vital* needs.
4 The flourishing of human life and cultures is compatible with a substantial decrease of the human population. The flourishing of non-human life requires such a decrease.
5 Present human interference with the non-human world is excessive, and the situation is rapidly worsening.
6 Policies must therefore be changed. These policies affect basic economic, technological, and ideological structures. The resulting state of affairs will be deeply different from the present.
7 The ideological change is mainly that of appreciating *life quality* (dwelling in situations of inherent value) rather than adhering to an

increasingly higher standard of living. There will be a profound awareness of the difference between big and great.

8   Those who subscribe to the foregoing points have an obligation directly or indirectly to try to implement the necessary changes.

REVIEW QUESTIONS

Look back over the chapter and check that you can answer the following questions:

- Explain religious approaches to the environment and Singer's objections.
- Make bullet point notes on the Gaia hypothesis. List reasons for and against it.
- Make a chart comparing deep (dark green) and shallow (light green) ecology.
- List the strengths and weaknesses of a utilitarian approach to the environment.

Essay question

**'Utilitarianism is the best approach to environmental issues.'
Discuss.** (OCR A2 Level 2772 June 2006 question 4)

In your answer to this question you will need to explain the main principles of Utilitarianism and how they might be applied to the environment. It would be better to concentrate on one or two environmental issues such as pollution or global warming or your essay may tend to be too much about environmental issues and not enough about ethical theories.

You will need to examine what is included in the greatest good principle – just humans or also animals and plants? You will need to consider the different forms of Utilitarianism to come to a conclusion about its usefulness.

However, you also need to ask if it is the 'best' approach and this means contrasting it with other approaches (e.g. religious ethics, deep ecology, Gaia hypothesis).

FURTHER READING

Benson, J. *Environmental Ethics*, London, Routledge, 2000.

Devall, B. and Sessions, G., *Deep Ecology*, Salt Lake City, Gibbs M. Smith, 1987.

Dregson, A. and Inoue, Y. (eds) *The Deep Ecology Movement: An Introductory Anthology*, Berkeley, North Atlantic Books, 1995.

Leopold, A. *A Sand County Almanac*, Oxford/New York, Oxford University Press, 1968.

Lovelock, J. *Gaia: A New Look at Life on Earth*, Oxford, Oxford University Press, 1979.

Pearce, D., Markandya, A. and Barbier, E.B., *Blue Print for a Green Economy*, London, Earthscan, 1989.

Singer, P. *Practical Ethics*, Cambridge, Cambridge University Press, 1993.

Singer, P. 'All Animals Are Equal' in Sterba, J. (ed.) *Ethics: The Big Questions*, Oxford, Blackwell, 1998.

Taylor, P. 'The Ethics of Respect for Nature' in Sterba, J. (ed.) *Ethics: The Big Questions* Oxford, Blackwell, 1998.

Walker, J. *Environmental Ethics*, London, Hodder & Stoughton, 2000.

For those who want to take the topic further than the limitations of A level, I suggest they look at ecological feminism – a good introduction is to be found in Warren, K. 'The Power and Promise of Ecological Feminism' in Sterba, J. (ed.) *Ethics: The Big Questions*, Blackwell, Oxford, 1998.

14 Sex and Relationships

WHAT YOU WILL LEARN ABOUT IN THIS CHAPTER

- Different ethical approaches to sex and relationships, both religious and secular.
- An understanding of the underlying principles and implications of these different approaches for making decisions about sex and relationships.
- How to assess the different approaches and to evaluate their strengths and weaknesses.
- The approaches of different ethical theories to the issues surrounding homosexuality.

KEY SCHOLARS

- Augustine of Hippo (354–430)
- Thomas Aquinas (1225–1274)
- Immanuel Kant (1724–1804)
- Jeremy Bentham (1748–1832)
- John Stuart Mill (1806–1873)

- Sigmund Freud (1856–1939)
- Joseph Fletcher (1905–1991)
- Richard Holloway (1933–)
- Michael Slote (1941–)
- Rosalind Hursthouse (1943–)

THE OCR CHECKLIST

Ethical theory (Natural Law, Virtue ethics, relativist views, Kant, various forms of Utilitarianism) and religious ethics as applied to:

- Sex and relationships.

From OCR A Level Religious Studies Specification 7877.

WHAT IS SEX AND RELATIONSHIPS?

Sex
Biological characteristics that
determine whether a person is
male or female.

Sex is an enormously wide term covering a range of issues from homo-sexuality to marriage, from pornography to prostitution, to the relational dimensions which are expressions of love and pleasure. It is part of being human and involves above all the question of how men and women should treat each other.

In spite of the fact that, or maybe because, sex and relationships are so natural to us, we hedge it with rules. As **Richard Holloway** put it: 'Human sexuality is like a runaway car.' It can be destructive or creative, but we are never quite in control of it.

HISTORICAL VIEWS OF SEX AND RELATIONSHIPS

Originally the Greek philosophers saw sex as something weakening to the mind. The Pythagoreans, who influenced Plato, believed that humans should refrain from physical activities and live a more ascetic life. In this way the soul, which is imprisoned in the body, is freed to move to a new form. This dualism between the physical and the spiritual may be seen in Plato's model

The Kiss, 1888–98
(marble) by Auguste Rodin
(1840–1917)

© Musée Rodin, Paris,
France/Philippe Galard/The
Bridgeman Art Library

of the soul as the charioteer with his two horses: the beautiful white horse that is a model of self-control and responds to the spoken word, and the ugly black horse that needs controlling with a whip. There are in this many levels of interpretation as far as sexual desire/pleasure is concerned – the desire needs controlling but it is allowed to exist; after all, the charioteer needs both of his horses.

The Cynics, on the other hand, saw no point in controlling sexual desire/ pleasure and saw no shame attached to the sexual act, even going so far as to perform it in public. The Stoics reacted totally against this and advocated overcoming any emotions that threaten self-control – the Stoics were the original 'stiff upper lips', and sex became linked to reproduction and the continuation of the human race.

So the early history of sex and relationships as far as philosophy was concerned was riddled with contradictions which have continued ever since. The same contradictions may be discerned in early Judaism as found in the Old Testament and later in Christianity. However, for the Greeks sexuality is naturally excessive and so the moral problem is not whether it is right or wrong but how to control it. This did not involve laws which prohibited certain sexual acts, but required individual self-discipline.

THE OLD TESTAMENT APPROACH TO SEX AND RELATIONSHIPS

The Old Testament is a reflection of its times and does not seem to have one particular view on sex and relationships. It includes moving love stories, such as the story of Ruth and Boaz; detailed accounts of incest, such as that concerning the two daughters of Lot in Genesis 19, whose incestual relationship with their father has the intention of assuring his line; and there are numerous tales of seduction and sexual revenge. Many of these are recounted in a factual way, without judgement. Sex is even celebrated in the Song of Songs.

In Genesis 1 and 2 there is an understanding that sex is created by God and meant for procreation. However, sex is not seen as wrong but good; yet the contradictions also appear, as sex should not be practised in sinful ways. Sexual involvement with non-Israelites was forbidden, as it would lead away from God (e.g. 1 Kings 11:1–13), and adultery was forbidden, seen as theft and punishable by stoning. This was a society in which women were not equal to men, but had to be part of the household of a man. Women should be virgins on marriage, but this was so the man could be certain that the children were his own and the line was assured.

THE NEW TESTAMENT APPROACH TO SEX AND RELATIONSHIPS

Jesus

Jesus himself said very little about sex; in fact he gave very few rules and instructions, but called his followers to live as part of the Kingdom of God, to reflect through their lives God's love for all people and to live justly with each other. As far as sex and relationships are concerned, Jesus seems to have left the issues open. Even in his teachings about marriage and divorce it is not possible to be sure what he said or what he meant. Jesus is quoted as saying: 'Whoever divorces his wife and (*kai*) marries another commits adultery (*porneia*) against her' (Mark 10:11). The wording here is not easy to translate into English; the word '*kai*' could mean 'in order to', not just 'and', and so depending on what the word means, the understanding of what Jesus meant changes. Similarly with the word '*porneia*' – it has three alternatives: it could refer to a woman who was not a virgin on marriage, in which case divorce would follow immediately after marriage; it could mean adultery, in which case a man could divorce his wife for her adultery, but she did not have the same right if he was adulterous; or it could mean 'fornication', which in the Old Testament means chasing after other gods – divorce is allowed if the partner is a non-believer. However, it is clear that Jesus is challenging the view of the wife as the man's property – he is talking more about equality than about sexual relationships. One thing is clear, however, and this is that Jesus is setting out an ideal and divorce falls short of it.

Paul

As we have seen, the New Testament does not have a great deal to say on the subject, and much of Paul's writing is influenced by his expectation of the imminent return of Christ and the end of the world. There was not much point in giving a detailed ethic on sex and relationships, as all human relationships were soon to end. Paul, influenced by Greek thinking, attempted to move the Christian people away from the body towards the soul. So he writes in 1 Corinthians 6:12–20 that Christians should not let their bodily emotions control them, that sexual activity is to be kept within marriage, that the body is a temple of the Holy Spirit and should be respected.

> 'All things are lawful for me,' but not all things are beneficial. 'All things are lawful for me,' but I will not be dominated by anything. 'Food is

meant for the stomach and the stomach for food,' and God will destroy both one and the other. The body is meant not for fornication but for the Lord, and the Lord for the body. And God raised the Lord and will also raise us by his power. Do you not know that your bodies are members of Christ? Should I therefore take the members of Christ and make them members of a prostitute? Never! Do you not know that whoever is united to a prostitute becomes one body with her? For it is said, 'The two shall be one flesh.' But anyone united to the Lord becomes one spirit with him. Shun fornication! Every sin that a person commits is outside the body; but the fornicator sins against the body itself. Or do you not know that your body is a temple of the Holy Spirit within you, which you have from God, and that you are not your own? For you were bought with a price; therefore glorify God in your body.

This whole passage shows Paul attempting to move people away from bodily pleasures to a more spiritual realm. Marriage was not forbidden, but considered only for those with no self-control.

Paul's views on sex and relationships, marriage and women are also inconsistent. Sometimes he was positive about women – all are equal:

> There is no longer Jew or Greek, there is no longer slave or free, there is no longer male and female; for all of you are one in Christ Jesus. (Galatians 3:28)

Yet elsewhere he argues that women should obey their husbands:

> Wives, be subject to your husbands as you are to the Lord. For the husband is the head of the wife just as Christ is the head of the church, the body of which he is the Saviour. Just as the church is subject to Christ, so also wives ought to be, in everything, to their husbands. (Ephesians 5:22–24)

Thus he returns to the Old Testament view of the wife as the property of the man. When he is positive about marriage and does not just consider it for the weak-willed, he compares marriage with the relationship between Christ and his Church:

> 'For this reason a man will leave his father and mother and be joined to his wife, and the two will become one flesh.' This is a great mystery, and I am applying it to Christ and the church. (Ephesians 5:31–32)

However, this still seems to say that the man is the head of the household, just as Christ is head of the Church.

Feminism
A way of thinking that seeks to emancipate women in society and give them equal opportunities.

Paul's views do seem more rigid than the equality message of Jesus, but he was a product of his times, and his focus on the imminent return of Jesus limited his teaching to preparation for that day.

Paul is credited with exerting great influence on the development of Christian thought, but he was also limited by his religious views and the attitudes of the times, especially on the value of **celibacy** and the inferior role of women. However, Platonic dualism and the views of the Greek philosophers were also important, as they stressed the spiritual above the physical – sex and relationships were part of the physical side of us.

Celibacy

Not having sexual relations with another person.

AUGUSTINE AND SEX AND RELATIONSHIPS

Augustine of Hippo lived in a world of multiple sects and 'heresies', one of which picked up on and emphasised the dualism of body and soul. This was Gnosticism, a mixture of the Greek traditions, some Judaism and Zoroastrianism. It was from Zoroastrianism that the extreme dualism sprang, along with a pessimistic fatalism. Central to Gnostic teaching was an intense dislike of the body and its needs, a total pessimism about sexuality which infiltrated the early Church. In this world, the views of Augustine were surprisingly liberal, and he considered that, far from abstaining from all sex, it was necessary for procreation, and that, like Paul and the Greeks, sex was a necessary evil. Augustine taught, after his many sexual relationships, that sex was to be restricted to marriage, but it was still 'dangerous'. The devil uses women to lead men away from reason, and pleasure in sex leads men away from reason. For Augustine the problem, and the solution, dated back to creation and the Fall. Adam and Eve, he concluded, must have been made for procreation, though they would not have needed to procreate before the Fall, or at least would have experienced no desire or pleasure. However, God knew that Eve would take the fruit and so he prepared for the consequences. For Augustine, then, sexual desire is a constant reminder of man's rebellion against God – it is our original sin. Augustine, unlike **Pelagius**, believed that we could not control sexual desire – he did not go in for 'muscular Christianity' like Pelagius, who thought that sexual desire could be controlled by the will. So, for Augustine, chastity was the ideal, but sex was allowed, so long as it was not enjoyed, within marriage.

Attitudes such as those of Augustine have had great influence on sexual attitudes and practices in the Western world.

THOMAS AQUINAS AND SEX AND RELATIONSHIPS

Thomas Aquinas' views on sex and relationships were accepted as right for Christians until they began to be questioned in modern times.

Aquinas based his thinking about sex and relationships on his understanding of Natural Law, in which he attempted to unite the thinking of Aristotle with Christian theology. Aquinas believed that human life had a purpose or *telos*; good acts developed our human nature and bad acts went against human nature. Aquinas assumed that humans shared a common human nature and so general principles could be applied to everyone, everywhere and at all times. Aquinas concluded that the purpose of the sexual organs and sexual activity was procreation, and any other use of sex was intrinsically wrong. Sex for Aquinas was to take place within the bounds of marriage, and must be open to the possibility of procreation. This became the view of the Catholic Church.

In the *Summa Theologiae*, Aquinas argued that sexual acts can be morally wrong in two different ways:

1   Sex is wrong when 'the act of its nature is incompatible with the purpose of the sex act [procreation]. In so far as generation is blocked, we have unnatural vice, which is any complete sex act from which of its nature generation cannot follow.' Aquinas gives us four examples: 'The sin of self-abuse' (masturbation), 'Intercourse with a thing of another species' (bestiality), acts with a person of the same sex (homosexuality), and acts in which 'the natural style of intercourse is not observed, as regards proper organ or according to other rather beastly and monstrous techniques' (foreplay?).
2   Sexual acts can be morally wrong even if natural; in these cases, 'conflict with right reason may arise from the nature of the act with respect to the other party'; for example, incest, rape or adultery.

Natural Law, however, raises two important questions:

1   Is an 'unnatural act' always wrong, even if it is consummated with mutual and informed voluntary consent?
2   Are there some non-procreative sexual acts that might be natural to human beings? Do we, in fact, share a common nature, but might God have created a variety of human beings with different forms of sexual expression?

KANT AND SEX AND RELATIONSHIPS

The categorical imperative causes **Immanuel Kant** to take a conservative attitude to sex and relationships in many ways. A husband who commits adultery cannot want extra-marital sex to be a universal law unless he wants his wife, children, parents and so on to also engage in extra-marital activities. Neither can homosexuality be universalised, since every homosexual is conceived through a heterosexual relationship – although artificial insemination could change this.

According to Kant, the pursuit of sexual pleasure is only allowed when serving more valuable goals, such as marriage, since 'Taken by itself sexual love is a degradation of human nature'. The categorical imperative does not allow people to be treated as a means to an end and so he claims that: 'As soon as a person becomes an object of appetite for another, all motives of moral relationship cease to function, because as an object of appetite for another, a person becomes a thing and can be treated and used as such by everyone.' The Kantian viewpoint seems to be that sexual acts are wrong in themselves, as they involve using another person for one's own pleasure, but this seems to apply to prostitution, not marriage. Kant calls marriage a contract in which two people grant each other reciprocal rights, and so it is not about one person using or abusing another. It seems a rather cold way of putting it, so perhaps it is just as well that he never tried it. However, Kant does not see sex within marriage as wrong, and the purpose of marriage, as he sees it, is not procreation, as in Natural Law, but the union of two people of different sexes. Husband and wife are equal partners in this and sexual enjoyment is a right to be permitted within the partnership.

Thus, Kant emphasises the contractual nature of sexual relationships and seems to find sex morally acceptable as long as one person is not using the other as a means to an end. Using Kant's arguments, it is possible to say that providing sexual services is morally acceptable as long as no coercion is involved. Some forms of prostitution would be allowed, although not if people engage in it against their will, or if they could be harmed mentally or physically by it.

A Kantian would be opposed to pornography because one is taking pleasure in looking at a person in such a way that they are thought of as mere things, mere means of obtaining sexual gratification. However, Kant emphasises the physical side of the 'sex', not the emotional side of the 'relationship'.

UTILITARIANISM AND SEX AND RELATIONSHIPS

Utilitarian reasons for having sex are:

- the value of pleasure
- the contribution which shared pleasure makes to the value of a relationship
- that consensual sex creates much good, and, if harm to another person is avoided, provides the greatest happiness for the greatest number.

Utilitarians want a happy society and sexual pleasure is an important element of human happiness, so utilitarians would want to maximise the good things about sex and relationships while minimising their downside. The utilitarian approach to sex and relationships is often called libertarian, as it allows consenting adults to do what they want and protects their freedom to do so. However, maximisation of sexual pleasure does not mean 'free love', as there are consequences of the latter such as unwanted pregnancies and sexually transmitted diseases like HIV and AIDS, not to mention 'broken hearts'.

Utilitarian arguments will include what many other ethical theories forget – the emotional aspect of a good relationship and the emotional suffering caused by unfaithfulness and deceit. Utilitarianism approaches sex and relationships with something more than the contractarian approach which emphasises the importance of mutual and voluntary informed consent. Under the contractarian approach sex is morally wrong if one or both of those involved lack a knowledgeable consent; for example, the under-aged, the mentally impaired or even the drunk. However, even when a contract is involved, it does not mean that the sexual relationship is necessarily moral. A middle-aged man may have a 'sexual contract' with a 15-year-old illegal immigrant who is desperate for money. He can pay her for having sex with him, and although a 'contract' has taken place, it is not a moral one because the girl, like many prostitutes, may have been forced into prostitution due to her status and poverty.

Jeremy Bentham may allow this kind of sex and 'relationship' as providing the greatest happiness for the greatest number. In 'Offences against One's Self: Pederasty', he argued that mutual consent for pleasure cannot make any sex act wrong if both partners are willing. However, he also asked whether such a relationship harmed society and caused unhappiness, either physical or moral (e.g. by undermining marriage, fidelity, family life or causing public offence).

John Stuart Mill also stressed the value of liberty, and in *On Liberty* suggested that this should be a matter of individual choice, without state interference, 'so long as we do not attempt to deprive others of theirs or

Gender
Cultural and psychological characteristics that determine whether a person is male or female.

Queer theory
The idea that there can be no fixed rules about what is or is not a legitimate sexual relationship. Being queer is the freedom to define oneself according to one's nature.

Harm principle
The belief that an act or consequence is morally permissible if no harm is done.

impede their efforts to obtain it'. However, he also argues that we should seek the 'higher pleasures', and that the goal of ethics is to seek the happiness of all by taking their needs and desires into account.

Utilitarians, therefore, should be tolerant of people with non-traditional sexual orientations, except in cases that do great social harm such as child molesters. Masturbation is permissible, assuming that it really does not make one go blind, although sex and relationships without two people involved may be seen as meaningless, so taking away the greatest amount of happiness for the greatest amount of people. Homosexuality and bisexuality can be tolerated, although if homosexuality were the norm, it would be harmful to society.

However, the **harm principle** is important to the utilitarian, especially in the case of extra-marital affairs, as very often the short-term pleasure they produce is not worth the ultimate pain and misery they can cause.

RELATIVE ETHICS (SITUATION ETHICS) AND SEX AND RELATIONSHIPS

Situation ethics is primarily associated with **Joseph Fletcher**, whose book *Situation Ethics* captured the mood of the 1960s when approaches to sex and relationships became more free, as the contraceptive pill almost eliminated the fear of pregnancy. Situation ethics has one primary principle – agape or unconditional love; not love as an emotion but the love that puts what is best for the other person first.

In principle, Situation ethics would seem to be a good approach to sex and relationships, as it seeks equal treatment of everyone and acts out of love. So the only basis on which a follower of Situation ethics can condemn any aspect of sex and relationships is if it is for mere pleasure or some other meaningless purpose, rather than a genuine expression of love and commitment. Situation ethics, therefore, rejects the 'free love' of the 1960s as thoroughly as any absolutist theory of ethics.

However, good as this sounds in theory, it is not so easy to apply in practice when strong emotions and physical drives take over.

VIRTUE ETHICS AND SEX AND RELATIONSHIPS

Virtue ethics stands apart from the approaches of most ethical theories and looks at moral choices from the standpoint of the individual and his or her personal qualities, virtues and ideals. Virtue ethics would consider what kind of sexual practices will tend to make a person more virtuous – those that involve taking pleasure in giving oneself to another and developing intimacy and commitment would make a person more virtuous, whereas those that use others for one's own pleasure would tend to make us less virtuous. In sex and relationships, Virtue ethics points to the enduring values of love and commitment, honesty and loyalty, friendship and pleasure, and away from harmful traits such as exploitation and selfishness.

According to **Rosalind Hursthouse**, Virtue ethics implies that an action is right if it is what a virtuous person, who has and exercises the virtues, would characteristically do in the circumstances. Many modern Virtue ethicists, such as **Michael Slote**, emphasise the ethics of care in relationships, which requires a sort of three-way balance as far as sex and relationships are concerned: care for those who are near to us (intimate care); care for other people in general (humanitarian care); and care for our own well-being (self-care).

This view implies tolerance towards others' approaches to sex and relationships, and it also accepts that we are responsible for our character and the moral choices we make. Virtue ethics also urges us to rediscover balance in human sexuality and in our relationships.

MODERN INFLUENCES ON SEX AND RELATIONSHIPS

Modern popular thinking, influenced by developments in psychology and sociology, began to question traditional views by asking such questions as: 'Why is sex within marriage for procreation more in accordance with human nature than sex outside marriage for pleasure?' and 'Why cannot sexual relationships be morally right if there is love, loyalty and intimacy?'

According to **Sigmund Freud**, each person's approach to sex and relationships is based on their upbringing and their relationship with their parents. He suggests that sexual personality may be found at the core of moral personality: how we behave towards sexual partners both influences and mirrors how we perceive and interact with people in general. So, the failure to learn to control the pursuit of sexual pleasure undermines the achievement of a virtuous character.

Freud says that we each have a super-ego, which is like an inner voice reminding us of the social norms inculcated in us by our parents and authority figures in society. We need this voice in order to live happily in a law-abiding society. Unlike Aquinas, Freud considers that being moral may not accord with our real natures at all and so it is not possible to base an ethical theory on what we essentially are.

Rules about sex and relationships have existed in every culture, as have disagreements about what is and what is not morally acceptable. Must morally permissible sex have only one function? Must it be heterosexual? Must it be limited to marriage? Does sex require love or just mutual consent? Conditions in the modern world are changing rapidly and, as a result, modern opinions towards sex and relationships are also changing. This has influenced traditional religious teaching also.

RELIGIOUS ETHICS (CHRISTIAN) AND SEX AND RELATIONSHIPS

Traditional Christian ethics about sex and relationships is based on the teachings of the Bible, Augustine and Aquinas. Marriage is seen as the norm and the purpose of marriage is seen as fidelity, union and procreation. The unitive role of love is a comparatively modern element, and the role of sex in marriage as an expression of that love is also now recognised. Even sexual pleasure is seen as a gift from God – but only within the context of hetero-sexual marriage.

Jack Dominion argues, and has done for the past thirty years at least, not that sex is dangerous and needs marriage and procreation to protect it; but rather that sex is so powerful and meaningful that justice can only be done to it in a continuous and enduring relationship. He does not see premarital sex, cohabitation or even one-off adultery as destroying this ideal and even considers that homosexual sex is fine within a permanent loving relationship. He sees society as moving forward and the Church as needing to rethink but not reject its fundamental truths.

One issue that has divided Christianity is that of homosexuality. Every religion is divided between fundamentalists and liberals, between what is revealed and what is discovered. In Christianity, the issue of homosexuality points up that division, with the literal interpretation of the Bible asserting that homosexuality is wrong, and the spirit of the New Testament holding that it is the quality of the relationships which matters. There are many other issues involved, such as homosexuality being not natural, as homosexual sex does not lead to the procreation of children, the question of the 'gay gene', and the actual translation of the words in the Bible.

The two Greek words that have traditionally been translated as homo-sexual may mean 'loose living' or 'prostitute', so in the New Revised Standard Version of the Bible the word 'homosexual' has been omitted from Paul's letters. The story of Sodom (Genesis 19:4–11) is not about sexuality but hospitality, and so the only references are in the codes of Deuteronomy (Deuteronomy 23:17–18) and Leviticus (Leviticus 20:13). The meaning of these codes was obviously important at the time they were written, but today laws about purity, including the types of animals and fish that could be eaten, which excluded shell fish, and about dress, which outlawed the wearing of garments made from more than one type of yarn, are just irrelevant to many people. One concept underlying the laws was the idea of the pure form of a man and a woman, which led to the prohibition of shaving in men so that they did not look like women, and also of cross-dressing and same-sex relationships. Almost all Christians ignore these prohibitions, except the one about homosexuality. So it seems as though the Bible is being used, as in the possible split in the Anglican Church over the ordination of gay bishops, to reinforce prejudices. As **Richard Holloway** points out, the impetus for social reform comes from society, not from within the Christian Church.

Within the Catholic Church the position is similar – there is no sin involved in having homosexual inclinations, only in putting them into practice. Following Natural Law, any sexual act that is not open to procreation is unnatural and wrong. Again the Catholic Church has done nothing to counteract prejudice against homosexuals.

REVIEW QUESTIONS

Look back over the chapter and check that you can answer the following questions:

- What does the Old Testament say about sex and relationships?
- What does the New Testament say about sex and relationships?
- Why/how did sex become linked with procreation?
- List the strengths and weaknesses of a utilitarian approach to sex and relationships.

Essay question

'Natural Law is the most reliable approach when making judgements about sex and relationships.' Discuss. (OCR A2 Level 2772 June 2006 question 1)

You could start by explaining the main teachings of Natural Law (e.g. purpose, potentiality and actuality, primary and secondary precepts), the deontological and absolute nature of Natural Law and its origins in Aristotle, and how it is a basis for Roman Catholic teaching.

You could discuss the nature of sexual morality (e.g. sex as procreative, sex within marriage, homosexuality, 'abuses' of sex), and apply Natural Law to sexual ethics. Using examples, you could show how some may see Natural Law as the best approach because, for example, it is universal and God-given, but for others Natural Law may appear out of date and inflexible.

To really get to grips with this question you need to ask what is meant by 'reliable' and from whose perspective this theory may seem reliable. You may then discuss whether there can be any absolutes in terms of personal relationships or whether some other theories such as Kant, Utilitarianism or Natural Law might be considered more reliable.

FURTHER READING

Bellioti, R. *Good Sex: Perspectives on Sexual Ethics*, Kansas, University Press of Kansas, 1993.

Blackburn, S. *Lust*, Oxford/New York, Oxford University Press, 2004.

Holloway, R. *Godless Morality*, Edinburgh, Canongate, 1999.

Hursthouse, R. *On Virtue Ethics*, Oxford, Oxford University Press, 1999.

Kant, I. *Lectures on Ethics*, Heath, P. and Schneewind, J.B. (eds), Cambridge, Cambridge University Press, 1997.

Moore, G. 'Sex, Sexuality and Relationships', in *Christian Ethics: An Introduction*, Hoose, B. (ed.), London/New York, Cassell, 1998.

Slote, M. *Morals from Motives*, Oxford/New York, Oxford University Press, 2001.

Vardy, P. *The Puzzle of Sex*, London, Fount, 1997.

15 War, Peace and Justice

WHAT YOU WILL LEARN ABOUT IN THIS CHAPTER

- The principles of Just War theory and its application.
- Realism and Christian Realism as an approach to war.
- The theories of ethical and religious pacifism.
- How different ethical theories approach issues of war and peace.
- How religious ethics approaches issues of war and peace.
- The strengths and weaknesses of these different approaches to issues of war and peace.

KEY SCHOLARS

- Plato (428–347 BCE)
- Ambrose of Milan (c.340–397)
- Augustine of Hippo (354–430)
- Thomas Aquinas (1225–1274)
- Francisco de Vitoria (1480–1546)
- Francisco Suárez (1548–1617)
- Hugo Grotius (1583–1645)
- Emerich de Vattel (1714–1767)
- Jeremy Bentham (1748–1832)
- John Stuart Mill (1806–1873)
- Bertrand Russell (1872–1970)
- Reinhold Niebuhr (1892–1971)
- Dietrich Bonhoeffer (1906–1945)
- Thomas Merton (1915–1968)
- Elizabeth Anscombe (1919–2001)
- Martin Luther King Jr. (1929–1968)
- Walter Wink (1935–)

WHAT IS WAR?

Most people are now totally familiar with war. It used to be something you learned about in history books, but now we see its horror every day on television in our own homes. Except for disease and natural disasters there is nothing else that brings home human suffering so forcefully. It is hard to imagine that any country would want to go to war with the population of another country; that any sane individual would want to attack another country to seize its land or change its political processes. Therefore, there must be very powerful motivations for going to war.

People go to war for greed, for excitement and adventure, for religion and politics. War is a peculiar human activity and can bring out some of our best traits such as courage and self-sacrifice, and yet it can also lead men and women to commit acts of cruelty and barbarism.

War cemetery

War is conflict among states where armed forces confront the armed forces of another state. It is generally conducted within certain customs or laws. By common consent war is 'just' if it is in self-defence and if it is sanctioned by the UN – it is difficult to argue the idea of 'just cause' if the war is against a state that poses no immediate threat, but which perhaps has an undemocratic regime.

Thought Point

1 What would make anyone want to go to war?
2 Under what circumstances would you be prepared to go to war?
3 Under what circumstances would you not be prepared to go to war?
4 Is the 'war against terrorism' truly a war?
5 Can you think of any circumstance in which someone would be justified in killing another person?
6 Why does it always appear that the enemy's justification for war is weaker than our own?

There are three main approaches to the issues surrounding war and peace:

1 **Just War theory** – states can have moral justification for going to war and sometimes war is morally right.
2 **Realism** – says that basically ethics has nothing to do with war. War is often necessary to promote security, survival and economic growth.
3 **Pacifism** – it is right to apply ethics to war and ask whether the war is just, but the answer will always be the same: war is always wrong and there is always some better solution than fighting.

JUST WAR THEORY

Just War theory is probably the most influential approach to issues of war and peace. It is constantly being refined and redeveloped and has even been codified into contemporary international laws governing armed conflict, such as the United Nations Charter and the Hague and Geneva Conventions. Just War theory, complete with a picture of Thomas Aquinas, was even discussed in *The Times* at the time of the first Gulf War.

Just War theory
The belief that war is morally justified if it meets certain criteria.

Realism
Normal moral rules cannot be applied to how states act in time of war.

Pacifism
The belief that violence is wrong.

St Ambrose
(c. 340–397)

Ambrose was born in Trier
and studied in Rome. He
became Bishop of Milan in
374. Here he defended the
Church against Arianism.
He also received the future
St Augustine into the
Church. His feast day is
7 December.

Francisco Suárez
(1548–1617)

Francisco Suárez was born
in Granada on 5 January
1548. He taught theology
and philosophy studies
privately and also at Ávila,
Segovia and Valladolid.
From 1580 to 1585 he
taught at the Roman
College in Rome. He was
eventually appointed to the
chair of theology at the
University of Coimbra
in Portugal. He died in
Coimbra on 25 September
1617.

Francisco de Vitoria
(1480–1546)

Francisco de Vitoria was
born at Vitoria, Álava,
Castile. He entered the
Dominican Order and
studied and lectured in
Paris for sixteen years.
    In 1523 he returned
to Spain and lectured in

continued

The origins of Just War theory

The origins of Just War discussion go back to philosophers such as **Aristotle** and **Cicero**, who wrote that a war in self-defence was just. The first significant Christian development of Just War principles came with **Ambrose of Milan** and his student **Augustine of Hippo**. The political situation had changed rapidly and the Roman Emperor Constantine began to use the Roman state to support the Church. According to an influential bishop named Eusebius, Christian pacifism was from then on to be strictly for clergy, monks and nuns; lay Christians, however, were obliged to defend the country with force.

Ambrose and Augustine stipulated that war must only be waged by a legitimate governmental authority; it must be intended to restore peace and justice; it should be a last resort. There were also limits on the conduct of war: reprisal killings and massacres were forbidden. Augustine drew on the existing Roman idea of *justum bellum* and the Old Testament tradition where wars on behalf of Israel and God were clearly commanded by God.

Thomas Aquinas drew together the thinking on Just War and listed right authority, just cause and just intention as the most important aspects. In the *Summa Theologiae* Aquinas presents the general outline of what became the Just War theory, and he discusses not only war's justification, but the kinds of activity that are permissible in war, who can fight a war and when a war can be fought. In spite of all this, he starts by saying that war in itself is sinful as it is contrary to peace.

In the sixteenth and seventeenth centuries **Francisco Suárez** and **Francisco de Vitoria** added the extra conditions of proportionality, last resort and reasonable chance of success.

Just War theory can be divided into three parts:

1 *Jus ad bellum* concerns the justice of resorting to war in the first place.
2 *Jus in bello* concerns the justice of conduct within the war.
3 *Jus post bellum* concerns the justice of peace agreements and the ending of the war.

Jus ad bellum

These rules are addressed primarily to heads of state and governments, as they are the ones that set the wheels of war in motion. Just War theory demands that for war to be justified a state must fulfil each of the following six requirements.

1 Just cause

This is seen as the most important rule which sets the tone for all the others. There must be a good reason to go to war. So what makes a good reason? According to some of the most influential thinkers on the subject these are some of the reasons:

- **Augustine**, quoted by **Thomas Aquinas**, said: 'A just war is wont to be described as one that avenges wrongs, when a nation or state has to be punished for refusing to make amends for wrongs inflicted by its subjects, or to restore what has been seized unjustly' (*Summa Theologiae II–II* Question 40).
- For the Dominican **Francisco de Vitoria** a nation has just cause when it tries to correct a violation of its rights.
- For the Jesuit **Francisco Suárez** the victim nation also has the right to punish those who are responsible for the injustice.
- For **Hugo Grotius** and **Emerich de Vattel** the prevention of injustice also constitutes a just cause. However, one has to be certain of the facts.

Based on these ideas it seems that just cause is essentially about the correction and/or punishment of an injustice that has been done, or about the prevention of an injustice that is about to happen. This is a little vague, as it does not explain what kind of injustice has to occur for the war to be just. It seems to involve *self-defence* and *defence of others*.

Is war justifiable only in response to armed attack, such as the German invasion of Poland in 1939 or the Iraqi invasion of Kuwait in 1990? Is it true that to know who was right and who was wrong in a war, you only need to know who fired the first shot?

However, an important point to consider when looking at just cause is whether it is permissible to launch a pre-emptive strike against anticipated aggression. After all, the presumed injustice has not yet taken place, so how can it be self-defence? The UN Security Council forbids pre-emptive strikes unless they have been clearly authorised in advance. This problem was highlighted in the run-up to the 2003 US-led pre-emptive strike on Iraq. The US still maintains it was right to strike first, in spite of there being no weapons of mass destruction, as part of its war on terror. Many other countries disagreed with this action.

Self-defence also allows the retaking of what has previously been wrongfully taken away.

According to Just War tradition, the 'others' does not need to be another state; it can also be a group of individuals belonging to another state whose fundamental rights are being violated. For Vitoria, Suarez and Grotius the concept of intervention for *humanitarian* reasons was not unknown and

Valladolid. In 1526 he was elected to the chair of theology at Salamanca. Vitoria is well known for his anti-colonial views; he doubted the justice of the Spanish conquest of the New World. He died on 12 August 1546.

Jus ad bellum
Justice in the decision to wage war.

Jus in bello
Justice in the conduct of war.

Jus post bellum
Justice in the ending of the war.

Hugo Grotius (1583–1645)

Hugo Grotius was born in Delft on 10 April 1583. He studied at the University of Leiden and then studied law at Orléans. In 1607 he was appointed Attorney-General of the province of Holland. One of his most significant works was *De Jure Belli ac Pacis* (On the Law of War and Peace) (1625). Following a shipwreck, he died in Rostock on 28 August 1645.

the idea that the responsibility of state leaders does not stop at their borders follows logically from their Natural Law perspective, that a universal moral code unifies all of humanity. This gives the right to intervene in the affairs of another state to protect the innocent citizens of that state. There are numerous examples of this in our recent history, when states massacred large numbers of their own citizens: Cambodia and Uganda in the 1970s, Rwanda in 1984, Serbia-Kosovo in 1998 to 1999 and the massacres in Sudan/Darfur which began in 2004 and seem to be still rumbling on today.

However, the situation is not as simple as it would seem, since when we intervene to provide humanitarian assistance we are violating the sovereignty of that state and so giving that state just cause in defending itself. In addition, how far should the intervention go? Should it be limited to humanitarian assistance or should the operation attempt to create an environment safe for democracy and human rights? **John Stuart Mill** advocated respect for the principle of self-determination: 'The members of a political community must seek their own freedom' and 'they cannot be set free by external force'. Others disagree and say sometimes we simply do not do enough – it is not enough to feed people while allowing them to be killed.

Just cause is found on both sides of a conflict – nobody engages in war without thinking they have just cause. Just cause, then, cannot be an absolute principle, as the US Catholic bishops wrote in their pastoral letter *The Challenge of Peace, God's Promise, and Our Response* (1983): 'Every party should acknowledge the limits of its Just Cause and the consequent

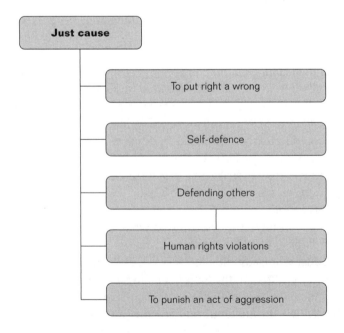

requirement to use only limited means in pursuit of its objectives.' Just War theory tells us not to exaggerate our own claims and to try to avoid the use of excessive force in pursuit of our own just cause.

2 Legitimate authority

A state may only go to war if the decision has been made by the appropriate authorities. When **Augustine** first framed the Just War principle, he associated it with the Roman Empire. In the Middle Ages, kings, nobles and cities claimed to have the authority to wage war, and throughout modern history revolutionary, secessionist and anti-colonial movements have challenged the right of established governments to be the only authority allowed to use legitimate force. After the Second World War the primary responsibility was given to the United Nations Security Council.

Just War principles have adapted to varying cultural and political needs.

3 Right Intention

The principle of Right Intention is closely related to the just cause principle and may be seen as its subjective element. Having a reason to go to war is not enough – the actual motivation must be moral. However, which intention is the right one? Reasons for going to war include the following:

- to kill and rob (barbaric wars)
- to seek glory in war (wars of chivalry)
- to promote commercial interests
- to promote colonial expansion
- to seize the land and resources of other countries
- for the sake of religion
- civil war
- revolution
- to retake something wrongfully taken
- to avenge a wrong
- in self-defence
- to prevent possible aggression in the future
- pre-emptive strikes
- to defend other states
- to protect people from genocide (humanitarian intervention).

Intuitively, most of us tend to think that some of the reasons in the above list are right and others wrong; for example, a war in self-defence is usually considered right. Intentions are often mixed and culturally influenced; for example, the Vikings would have found the intention to kill and rob perfectly acceptable, and a medieval knight would be happy to seek glory in war. So the principle of Right Intention needs to be based on more solid ethical grounds than our intuitions.

Augustine was the first to propose this principle, and for him just wars should be waged with the intention of achieving peace. He taught that if we go to war with the intention of achieving peace with the assistance of God, we would avoid such lower motives as revenge, cruelty and lust for power. However, the peace needed to be a just peace – wars, according to Augustine, were just when they aimed at restoring justice. This view is also criticised as being subjective, as it leaves people free to wage war because they believe they are following God's command. Augustine justified the use of force for the general good, but said that an individual Christian is not justified in using force for his own self-defence, for instance when being attacked by robbers. Augustine said that such an act is motivated by self-love and so is wrong.

Hugo Grotius opposed the Right Intention principle as too subjective, but it was interpreted again by the US Catholic bishops in 1983, who stated that good intentions in the use of force should aim at achieving a just cause, which is 'confronting a real and certain danger'. It is not always possible to know what the real intentions are of those who use military force and this principle is always open to abuse, so perhaps Grotius was right to be sceptical.

4 Likelihood of Success

Deaths and injuries incurred in a hopeless cause are not morally justifiable. This idea was identified explicitly as a Just War principle by **Hugo Grotius** early in the seventeenth century. What is actually meant by success? For some it will mean victory, for others stopping the enemy near the border; it may even be respect for having fought with courage. The likelihood of success principle is closely linked to the following one: proportionality.

5 Proportionality

Proportionality

In war weapons should be proportionate to the aggression.

Proportionality is a relational principle; nothing is proportional by itself, but always in relation to something else. It is often said that punishment should be proportional (i.e. related in some way) to the crime.

When it comes to the *Jus ad bellum* part of Just War theory, it is easy to find real and imaginary examples of disproportionality. It would be disproportionate for a nation to start a war because a few drunken soldiers went across a border, or over fishing rights. It is harder to find examples which are proportional – it is proportional when a relatively strong nation is attacked by an equally strong nation, and when a very strong nation responds to an attack by another relatively strong nation on a weak ally, such as in the 1990 to 1991 Gulf War.

Does this mean that the good consequences of going to war must be equal to or greater than the bad? Is it possible to anticipate that the costs of war would be higher than the benefits? National pride can often get in the way, as can the excitement of war, or events may simply run out of control so that one step in the direction of war leads to another.

The principles of likelihood of success and proportionality are different principles, but they both share the idea of taking *everyone's* consequences into account and they are both difficult to apply. They both attempt to measure benefits and harms based on the just cause principle.

6 Last resort

According to Just War theory, the use of force can only be justified as a last resort, when all other means of resolving the conflict have been tried. This idea dates from **Cicero**, who said that, according to Roman legal practice, a certain time period should pass between the demand for reparations and the initiation of hostilities. **Thomas Aquinas** also thought of war as a kind of sanction for an injury in case there was no other way to right the wrong. Alternatives to war were explored by **Hugo Grotius**, who proposed peace conferences, arbitration and even favoured methods of solving conflict that seem odd today, such as drawing lots and individual combat. He considered that both sides should do all they can to avoid war.

Last resort is often risky – sometimes an unjust peace may be preferred to the horrors of war, but at other times it may be seen as a sign of weakness; for example, the policies of appeasement of Britain and France towards Nazi Germany just allowed Hitler to build up his armaments and strengthen his military position in Europe.

Economic sanctions are the favoured method of trying to persuade an offending state to alter its policies. They do not always work; for example, the economic sanctions against Iraq were insufficient to make Saddam Hussein remove his troops from Kuwait and they also failed to force the Iraqi government to comply with UN resolutions following the Gulf War. Sanctions may also go against the *Jus in bello* principles of discrimination and proportionality as they usually have as bad an effect on the civilian population as war itself.

Just War theory insists that all six criteria must be fulfilled for any declaration of war to be justified. The criteria are a mixture of deontological and consequential requirements.

Jus in Bello

Jus in bello refers to justice in war, to right conduct in the midst of battle. In Western culture these rules can be traced back to Greek warfare, when there were a number of unwritten conventions covering things such as the ransoming of prisoners of war, the pursuit of a defeated enemy, and an agreement that battles should only be fought during the campaigning season (the summer).

Plato introduced the idea of not touching those who were not to blame for the conflict, in other words the non-combatants. However, these rules only applied to warfare among Greeks, not foreign enemies.

Today, responsibility for keeping the *Jus in bello* rules is mainly that of the military commanders, officers and soldiers. They are accountable for any breaches and may end up being put on trial for war crimes.

There are several rules of *Jus in bello*, but the first two are considered the most important.

1 Proportionality

In the context of *Jus in bello*, the term 'proportionality' refers to soldiers using proportional force to achieve the end they seek. The issue is one of weighing the evil of war against the good results gained by war. According to this guideline, each act in a war, each battle, each campaign, must adhere to the principle of proportionality.

However, this does not give any direct guidance to those who have to make the decision in time of war as to how to apply the principle of proportionality. Consider, for example, the bombing of Dresden during the Second World War: tactically the bombing accomplished little militarily, yet it did much to harm many people who had little or nothing to do with the German war effort. It is estimated that between 35,000 and 135,000 people were killed, many of whom were refugees fleeing the advance of the Soviet army. Tactically, then, the bombings were immoral. Some argued that a broader strategic look needed to be taken at the bombings of the German cities which could make these raids morally legitimate, as the principle of discrimination can be overruled by the principle of proportionality. However, the Dresden raids happened so late in the war that they fail the strategic tests and were, therefore, immoral.

The principle of proportionality as a *Jus in bello* criterion is in itself easy enough to understand, but it is difficult to employ in concrete situations. This is partly due to the uncertainty of war, and partly because rational calculations are difficult to make.

It is useful, however, as a restraint on some of the horrible effects of war, and it does encourage those who have to make decisions in the heat of battle to consider the costs and benefits impartially. It asks commanders not to forget the sufferings of those 'on the other side' and not just to look at immediate consequences. Thus to most people the use of nuclear arms on a large scale is seen as violating the principle of proportionality, because of the future effect of radioactive fall-out on the environment and on both present and future generations.

2 Discrimination and non-combatant immunity

Broadly speaking this means that those at war have an obligation to distinguish between appropriate and inappropriate targets of destruction, and between innocent civilians and those involved in waging the war.

Since the twentieth century the principle of Discrimination has focused on non-combatant immunity – usually to no avail, as civilian casualties, especially those of children, have been a painful feature of every conflict in the twentieth and twenty-first centuries. Such casualties are often referred to as 'collateral damage'. In 1983 the US Catholic bishops said: 'The lives of innocent civilians may never be taken directly. Regardless of the purpose alleged for doing so.' However, what exactly does 'taken directly' mean? In the Gulf War, the Iraqi military placed their command posts over schools so that the allied forces would have to kill children in order to destroy them – would this mean that innocent civilians were 'taken directly'? Again, is it morally right to bomb roads, bridges, airport runways, water supplies and power stations as Israel did in Lebanon in 2006?

A further complication is recognising who exactly is a non-combatant. Soldiers who are taken prisoner are no longer combatants, since they do not pose any threat, and nor are soldiers who are wounded. However, many wars in recent history have been fought by soldiers who do not wear uniforms or any distinctive signs. Guerrillas blend in perfectly with the civilian population, and guerrilla movements often rely on some measure of support from local people, as they try to avoid local casualties or attack local property in order to build up this support.

So who exactly are the 'innocent' in war? According to **Hugo Grotius**, if state A is justly fighting against state B, then all those in state A are innocent and all those in state B are guilty of aggression. This is now considered too simplistic, as wars do not always have the consent of the whole population. **Robert Holmes** suggests categorising people depending on their involvement in the war:

1   The initiators of the war: the government or leaders.
2   The agents of the war: the military commanders and the combatants.
3   Contributors to the war effort: those who work in munitions, military research or propaganda. This could also possibly include taxpayers

whose taxes pay for it – though taxpayers do not have much say in how their money is spent.

4   Those who approved of the war without actually encouraging it.
5   Those who neither contribute to nor support the war: children, some elderly people, people in mental institutions or in prison.

However, this approach is also fairly simplistic, as it does not include the question of the conscription of those who have no wish to be soldiers but are forced to fight, or even the use of child soldiers.

Discrimination also concerns the question of nuclear weapons which is dealt with below, but more important today is the problem posed by the proliferation of landmines. A UN report written in 2000 states that landmines have an appalling individual impact, and also create long-term economic and social destruction for generations to come, as they are active for years and the minefields are often unmarked.

The principle of discrimination provides much guidance on approaching modern methods of warfare, including terrorism. Terrorism is always aimed at innocent victims (non-combatants), and the seeming randomness of terrorist attacks puts pressure on governments to yield to terrorists' demands. However, without even looking at other issues, the principle of discrimination will conclude that terrorism is unjustified.

3 Obey all international laws on weapons

There have been various attempts in the past to rule out certain weapons, ranging from crossbows to gas. In 1054 at the Council of Narbonne the Church decided certain days on which fighting could not take place. In 1139 the Lateran Council banned crossbows, bows and arrows and siege machines as unethical. However, these restrictions were rather like those of Plato and the Greeks, as they only applied to warfare between Christians. Chemical and biological weapons are forbidden by many treaties. Nuclear weapons are not so clearly prohibited, but any use of them would be met by incredible hostility from the international community. As far as nuclear weapons are concerned, we need to weigh up the principle of discrimination against the principle of proportionality, and the principle of proportionality seems to dominate, which is why many support nuclear deterrence, even though they recognise that the threat to use nuclear weapons is a threat to cause non-combatant casualties. However, given the destructiveness of nuclear weapons, could their use ever be proportionate to the final goal?

4 Fair treatment of prisoners of war

Enemy soldiers who surrender or who are captured no longer pose a threat. Therefore, it is wrong to torture them or otherwise mistreat them. The Geneva Convention says they should be kept in benevolent quarantine, away from the battle until the war ends, when they should be exchanged for one's own POWs. The question is whether terrorists also deserve such protection, and controversy continues about the aggressive questioning of terrorist suspects held in US detention centres.

5 No means mala in se

Soldiers may not use weapons or methods of warfare which are 'evil in themselves', such as mass rapes, genocide or ethnic cleansing, forcing soldiers to fight against their own side, and using weapons whose effects cannot be controlled, such as biological weapons.

6 No reprisals

A reprisal is when country A violates *Jus in bello* while at war with country B. Country B then retaliates with its own violation of *Jus in bello*, seeking to make country A obey the rules. Reprisals do not seem to work, but just escalate violence and make the destruction even more indiscriminate.

Jus in bello also requires a state to respect the rights of its own citizens, even though it is engaged in war. This includes issues such as conscription and censorship of the press. Some states have used the cover of war to engage in massive human rights violations, usually against some disliked minority group.

Jus post bellum

Jus post bellum refers to justice during the ending of war. It helps to ease the move from war to peace. This is a new approach to war and, if applied correctly, could lead to fewer wars.

1 Proportionality

The peace treaty should be reasonable and not seek to humiliate – so this rules out unconditional surrender. The settlement should not be able to be used as a source of revenge in the future.

2 Discrimination

A distinction needs to be made between the leaders, the soldiers and the civilians in the defeated country. Civilians should be protected, which rules out any economic sanctions after the war.

3 Rights vindication

The settlement should secure the rights to life and liberty, territory and sovereignty, especially any violations which may have been a trigger for the war. This means that the war and the subsequent peace treaty will actually have an improving effect on the country.

4 Punishment

Where necessary any leaders of an oppressive regime who engaged in massive human rights violations should face international war crimes tribunals. Soldiers from all sides of the conflict should also be held accountable for their actions and face investigation and possible trials.

5 Compensation

Financial restitution may be necessary so that the defeated country can get back on its feet and repair its infrastructure: roads and transport links, hospitals, and schools and institutes of further and higher education.

6 Rehabilitation

The postwar environment provides an ideal chance to reform an aggressive regime. This may involve disarmament, the rehabilitation of the military, retraining of police, working with local people on new constitutions, education, helping people to see that the new order is better than the old and leaving the new regime to govern its own affairs when it is ready.

Finally, *Jus post bellum* requires **time**; it cannot be achieved overnight or even in a few years, as the situation in Iraq shows, but it can be achieved in the end, as modern Germany and Japan testify.

Just War theory may be an ancient one, but it still provides rules to guide decision-makers on starting wars, conduct during war and the ending of the war. It tries to ensure that wars are only started if they are just, that is, for a few defensible reasons, that they are fought in a responsible and controlled way and that the dispute is ended justly.

Strengths of Just War theory

- Just War theory defines the conditions under which violence may be used and it combines the wisdom of thinkers and philosophers from many centuries.
- It is a flexible theory, and grows and develops with the times.
- Just War theory recognises the necessity of action against an aggressor.
- Just War theory allows defence of the defenceless.
- Just War theory does not allow acts of war simply because they are thought to be in the interest of one nation.
- Weapons of mass destruction may change Just War theory, but we still need to consider their use within a moral framework.
- In spite of difficulties with the individual principles, Just War theory remains a universal theory.

Weaknesses of Just War theory

- Just War theory says that violence is permitted, but morality must always oppose deliberate violence.
- Just War theory is unrealistic, as the strong and powerful will always win.
- The conditions are too simplistic and ambiguous to apply in practice.
- Weapons of mass destruction demand a different approach, as they break all the basic rules.
- Terrorism demands a different approach, as terrorists take no notice of the rules.
- Many wars are only considered just in hindsight.

Thought Point

Is it morally defensible to have rules for war?

- What problems can you see with the following imaginary press release? During a recent action against terrorism, the ground troops called up air support who carried out a targeted strike using smart missiles. Collateral damage was kept to a minimum, with the loss of a few to friendly fire. There were few casualties.

continued

> • In July 2003 the sons of Saddam Hussein, Uday and Qusay, were killed by US troops. The US had offered a reward for their capture 'dead or alive'. There was, it seems, no attempt by the US troops involved in the action to try to capture the men alive so that they could be brought to trial.
>
> What rights were violated here and could this violation be justified?
>
> • Is it right for a state to treat prisoners of war according to how 'evil' that state considers the enemy to be?

REALISM

Realists fully appreciate the horrors of war and so, like others, try to assess its costs, but they also respond to war in terms of its benefits. War sometimes gives a state extra land or resources.

Realists argue that war is a **non-moral activity** – actions such as killing, maiming or stealing may be wrong for individuals, but have no application to nations in times of war. So if a state is thinking of going to war with another state, it does not have to have moral reasons before actually starting a war. Neither can the warring nations be criticised for how they fight the war.

So how can Realists justify this point of view? They give a number of reasons, including:

- There is no real moral authority over nations telling them how to act.
- To survive, a nation has to look after its own interests.
- The threat of war and war itself make it impossible for any nation to do anything but act in its own interest – there is no time to do anything else.

However, even if Realists do not accept moral principles, they can still act in line with them, as it is often more practical to do so (e.g. treat prisoners of war well). In addition, a nation often cannot afford to alienate a nation which does follow the Just War principles. Realists also say that it is important to protect the state's citizens.

Realists really say that anything is fair when it comes to war, and only self-interest matters. Ethics and war do not mix.

Christian Realism

Christian Realism gives the term a different meaning. According to **Reinhold Niebuhr**, whose Christian Realism was influential in the USA from the late 1930s to the 1960s, it is impossible fully to achieve ethical ideals because sin is present in everyone and in every action, especially self-interest and the desire to control other people. He saw war as evil and the result of human sinfulness, but it may be necessary to prevent greater evils. Niebuhr's views need to be understood within the context of the post-First World War period, and the failure of idealism to prevent that conflict and the conflicts which followed. He saw the importance of justice in society and the importance of creating systems of justice; so Christians sometimes have to support the use of force to restrain evil and prevent greater injustices. He also warned against overestimating our power to do good and the fact that we try to do things without full knowledge and awareness of our limitations. Niebuhr saw the rise of fascism as an evil which demanded the use of force, even by Christians, to get rid of it. Niebuhr thought that although individuals may sometimes rise above self-interest, the same was not true of states, and therefore he opposed pacifism.

PACIFISM

Pacifists reject all war in favour of peace. Conflicts between nations should be settled by international gatherings such as the UN. The use of force is always wrong, even in self-defence, and so pacifism rejects both the Just War theory and Realism.

Pacifism is a broad term and may be roughly divided into Absolute Pacifism, which sees all war as wrong, and Consequentialist or Contingent Pacifism, which sees the costs of fighting the war as always greater than the benefits. However, both forms place great emphasis on the importance of respecting human life, and so reject killing.

Absolute Pacificism

Absolute Pacificism says it is never right to kill another human being, no matter what the consequences of not doing so might be, even loss of life. This may be a religious belief or even a secular one. Absolute pacifists see violence as totally unacceptable.

This position is a difficult one to keep in practice, as they would see it as unethical to use violence in any situation, even to rescue an innocent person who is being attacked and may be killed. It is even more difficult to try to

Christian Realism
The belief that Christianity may use violence to bring about the Kingdom of God and secure peace on earth.

Reinhold Niebuhr (1892–1971)

Reinhold Niebuhr was born in Wright City, Missouri, on 21 June 1892. In 1915 he became pastor of the Bethel Evangelical Church of Detroit. From 1928 he taught at the Union Theological Seminary in New York. Niebuhr is best known for his work on the interrelationships between religion, individuals and modern society. He died on 1 June 1971.

persuade others to do likewise. However, once accepted, it does provide a straightforward way of making decisions – there is certainly no need to work through a whole load of criteria like the follower of Just War theory.

Religious Pacifism

In the West, pacifism is rooted in Christianity and was particularly strong in the early Church. It looked to the Gospels, which record that Jesus called his followers not to violence, but to sacrificial love. Jesus taught that we must love our enemies, do good to those who hate us and 'Blessed are the peace-makers' (Matthew 5:9). These themes are rooted in the Jewish prophetic tradition, and followers of Jesus see both his ministry and his sacrificial death as a continuation and a fulfilment of that tradition, which must be carried on by his followers. The early Christians saw Jesus' commands as a prohibition on the bearing of arms, and so they refused to join the Roman army. As explained earlier, a profound change in the Christian attitude to war came at the time of the emperor Constantine, and from this time pacifism has been a minority view within the Christian Church.

However, there have been influential peace churches which continue the original Christian position, such as the Quakers, the Mennonites, the Amish, the Bruderhof Brethren (a community now living in East Sussex) and the Dukhobors (originally from Russia, but now living mainly in Canada). The **Quakers** are the most familiar group in the UK and, having been founded at the time of the civil war, they consider that violence only leads to more violence, and also that it is important that each person actively works to overcome anything which causes conflict between peoples. Most of these pacifist Christian communities were not against state military service, or the idea that a state should be able to defend itself, as they saw the state as a necessary vehicle for social order, but they themselves would not serve in the military. These Christian pacifists follow the teaching of Paul in Romans 13, where he wrote: 'Let every person be subject to the governing authorities; for there is no authority except from God, and those authorities that exist have been instituted by God' (Romans 13:1).

Paul saw those in authority thus: 'It is the servant of God to execute wrath on the wrongdoer' (Romans 13:14b). The state seems permitted to use force, but not the individual Christian. Peace churches see a complete separation between the 'church' and the 'world', and take the stance of *conscientious objectors*, often being persecuted by the authorities who do not share their view.

However, this pacifism does not mean doing nothing, but often encompasses *non-violent direct action*. The most well-known example of this was **Martin Luther King Jr.**, who used forceful language, non-violent resistance, strikes, peaceful protest and civil disobedience, eventually culminating in his assassination, in the struggle for racial equality in the USA. He was influenced by the campaign for Indian independence led by **Gandhi**, who advocated *ahisma* or non-violence and *satyagraha* or zest for truth. Other examples include the transformation of Polish society by the *Solidarity* movement led by **Lech Walenska**. However, whether such action will work in a war situation is another question.

Christian pacifism is not, however, limited to small Protestant groups but is followed by many in mainstream Christian denominations. Influential among these was the Catholic monk **Thomas Merton**, who influenced many with his prolific writings. He renounced violence as a way to peace and wrote that the task of the Christian is to work for the total abolition of war.

Merton advocated of non-violence as a realistic alternative to violence and killing; the task was to try to win people's minds instead of destroying their bodies. In the Preface of his autobiography he wrote:

> It is my intention to make my entire life a rejection of, a protest against the crimes and the injustices of war and political tyranny which threaten to destroy the whole human race . . . and the world with it. By my monastic life and vows I am saying NO to all the concentration camps, the aerial bombardments, the staged political trials, the judicial murders, the racial injustices, the economic tyrannies and the whole socio-economic apparatus which seems geared for nothing but global destruction in spite of all its fair words in favour of peace.

Merton was censored by his superiors, but partly due to him Catholic pacifism is now more common and is even supported by the Vatican as an appropriate faith response to issues of war.

On the mainstream Protestant side **Walter Wink** criticises Augustine's support of violence to defend the innocent, and the whole Just War theory, as it has led Christians to be one of the most warlike factions on Earth. He says that Christians should be non-violent pacifists who resist evil, but reject any idea of just war.

Contingent Pacifism

Contingent Pacifism is not opposed to war on absolute grounds, but on contingent grounds – war as we know it cannot be waged in a morally acceptable way. In other words, all wars today involve killing of the innocent, and this is morally unjustifiable.

Contingent pacifists accept wars in some circumstances, such as self-defence and defence of others, but the innocent must always be protected. So wars are justifiable in theory, but not in practice. Contingent pacifists

Martin Luther King, Jr. (1929–1968)

Martin Luther King, Jr. (b/w photo) by American photographer (twentieth century)

© Private Collection/Peter Newark

American Pictures/The Bridgeman Art Library

Martin Luther King was born on 15 January 1929 in Atlanta. He was ordained as a Baptist minister at the age of 18. In 1954 he was appointend pastor of the Dexter Avenue Baptist Church in Montgomery, Alabama. In 1960 he became co-pastor (with his father) of the Ebenezer Baptist Church in Atlanta. In 1963 he led a civil rights campaign in Birmingham, Alabama, working for black voter registration, desegregation, and better education and housing. He led the march on Washington on 28 August 1963 and gave his famous 'I Have a Dream' speech. On 4 April 1968 he was shot and killed in Memphis.

continued opposite

need to look at each case to see if there are justifiable ways to fight the war. However, it is not possible to know in advance whether a proposed war will be able to be conducted rightly – without killing the innocent.

Finally, Contingent pacifists are against violence and war in principle, but accept that there may be times when war is the lesser of two evils. **Bertrand Russell** could be considered a Contingent pacifist, although he himself called it 'relative political pacifism', as he believed the Second World War to be a necessary evil to rid the world of Hitler and fascism. This is basically a utilitarian view: it is bad consequences that make violence and war wrong.

Preferential Pacifism

Preferential Pacifism is a preferential option over violence. Preferential pacifists choose this option partly because war has been so destructive historically. This position in the twentieth century has been linked to economic justice as a basis for peace. In *Populorum Progressio* in 1967 Pope Paul VI wrote: 'To struggle against injustice is to promote the common good. Peace is not just the absence of war.' This was also the basis of the Catholic Workers' Movement and the views of its leaders, such as Dorothy Day, and led to what has become known as 'the preferential option for the poor' – social injustices, inequality and lack of human dignity are seen as militating against social and international peace.

Sometimes pacifism as a preferential option has to take a back seat to the welfare of the oppressed. This is shown in the actions of the Christian pacifist Dietrich Bonhoeffer, who, in spite of his pacifist stance, took part in a failed assassination plot against Hitler and was later hanged at Birkenau for his part in the plot.

So, for the Preferential pacifist, pacifism is about how to live life, but sometimes it is either impossible or immoral to maintain a pacifist stance.

Pacifism, therefore, is not just one view. There are different sorts and degrees of pacifism, but they all include the view that war and violence are unjustified and that conflicts should be settled in a peaceful way. Pacifism is also seen as more than opposition to violence and war; it must also include the promotion of justice and human rights.

Strengths of pacifism

- Pacifism is clear-cut – it opposes all forms of violence.
- Pacifism follows the teachings of Jesus, which pacifists see as ignored by Just War theory.

- It follows the historical position of the early Christians.
- It promotes the absolute value of human life.

Weaknesses of pacifism

- We do not live in a world based on pacifism and, as **Elizabeth Anscombe** points out, pacifism is wrong because it denies the right of self-defence.
- The state has a duty to protect its citizens.
- Pacifism allows evil to dominate.

APPLYING ETHICAL THEORIES TO ISSUES OF WAR AND PEACE

Utilitarianism

Utilitarianism approaches war not by asking if it goes against moral principles or rules, but by assessing the results it produces. If war produces more happiness or pleasure than unhappiness, then the principle of utility allows it. It depends on whether the loss of life, the number of injured and bereaved etc. outweigh the benefit.

Utilitarianism is difficult to apply to war, as the results are even more unpredictable than those of many other moral dilemmas. Perhaps it would be easier to say that wars should only be fought when it is at least possible that the outcome and the just purpose can be achieved – the Just War criterion of likelihood of success. There are too many 'what ifs?' to be weighed up against each other.

Preference Utilitarianism requires that the preferences of all those involved be taken into account – so in the war in Iraq does an Iraqi count as much as an American or British soldier? What of people in the future – what if in ten years' time Iraq is a free, democratic and prosperous country?

Utilitarians can also oppose war if the loss of human life looks too great, and can reassess their position as events change. Ultimately, though, Utilitarianism approaches issues of war and peace by asking if the end justifies the means.

Kantian ethics

The many strands of Kantian ethics can be fruitfully applied to issues of war and peace. Kant's focus on the 'good will' has parallels with Aquinas'

and then travelled across Europe and the USA. His specialist fields were logical and mathematical questions but he also had a strong sense of social consciousness. In *The Problems of Philosophy* (1912) Russell used sociology, psychology, physics and mathematics to argue against idealism. Russell believed that 'objects perceived by the senses have an inherent reality independent of the mind'.

Dietrich Bonhoeffer (1906–1945)

Bonhoeffer was born in Breslau on 4 February 1906. He studied theology at Tübingen and Berlin. He became a lecturer in theology in Berlin in 1931. Bonhoeffer was a leading critic of the Nazis and, in 1933, joined the Lutheran Confessing Church which opposed anti-Semitism. After a period in England he returned to Germany as a seminary director for the Confessing Church. He was imprisoned in Berlin in April 1943 and was hung at the Nazi concentration camp at Flössenberg on 9 April 1945.

contribution to the *Jus in bello* condition which requires there to be right intention.

However, applying Kant's categorical imperative is not so straightforward – it is difficult to find a maxim that could universalise killing, as it is a contradiction *of the will* and the *law of nature*.

Equally, when comparing Kant to Utilitarianism, killing others for a greater good or to reach some ultimate purpose does not meet Kant's requirement to treat people as ends in themselves and not as a means to an end, although a humanitarian intention could be possible.

However, Kant was fairly pessimistic about the human race and believed warfare to be morally permissible in the less than ideal world in which we live. Kant universalises the maxim to preserve one's life, so justifying violence in self-defence. If everyone adopted this maxim and fought only to preserve his or her own life, then Kant's theory of duty would have successfully eliminated war.

Finally, the third part of the categorical imperative, that we should act as though legislating for a Kingdom of Ends, influenced another of his writings, *Perpetual Peace*, written in 1795. Here he recommends a federation of free states, bound together by a covenant prohibiting war – war is a problem which only an international government could solve. This idea was fundamental to the League of Nations (1919–39) and then the more effective United Nations (1949–). However, Kant saw the importance of some sort of world federation – even if it was necessary to wage war to achieve it.

REVIEW QUESTIONS

Look back over the chapter and check that you can answer the following questions:

1   Make brief bullet point notes on each of the following:

   * *Jus ad bellum*
   * *Jus in bello*
   * *Jus post bellum*

2   Make a chart of the strengths and weaknesses of Just War theory.
3   Explain Realism as an approach to war in one short paragraph.
4   List the different types of pacifism and write one or two sentences explaining each.
5   Make a chart of the strengths and weaknesses of pacifism.

Essay question

Discuss the claim that killing in warfare is more justifiable than other kinds of killing. (OCR A2 Level 2772 June 2005 question 3)

You will need to consider whether killing is always wrong in an absolute sense or whether it can be justified in some circumstances. You could consider the issues surrounding abortion or euthanasia compared with killing in war. Or you could concentrate on the ethics of war, exploring the Just War theory and arguing for or against it. You may need to consider the situation in the world today and look at varieties of pacifism (e.g. religious, contingent). You could also consider Christian Realism as an alternative approach and conclude that killing in warfare is necessary as the lesser of two evils. You may want to contrast the impersonal killing in war or the obeying of orders with the more personal nature of euthanasia. You may simply wish to argue ultimately that all life is sacred.

There is no one perfect way of answering a question such as this – it is all about you justifying your approach and showing your knowledge, understanding and evaluative skills.

FURTHER READING

Anscombe, E. 'War and Murder' in *Moral Problems*, Palmer, M., Cambridge, Lutterworth Press, 1991.

Aquinas, Thomas. *Summa Theologiae II–II q.40* (Dominican translation), London, Burns & Oates, 1936.

Coates, A. *The Ethics of War*, Manchester, Manchester University Press, 1997.

Coppieters, B. and Fotion, N. (eds) *Moral Constraints on War*, New York/Oxford, Lexington Books, 2002.

Glover, J. *Humanity: A Moral History of the Twentieth Century*, New Haven, CT, Yale University Press, 2000.

Holmes, R. *On War and Morality*, Princeton, NJ, Princeton University Press, 1989.

Niebuhr, R. *Moral Man and Immoral Societies*, New York, Scribner, 1932.

Norman, R. *Ethics, Killing and War*, Cambridge, Cambridge University Press, 1995.

Rawls, J. *A Theory of Justice*, Harvard, MA, Harvard University Press, 1971.

Wilcockson, M. *Issues of Life and Death*, London, Hodder & Stoughton, 1999.

CONNECTIONS IN PHILOSOPHY OF RELIGION AND RELIGIOUS ETHICS

PART IV

The following chart lists the connections themes and which philosophy and ethics topics they relate to. It also shows possible connections that you could explore. Remember that the connections paper draws on topics you have studied at both AS and A2 level.

1 The concept of free will and determinism in relation to the problem of evil

   (a) Philosophy and ethics topics

      (i) Life after death
      (ii) God the Creator
      (iii) The goodness of God
      (iv) The problem of evil
      (v) Determinism

   (b) Possible connections to explore:

      (i) Is life after death a solution to the problem of evil?
      (ii) Is the goodness of God and creation challenged by the existence of evil?
      (iii) Does determinism negate our responsibility for evil?

2 Conscience or a sense of moral responsibility as possible evidence for the existence of God

   (a) Philosophy and ethics topics

      (i) The moral argument
      (ii) Conscience
      (iii) Psychology and sociology of religion

(b) Possible connections to explore:

    (i) Is conscience evidence for the existence of God?

    (ii) Is morality a matter of social convention or psychological conditioning?

    (iii) Is conscience innate or learnt?

3 The implications for ethics of the theories of psychology and sociology

(a) Philosophy and ethics topics

    (i) Psychology and sociology of religion

    (ii) Ethical theory (Kant, Utilitarianism, Virtue ethics, Natural Law, Situation ethics)

    (iii) Meta-ethics

(b) Possible connections to explore:

    (i) Is ethics really a branch of psychology/sociology?

    (ii) Is there any certainty in ethics?

4 The relationship between ethical language and religious language

(a) Philosophy and ethics topics

    (i) Meta-ethics

    (ii) Religious language

(b) Possible connections to explore:

    (i) Is religious language meaningful?

    (ii) Is the use of symbolism falsifiable?

    (iii) Is ethical language more meaningful than religious language?

5 The relationship between moral behaviour and life after death

(a) Philosophy and ethics topics

    (i) Life after death

    (ii) Kant and the categorical imperative

    (iii) Utilitarianism

    (iv) Religious ethics

(v) Natural Law

(vi) Virtue ethics

(b) Possible connections to explore:

    (i) Are life after death and virtuous life related?

    (ii) Is ethics meaningless if there is no life after death?

6 The concept of free will and determinism in relation to the nature of an omniscient God

(a) Philosophy and ethics topics

    (i) Free will and determinism

    (ii) God the Creator

    (iii) Life after death

(b) Possible connections to explore:

    (i) Is God's foreknowledge a problem for belief in free will?

    (ii) Is belief in God's omniscience and free will incoherent?

16 Connections in Religious Studies

THE ISSUES

1   What is different about the connections paper?
2   How do I prepare for the connections paper?

WHAT YOU WILL LEARN ABOUT IN THIS CHAPTER

In this chapter you will be introduced to the themes of the connections paper and study some ways in which to prepare for it.

STARTER

Examine the following arguments. How could each argument be defended? What evidence could be presented to support the argument? What are the weaknesses of each argument? What counter-arguments could you present?

Argument 1	Argument 2
1 God is omniscient 2 God knows what will happen tomorrow 3 If God knows, God is not mistaken because God is perfect 4 Therefore, human beings cannot choose what they do tomorrow.	1 God gave Moses the Ten Commandments 2 The Ten Commandments come from God 3 Anyone who disobeys the Ten Commandments is disobeying God and will not go to heaven.

THE OCR CHECKLIST

You will explore connections and aspects of human experience related to the following issues:

1   The relationship between free will and the problem of evil.
2   Conscience or sense of moral responsibility as possible evidence for the existence of God.
3   The concept of free will and determinism in relation to the nature of an omniscient God; issues of the extent to which God knows the future, and the implications for human responsibility of God knowing the future.
4   The implications for ethics of the theories of psychology and sociology.
5   The relationship between ethical language and religious language.
6   The relationship between moral behaviour and life after death.

From OCR A Level Religious Studies Specification 7877.

INTRODUCTION

The connections examination paper is different from all the other parts of your course because the paper is 'synoptic'. By 'synoptic' OCR mean that the questions on this examination paper require you to be aware of the links between different topics you have studied.

The good news is that you do not have to learn new information for the connections in religious studies paper. What you must be able to do is understand the relationship between the different topics you have studied. For example, the first argument in the starter activity drew your attention to possible links between three philosophy topics you have studied: the problem of evil, God the Creator and the goodness of God, as well as the ethics topic: free will and determinism.

It is important that you understand all the topics you have studied. If you do not, you will find it very hard to understand and evaluate the links between the topics you have studied. So, if you are unsure about a topic you have studied, make sure you discuss your difficulties with another student or teacher.

The connections paper focuses on the links between philosophy of religion and religious ethics and, as indicated above, there are six themes to explore.

THE STRUCTURE OF THIS CHAPTER

In this chapter there is a short introduction to some of the issues raised by each theme and some recommended reading. The recommended reading is important, as the articles and texts indicated explore one or more ways of understanding the relationship between philosophy and ethics for the topics you are studying. It is a very good idea to discuss the ideas raised by the recommended reading with other students; to help you with this, some discussion questions are suggested below each recommended article.

This chapter assumes that you have a good understanding of the topics you have studied, and the suggested reading is based on this assumption. If there is a topic you have not understood properly, discuss it with other students and/or your teacher.

RECOMMENDED READING

For each theme examined in this chapter some additional reading is recommended. You do not have to read all, some or any of these items. The recommended reading contains suggestions to help you explore the issues. There are many other books that you could explore or that your teacher may recommend. These will be equally valuable. What is most important is that you understand the topics you have already studied during your religious studies course.

It is important to note that the recommended reading suggested in this chapter supplements the reading suggested in the further reading sections at the end of each chapter. It is a good idea to look at some of these suggested items before studying the recommended reading in this chapter.

PREPARING FOR THE CONNECTIONS PAPER

The connections paper tests your skills of selection, comparison and evaluation, drawing on the knowledge you have gained throughout the course. Do not expect to spend the same amount of class time on this paper as on other A2 papers, because the content you will need to use comes from the other AS and A2 modules you have studied. Therefore, your teacher will quite likely spend more time presenting these modules before you devote time to practising the skills required to complete the connections paper.

If you have enjoyed your religious studies course and worked hard at it, you will find that the connections paper gives you an opportunity to explore topics and issues in a broader, deeper and more mature fashion. Many students enjoy preparing for this paper, as it gives them the opportunity to explore the links between issues.

THE RELATIONSHIP BETWEEN FREE WILL AND THE PROBLEM OF EVIL

KEY ISSUE

Is free will a price worth paying for the existence of evil?

Thought Point

How do you solve this old dilemma?

1   God is the omniscient, omnipotent, omnibenevolent and just creator.
2   The universe is God's creation.
3   Evil exists in the universe.

This theme explores some of the fundamental difficulties in believing that God is omnipotent, omniscient and omnibenevolent, even though evil exists. Traditionally, God is defined in the Judaeo-Christian tradition as omnipotent, omniscient and omnibenevolent. If God has these qualities, the fundamental problem is why can God not prevent evil?

The challenge for believers is to explain how the belief in the omnipotent, omniscient, omnibenevolent God can be maintained in the light of the existence of evil.

The challenge that is presented by the problem of evil is twofold. One aspect of the challenge is the problem of evil acts committed by human beings, such as murder, rape, genocide and theft. Traditionally, these actions are blamed on human beings exercising their free will, as illustrated in the work of Augustine, Irenaeus or more modern writers such as Hick and Swinburne. However, the work of people such as Skinner, Watson and Darrow challenges the idea that human beings can be free in a libertarian sense. More modern work on genetics points to the complex interrelationship between genetics and the environment which affects the way humans behave.

The other aspect of the problem is the nature of the world: many people's experience of the world is that it is a harsh and inhospitable place in which to live. For example, every year many people die of famine or malnutrition. An additional issue is: what counts as an evil? If evil is defined as privation (following Augustine and Aquinas), the fundamental problem is that of human behaviour. However, if evil is an experienced reality, then should it only be human beings who are considered in respect of the problem of evil? Dawkins and Mill have both pointed to the large amount of suffering in the natural world. If this suffering is included in the problem, the amount of evil experienced in the world is far greater.

Christian responses regarding free will and the problem of evil come in three forms:

1   The definition of God is clarified or modified.
2   Evil is not God's will.
3   Evil is necessary.

Many philosophers since the time of Epicurus have pointed to the apparent problem of or contradiction between belief in an omnipotent, omniscient and omnibenevolent God and the existence of evil. One way in which these problems have been resolved is to clarify or rethink what exactly the 'omni' terms mean. Some thinkers, following the ideas of Avoroes, have suggested that God omnipotently creates free human beings, so God cannot then override their evil choices. However, this concept of omnipotent creation of free human beings has been criticised as suggesting a limitation in God, which contradicts belief in God's perfection. Mackie has suggested that free will and God being omnipotent ends in a paradox.

For many Christians evil is not God's will. This approach may be seen in the work of Augustine, Aquinas and Swinburne. The free will defence suggests that evil is a privation, a lack of goodness in something. God's call is for all to choose to be good. Great value is placed on the importance of free will and choosing to be good as opposed to being made good.

There are a number of problems related to free will defences. First, is free will really a price worth paying for the existence of evil? For some people, free will is clearly not a price worth paying. This is the famous challenge presented in Dostoevsky's *Brothers Karamazov*. Second, the concept of free will can be debated. If the claims of determinists are true, the free will defence is undermined, as free will is a fiction – it is an idea about how we see ourselves, but it is not reality. If this is so, the question remains: if God made the world and God determines how it is, why is it like this? The answer of course may be impossible, which is Job's ultimate response to the problem of evil.

Hick has suggested that creation is about soul-making, and the result of actions having consequences is that we can learn from them. The problem is whether the whole range of evils that exist is necessary for us to learn and to grow into relationship with God. Equally, if you start to decide that some evils are unnecessary, where do you draw the line?

For other thinkers, the existence of evil provides an opportunity for human beings to develop higher order goods or qualities such as charity and mercy. This line of thought is represented in the work of Swinburne. However, other people question what this says about the nature of God: great evil is permitted so that people may learn from their mistakes.

Many Christians over the centuries have pointed to belief in God's judgement at the end of time. This judgement will separate the just from the unjust. The belief centres on the fact that good and evil are a reality, and people are judged according to which reality their life embodies. In this sense, evil is not the will of God, but people will be held to account for how they use their freedom.

Finally, a question to consider is whether evil is a reality or not. Sociology of religion in particular points to the interrelationship of religious beliefs and society, suggesting that the two are intertwined, growing and influencing each other. It is certainly the case that some things which were considered evil in the past are not viewed in the same light today. For example, consider attitudes to marriage, divorce and sexuality. If the problem of evil is a problem of society's creation, it can be resolved as society's views and ideas develop.

It is important to realise that the problem of evil is only a problem that requires solving if you are a religious believer. There is no doubt that evil is experienced by theists and atheists. Both groups have to learn to cope with their experiences and learn from them. However, for a religious believer an additional challenge is to justify continued belief in God in the light of evil experiences. Ultimately, whether a solution to the problem of evil is convincing or not is actually a choice of interpretation, i.e. a faith choice, just like believing in the first place.

RECOMMENDED READING

Richard Swinburne (*Providence and the Problem of Evil*)

(The Introduction, pp. ix–xiii and Chapter 9)

In chapter 9 Swinburne presents his argument that natural evil plays an important role in God's creation. It is worth reading this argument because it is often summarised in textbooks and, inevitably, summaries sometimes lack the nuances and detail of the author's own words.

continued

It is also worth remembering that Swinburne himself suggests that his writings are an academic response to the problem of evil; they are not necessarily what should be offered to people who are suffering evil. This point is made at the end of the introduction.

Discussion questions

1   Why might Swinburne's argument distress people and religious believers?
2   Why is the fact that God permits natural disasters important in Swinburne's argument? Do you agree with him?
3   Should animal suffering be considered when people discuss the problem of evil?

J.L. Mackie (*The Miracle of Theism*)

Mackie argues that talk of God's omnipotence and free will ends in a paradox – a philosophical dilemma that cannot be solved. Do you agree with him?

1   Summarise Mackie's argument.
2   Is omnipotence a paradox?

Matt Ridley (*The Origins of Virtue*)

(Prologue and Chapter 13)

Matt Ridley's book explores the way in which insights from modern biology can help to inform debates about the origins of values and ethical systems. The Prologue reviews what we know about human nature from scientific research. In particular, it emphasises the characteristics of human beings to cooperate, to be social animals and the evolution of society.

The final chapter of the book explains Ridley's conclusion that human minds have been evolved to be '*social, trustworthy and cooperative*' and that '*our minds have been built by selfish genes*'. It reviews the various ways in which explanations of the origins of values have been mistaken over the centuries.

The book explores whether our character and behaviour are genetically determined. If this is the case, can a free will defence resolve the problem of evil?

The origins of human nature

If these extracts from Matt Ridley's book interest you, it is well worth exploring his thinking in greater detail. You could read the whole of *The Origins of Virtue*, but if you are thinking of doing this it is well worth reading its predecessor volume first: *The Red Queen: Sex and the Evolution of Human Nature*.

Discussion questions

1   Are human beings, by nature, selfish or society-minded individuals?
2   Do human beings have 'instincts'? If so, give some examples and think about where they come from?
3   Is saying people are 'nasty' a problem or 'a statement of fact'?
4   What, according to Matt Ridley, is the cause of the loss of community values in modern societies? Can you think of examples to illustrate his point? Do you agree with him?

CONSCIENCE OR A SENSE OF MORAL RESPONSIBILITY AS POSSIBLE EVIDENCE FOR THE EXISTENCE OF GOD

KEY ISSUE

Is a person's moral sense or conscience evidence for the existence of God?

Thought Point

Making decisions

1   Make a list of the most important influences or events that have shaped your value system.
2   Think of an important decision that you have made, such as a choice of university, job or relationship. Try to think of the process you went through to make the decision. Did you consult other people? How did you reach your final decision?

The fundamental issue to explore is whether conscience provides evidence for the existence of God. There are two aspects to this issue: first, what is the source of people's conscience or moral sense, and, second, is conscience evidence for God's existence? In order to explore these questions you will need to draw on your work on Butler, Newman and Aquinas, as well as your studies of sociology and psychology of religion.

Thought Point

What do you mean by conscience?

In order to answer questions on this paper successfully, you must make sure you clearly define what is meant by conscience. In addition, if you refer to different philosophers, make sure that you clearly identify their definition of conscience.

The starting point for exploring this theme is the importance of conscience in human moral decision-making. People emphasise the importance of acting in good conscience, and sometimes of following one's conscience even if it conflicts with society's values. For example, in wartime soldiers sometimes refuse to fight because they believe the war to be immoral. Conscience becomes important in cases such as this. Sociology of religion suggests that the formation of moral sense relates to one's culture and society; this may be explored in contrast to religious beliefs that moral sense comes from God and suggests the existence of God.

The claim that moral sense leads to the existence of God may be examined by considering whether morality is possible without God. There are many ways to investigate this; for example, by considering whether relativism can actually provide value systems, or whether the basis of conscience is to be found in society or by psychology. If this is the case, conscience is clearly not a satisfactory argument for belief in God.

Thought Point

Test yourself

Explain simply (in one paragraph or less) what the following thinkers meant by:

1   *Synderesis* and *conscientia* (Aquinas)
2   Super-ego (Freud)
3   Our natural guide (Butler)
4   The law, engraved on their hearts (Paul)
5   Conscience (Newman).

Conscience and the sense of moral responsibility as evidence for the existence of God provide you with an opportunity to review the various different moral arguments for God's existence. Kant's moral argument suggests that God's existence is a postulate of reason. The strengths and weaknesses of this argument are one aspect of this theme that needs to be explored.

However, you can also explore other arguments for God's existence. Particularly relevant is John Henry Newman's work on conscience, which suggests that through reason people can understand the universe and be led beyond the universe to God. Newman himself suggested that the moral feelings we have in our conscience suggest a cause: God.

> These feelings are such as require for their existing cause an intelligent being. (J.H. Newman, *An Essay in Aid of a Grammar of Assent*)

Conscience for Newman was an ability to make decisions about right and wrong and also an emotional awareness of what is right and wrong. Newman's claim that feelings arise in relation to a person, and moral feelings lead one to suggest the existence of God as a cause of the feelings, could be explored.

An alternative approach is to consider Butler's claim that conscience is the absolute authority and guide in life that reveals God's will. An interesting comparison may be made between Butler's ideas about conscience and Freud's suggestion that conscience is a particular activity of the super-ego that originates from the upbringing a child received from his or her parents.

Psychologists of religion have suggested that the origins of conscience are to be found in human psychology, perhaps relating to the experiences of childhood, upbringing or society. The work of Freud on religion is particularly relevant as a reason to suggest that there is no link between moral sense and God's existence. Freud's thinking concerning the neurotic nature of religious belief and its origin both in the primal horde and childhood experiences may be explored. Equally the weaknesses of Freud's ideas may also be considered.

An alternative approach is to consider the work of Jung and his suggested God archetype. You could consider whether conscience does lead a person to the God archetype, but if it does, is this actually the God of the religious believer's faith?

In order to gain high marks you will need to explore both the strengths and the weaknesses of philosophers' and psychologists' thinking about conscience and a moral sense. In particular, Freud and Jung's work should not be seen as a definitive response to the religious believer's claims, as their work is widely disputed by philosophers and psychologists.

Finding ancient texts to read

Most ancient texts are available in libraries and a large number of different editions of this text can be obtained from bookshops or on the internet from companies such as www.amazon.com. If you are looking for a text to read, it is a good idea to get a modern translation; editions written for the general public or students are often more accessible for people who are new to reading classical writings.

Reading classical texts

In order to make the most of classical texts by people like Plato it is a good idea to do the following:

1   Read the text at home. Highlight or note down what you think are the main points.
2   Read the text aloud. If it is a dialogue, read it with other people.
3   Discuss what you think are the main points the text makes. Do not be afraid to suggest ideas other people have not said or disagree with. The meaning of classical texts can be hard to work out.

RECOMMENDED READING

John Henry Newman (*An Essay in Aid of a Grammar of Assent* – Part 1, Chapter 5, Section 1)

(The whole of the *Grammar of Assent* text is available at www. newmanreader. org/works/grammar/index.html)

In this extract, Newman presents his explanation of the link between moral feeling and conscience, and he also explores the two senses in which he uses the word 'conscience': as a sense of duty and as something which judges one's actions. Second, Newman points out that conscience reaches beyond itself to God.

Discussion questions

1   How would you summarise Newman's ideas in:
    (a) a paragraph?
    (b) a sentence?
2   Newman suggests that the world reflects truths about God. What do you think he was thinking of? Do you agree with him?
3   Do you think that human beings' sense of moral responsibility always looks to some higher source of authority?

The Euthyphro dilemma (Plato, *The Last Days of Socrates*)

Plato's classic writing about whether morality depends on the gods is well worth reading. It considers whether goodness is dependent on the gods' commands or whether goodness is something independent of the gods. Two important things to remember are that Plato has in mind the concept of gods as presented in Greek mythology (not the Monotheistic God of Judaeo Christian tradition). Second, the debate takes place between two people: Socrates and Euthyphro, both of whom are on their way to court, charged with disrespecting the gods. At the end of his trial Socrates is condemned to death.

If you want a short piece of background information about the text, have a look at the Introduction to the book.

Discussion questions

1   What different definitions of goodness are presented?
2   Does Socrates believe that there is a link between goodness and the gods? Do you agree with his reasoning?

Sigmund Freud (*The Future of an Illusion*)

(Chapters 6 and 7. A useful set of extracts from these chapters may be found online at www.pbs.org/wgbh/question ofgod/ownwords/future2.html)

This extract from Freud's work suggests that religious belief is an illusion that relates to the Oedipus Complex. It also discusses the neurotic nature of religious belief. Freud's argument suggests an alternative explanation of the source of values in society. If correct, Freud's argument would suggest that there is no link between a sense of moral responsibility and belief in God.

Discussion questions

1   Is religion an obsessional neurosis? What evidence can you present to support your view?
2   Is murder wrong? If it is, why is it wrong?

THE IMPLICATIONS FOR ETHICS FROM THE THEORIES OF PSYCHOLOGY AND SOCIOLOGY

KEY ISSUE

Does our understanding of ethics have to change as a result of the discoveries of sociologists and psychiatrists?

Thought Point

1   How does each of the following influence your moral decision-making process? Is their influence conscious or subconscious? Is their influence strong or weak?

(a) Parents
(b) Friends
(c) Television, magazines, internet and the media

continued

(d) Religious organisations
(e) Genes
(f) Upbringing
(g) Education
(h) Culture

2 Discuss your thoughts.

Ethics is concerned both with analysing why people behave as they do and putting forward theories to guide people in how they behave. This particular theme invites you to consider how the insights of psychology and sociology may affect people's understanding of ethics.

For example, Kant's theory of ethics places great emphasis on human beings as rational, autonomous, moral decision-makers. The basis of moral decision-making in Kant's thought focuses on human beings making a rational choice. However, the insights of psychology and sociology suggest factors which affect or motivate moral behaviour that are rather different from Kant's emphasis on reason.

The findings of sociologists suggest that society has an important and perhaps determinative role in forming people's moral value systems. This claim challenges the Kantian view that morality is based on reason, but also the notion in ethics that there are absolute values. One area to explore is whether sociology actually suggests that a relativist approach to ethics is perhaps the correct one. Alternatively, it is possible to argue that ethical values are something that cross societies and are thus not explained by sociology. For example, murder, rape and theft are wrong in different societies and cultures all around the world. This leaves open the question of whether there is an underlying absolute order of morality, such as Natural Law, that holds independently of society's values, or whether the development of moral theories can be explained by human psychology.

Psychology suggests that scientific enquiry can explain some aspects of how the human mind works and makes decisions, and that it can explain moral behaviour in a different way from ethical theories. In particular, it might point to the important role of upbringing and education in shaping a person's moral reasoning abilities.

Freud's emphasis on the role of parents in shaping children's character, the Oedipus complex and the primal horde theory all suggest a different set of factors which affect moral behaviour than those which ethics traditionally claims. If the claims of Freud are correct, it would suggest that human beings are not autonomous in the manner in which Kant perceived them to be.

The role of conscience in decision-making provides an interesting contrast between the insights of psychology of religion and ethical theory. In particular, if psychologists can demonstrate that a sense of moral authority or conscience comes from a person's subconscious or psyche, this undermines the role of conscience as an authoritative decision-maker that ultimately reaches to God. If the claims of psychologists like Freud are correct, other factors such as the influence of parents on a person's upbringing take on new importance when it comes to evaluating moral responsibility for an action.

However, it is equally important to consider the variety of different views of human psychology and the lack of agreement between them. The extent to which this lack of agreement limits the impact of psychology regarding ethics is an open question.

RECOMMENDED READING

Matt Ridley (*The Origins of Virtue*)

Matt Ridley's book explores theories regarding the origins of feelings about morality. As well as considering some sociological ideas, he presents some insights from biology concerning the origins of value systems.

Discussion questions

1   Is revenge irrational?
2   Does fairness matter?
3   Does virtue matter?

THE RELATIONSHIP BETWEEN ETHICAL LANGUAGE AND RELIGIOUS LANGUAGE

KEY ISSUES

Is the language used in religious and ethical debates:

1   Meaningful?
2   Comparable?

Thought Point

1   How would you explain what these words mean to an alien who has never
    heard them before?

    (a) Good
    (b) Evil
    (c) God
    (d) Incarnation

2   What physical evidence, examples and arguments could you give to help
    explain the meaning of these words?
3   Compare your answer with that of another person.

This theme provides you with an opportunity to explore philosophers' ideas
about the use of language. Particularly important are your studies of religious
language and meta-ethics. At the heart of the issue is the question of whether
religious and ethical language is meaningful.

There are many ways in which language is used in both religious and
ethical thinking. Broadly speaking you need to be able to explain, compare
and contrast the use of symbols, myth and analogy to communicate truth in
religious belief, with contrasting theories of ethical language, such as naturalism, intuitionism, emotivism and prescriptivism.

One starting point for exploring this theme is the fact that people do use
both ethical and religious language. They make statements such as 'God is
good' and 'murder is wrong'. These make sense, but what this theme concerns
is what exactly is meant by 'murder is wrong' or 'God is good' and if there is
any way to demonstrate the truth of these statements.

When religious believers make statements about God they are suggesting something which is meant in a factual, analogical or symbolic sense.
For example, if God is described as a warrior, what does this mean? Clearly
it could be literal, but it is perhaps more likely meant symbolically or
analogically. Whatever particular position is adopted, the language is com-
municating something about God. However, in the thinking of verification
or falsification theory, describing God as a warrior is not meaningful, because
it is not a statement that can be justified or falsified by sense observation. No
sense can be made of the qualities of God in the theories of Ayer or Flew.

However, is ethical language any different from religious language in this
respect? For some thinkers, sense can clearly be made of ethical language.
In Kant's work an action is wrong if it is not according to reason and in

Know the terminology

It is impossible to answer
questions on this theme
successfully unless you
know the terminology used
in debates about both
meta-ethics and religious
language. Revise these
topics before starting work
on this theme.

accordance with good will. So ethical language could be argued to have some sort of rational basis that perhaps distinguishes it from religious language about God.

An interesting contrast to draw here involves **G.E. Moore**'s moral intuitionism. According to Moore, when you say something like 'Martin Luther King was a good person' the word 'good' is not verifiable, but it is still meaningful because it is clear that Martin Luther King had the property of being 'good'. Moore's reference to these properties as 'non-natural' suggests that they are not observable and testable (putting ethical language on the same level as religious language) but also that these non-natural properties are 'simple notions' that you can recognise a person has. If Moore is right, moral language is meaningful in a different way from symbolic religious language.

Also significant is the application of A.J. Ayer's aforementioned verification theory. If you consider the strong and weak senses of verification, can a case be put together to suggest a weak form of verification for religious and/or moral language? This issue provides a good opportunity to explore not only the application of verification (and falsification) to moral and religious language but also the limitations of the theories of Ayer and Flew.

RECOMMENDED READING

A.J. Ayer (*Language, Truth and Logic*)

Language, Truth and Logic is Ayer's famous presentation of the theory of verificationism. In this book Ayer argues that language that cannot be verified is meaningless. When this theory is applied to ethical and religious language, both are found to be meaningless. Ayer suggests later that ethical language is an expression of feeling; it is not something which communicates an absolute truth.

Discussion questions

1   According to Ayer, what conditions need to be met if a statement is to be verified?
2   What is meant by emotivism according to Ayer?
3   Ayer suggests that '*ethics, as a branch of knowledge, is nothing more than a department of psychology and sociology*' (Ayer, *Language, Truth and Logic*). What reasons are there to agree with Ayer? Is his argument convincing?

continued

Peter Vardy (*What Is Truth?*)

Peter Vardy argues that the debate about what is truth is important and that it matters. He also suggests that denying there is any moral truth or claiming to have it can both be problematic. This leads Vardy to consider if and why the search for truth matters for society and people.

Discussion questions

1   Is there any such thing as truth when it comes to religious and ethical language? If there is, what does truth mean?
2   Why does the truth matter?

THE RELATIONSHIP BETWEEN MORAL BEHAVIOUR AND LIFE AFTER DEATH

KEY ISSUE

Is there any relationship between moral behaviour and life after death? If there is, what is the nature of the relationship?

Thought Point

Good deeds and life after death

Look up the following passages in the Bible. What do you think they communicate to Christians about the relationship between actions in life and life after death?

1   Mark 13:33–37
2   Luke 12:35–48
3   Matthew 25:14–30
4   Matthew 25:31–46

Within many religious traditions a clear link is made between your actions in life and God judging you after death. In Christianity, the traditional belief has been that good people go to heaven and bad people go to hell. This is clearly seen in Jesus' teaching in stories such as the Last Judgement or the parables of the Vineyard or the Talents, as well as in the ethical teaching of the New Testament.

Ethical theories, such as Virtue ethics, Utilitarianism and Kant, all rely on the assumption that human beings are capable of choosing how they behave and that they are morally responsible for their choices. In religious belief, these moral choices are significant because they also shape your relationship with God in both physical life and life after death, be that in heaven (e.g. Christianity and Islam) or in your next incarnation on Earth (Hinduism).

Two important issues arise from this:

1   What is meant by life after death?
2   What is the motivation for moral behaviour?

The nature of life after death could be interpreted as a motivating factor for behaviour. You could consider the historical descriptions of hell in the Christian tradition and whether these images could be used to motivate behaviour. Equally, the idea of something attractive, such as heaven, motivating behaviour could be considered. In both cases, what exactly is meant by heaven and hell can be investigated as an aspect of whether beliefs about life after death do motivate behaviour.

The motivation for moral behaviour can be explored through work you have carried out on life after death or on ethical theory. The link between life after death and moral behaviour in life may be explained and contrasted with the moral motivation for action such as in Kant's theory or Utilitarianism. In particular, you can consider whether the immediate motive for behaviour in religious belief or ethical theories is life after death.

An alternative approach is to deny that there is life after death and thus assert there is no relationship between moral behaviour and life after death. An atheistic approach to ethical decision-making could be used to illustrate why there is not necessarily any link between moral behaviour and life after death. You can explore reasons why people behave morally, and the fact that it is not necessarily because people seek a life after death. Many people favour utilitarian approaches to decision-making and aim to promote the greatest good, and try to act morally according to this theory, even though this approach does not involve a belief in life after death.

Denying a relationship between life after death and moral actions can also lead you into debating whether values are subjective. As people act morally for reasons other than seeking life after death, does this therefore suggest that moral values are subjective? J.L. Mackie (*Ethics: Inventing Right*

Life after death and different religions

Remember that it does not matter which world religion you refer to when discussing life after death. However, it is important that you make clear to the examiner which particular religious beliefs you are referring to, and in some cases you may have to be quite specific. For example, within Christianity hell could be a place of physical suffering, an experience of other people or something else.

and Wrong) has suggested that moral values are subjective, but this is not the same as saying people do not act morally just because their value system is perceived to be subjective.

RECOMMENDED READING

The Cathechism of the Catholic Church

(Paragraphs 1021–41)

The Catholic Catechism is the official book of teachings of the Roman Catholic Church. This section of the Catholic Catechism is an example of traditional Christian beliefs concerning heaven and hell, and the link between behaviour in one's physical life and later judgment by God.

Discussion questions

1   How are heaven, purgatory, hell and the Last Judgment defined? Do you agree with these definitions? (1021–35, 1038–41)
2   Does the justice of God demand that people are judged and punished according to how they behaved in physical life?

Richard Swinburne (Providence and the Problem of Evil)

Swinburne explores what is meant by life after death in Christian belief, and he argues that it is good that God deters people from sinning; part of that deterrence is the reality of punishment by God for one's wrong actions in life.

Discussion questions

1   How would you define what is meant by life after death?
2   Do you think it is necessary for there to be a possibility of sin?
3   Are heaven and hell motivating factors that drive moral behaviour?

J.L. Mackie (Ethics: Inventing Right and Wrong)

Mackie presents a philosophical account of ethics. He discusses whether moral values are subjective, and examines what is meant by moral scepticism. This is an interesting example of ethics being discussed where the motivation for ethical behaviour is not found necessarily to be religious belief.

The *Catechism*'s index

If you use the index in the *Catechism* remember that the numbers next to an entry refer to the paragraph number, not the page number.

Discussion questions

1   What does Mackie mean by moral scepticism? Do you agree with his views?
2   Do you think that there are no objective moral values?

THE CONCEPT OF FREE WILL AND DETERMINISM IN RELATION TO THE NATURE OF AN OMNISCIENT GOD

KEY ISSUE

If God is omniscient, is free will real or an illusion?

Thought Point

God's foreknowledge

1   Complete the conclusion to the argument below.
2   Is the argument valid?

The argument

Belief 1: God is omniscient
Definition: Omniscience concerns knowledge of all that it is logically possible to know
Belief 2: God is perfect and therefore cannot be mistaken
Belief 3: God made human beings and gave them free will
Conclusion: God has/does not have foreknowledge of human actions. If God has foreknowledge of human actions there is/is not free will.

Know your terminology

Can you explain the meaning of the following words without looking at your books and notes?

1   Foreknowledge
2   Omniscience
3   Omnipotence
4   Libertarian
5   Hard determinist
6   Soft determinist

In philosophy of religion, the problem of God's foreknowledge is a challenging topic. The heart of the problem lies in the religious believer's emphasis on free will. The argument runs that people are responsible for their actions and omissions if they have free will. If hard determinism is true, human beings can be held causally responsible for their actions but not morally responsible for their actions. The problem is that if free will is defended in a libertarian sense, how can religious believers, such as Christians, make sense of claims that God knows the future? Certainly, in the Bible, God states what will happen and it happens. According to the traditional Christian understanding of God, God cannot be mistaken, as this would imply that God is lacking in some way (i.e. not perfect).

One approach to solving this problem is to explore the ideas of **Boethius** and **Aquinas**. The solution offered by Boethius and Aquinas suggests an understanding of human freedom that some people might describe as soft determinism. However, you could explore the problem using the suggestion from this tradition that events are simultaneously present to God. Anthony Kenny (*The God of the Philosophers*) in particular has criticised the logic of this type of argument.

An alternative approach to the problem of God's foreknowledge is to argue that the future does not exist to be known. However, this entails changing the definition of God to one where God is mutable (changeable) and in time, as it suggests that God acquires new knowledge as future events happen. Swinburne (*Coherence of Theism*) has written about this issue. The difficulty for Christian believers is that the traditional understanding of God sees God as transcendent, perfect and unchanging (immutable).

In ethical theory the problem of God having foreknowledge of our actions is twofold. First, if God's knowledge cannot be mistaken as God is perfect, does God actually know what we will do before we do it, and if God does, do we have a real choice or is the choice illusory? One way to examine this problem is to consider Aquinas' analogy concerning walking along a road. Second, many Christian theodicies rely on the free will defence to explain natural and moral evil. If, however, God has foreknowledge because he is omniscient, and power because he is omnipotent, the problem concerning God not preventing evil arises once more.

The importance of free will in the debate about God's omniscience concerns the extent of moral responsibility for one's actions. If God sustains everything (God is the creator), knows what will happen (God is omniscient) and has the power to effortlessly manage what happens (omnipotence), is God responsible for what happens? In which case, are human beings responsible for their actions? Moral philosophy clearly relies on the idea of human beings being in some way morally responsible for their actions. This leads into the debate concerning whether God can limit his omniscience or omnipotently create beings beyond his control – the idea of human beings being beyond God's control does not fit in very well with traditional belief in God the omnipotent creator. If God is in control, is God responsible for evil happening?

Finally, the question of God's omniscience and free will is significant in relation to religious beliefs about life after death. In many religious traditions,

God judges people after death, based on their actions in life. The justice of God involves God punishing people if they deserve it. The belief in God's judgement of people therefore relies on the belief that human beings have free will and are morally responsible for their actions. If human beings are not free, this suggests that God's omniscience entails predestination. Both of these views may be explored; for example, within the Christian tradition the Protestant doctrine of election has led some people to believe in predestination, although most Christians believe that particular judgement follows death, based, for example, on Jesus' teaching (cf. Matthew 25:31–46).

Ultimately, the definition of omniscience that you adopt defines whether determinism or free will is accepted. Conversely, your understanding of the nature of God may be affected by your attitude to the free will and determinism debate. This theme provides you with an opportunity to explore these issues.

RECOMMENDED READING

Quentin Smith and L. Nathan Oaklander
(*Time, Change and Freedom*)

(L. Nathan Oaklander, *Dialogue 10*: 130–40)

Smith and Oaklander's book is an introduction to philosophical problems concerning belief in God and questions about free will and determinism. It is written as a series of dialogues between four people. Alice and Phil are philosophy degree students, while Sophia and Ivan are philosophy professors. Each one of the characters defends a particular philosophical view. In this chapter the topic is whether free will is possible if God exists.

Since it is written as a dialogue, it is a good idea to read the text in a group. In addition, if any of the terminology in the chapter is unclear, have a look at the glossary at the end of the chapter.

Discussion questions

1   What can be meant by the foreknowledge problem? Is there any way to solve it?
2   Are you convinced by Boethius' argument? Explain your thoughts.

continued

The Cathechism *of the Catholic Church* (1994)

(Paragraphs 1036–7)

Paragraphs 1036–7 of the Catholic *Catechism* explain the Catholic Church's position regarding predestination and free will. It is a good example of one religious tradition's approach to the problem of God's omniscience and human freedom, and the implications of this belief for human freedom.

Discussion questions

Why is predestination rejected?

Michael Clark (*Paradoxes from A to Z*)

('The Paradox of Foreknowledge' (pp. 54–6) and 'The Paradox of Omniscience' (pp. 130–1)

Michael Clark sets out two classical problems concerning how you can make free choices if God knows the future omnisciently. Discuss the paradoxes.

Discussion question

Do you think these two paradoxes undermine religious believers' claim that God is omniscient and that people have free will?

REVIEW QUESTIONS

Try to talk for two minutes about the relationship between each of the following topics of study. Highlight similarities and differences, and explain them.

1   Freud and Aquinas on conscience.
2   Butler and Jung on conscience.
3   Ayer and Ramsey on religious language.
4   Aquinas and Flew on moral language.
5   Kant and religious beliefs explaining motivation for moral behaviour.
6   Boethius and Swinburne on God's foreknowledge.

Examination Questions Practice

EXAM MISTAKES TO AVOID

This examination paper requires you to select relevant information to answer a question, compare it with other information and then assess and evaluate the information you have selected. Make sure that you avoid just describing what philosophers have said, because if you do not focus on the question and present an argument that responds to it, you will only score a maximum of level four on the mark scheme.

Remember that you need to explore and assess the various connections between topics you have studied. Make sure you understand the topics you have studied before entering the examination.

PAST PAPER QUESTION

'Belief in reward after death encourages people to perform the right actions for the wrong motives.' Discuss. (OCR A2 Level 2791 June 2004 question 3, 60 marks)

To complete this question you need to demonstrate a good understanding of a religious tradition's belief in an afterlife and then consider whether a wish to enter the afterlife is a good or bad motive for someone's actions. You will need to refer to religious beliefs, but you can choose which religion to talk about.

1 Discuss whether life after death is a reward.

(a) You could refer to Christian belief in the beatific vision of God and life after death and its link to actions in life. You could discuss Paul's notion of seeing God face to face and the idea of the afterlife as a reward which fits in with Jesus' story of the Last Judgement. The link between obedience to God's commands and eternal life is important. The link between conduct and reward can be explored.

(b) Alternatively the idea of divine election could be discussed, particularly the fact that election is not a reward for good actions. In which case, is divine election actually a motive for behaviour?

(c) Another approach would be to consider a different religious tradition such as Hinduism, and to explore the link between Karma and eventual Nirvana.

2 Assess whether seeking the reward of life after death is a right or wrong motive for action.

(a) Kant's ethical theory could be used to suggest that seeking reward is an inappropriate motive for moral action. Instead, good moral action is that carried out from a sense of duty. However, one reply from Christianity could be to suggest that it is the Christian's duty to follow God's commands. Life after death is a gift from God, but not a right or reward for doing one's duty. Christian teaching about repentance, forgiveness and salvation could be referred to here.

(b) Utilitarianism or other ethical theories could be used to suggest that part of the motive for an action is always its consequence. Thus what then becomes an issue is which theory of ethics you choose. Utilitarians would of course suggest that maximising happiness is the most important motive for action.

(c) Virtue ethics could be discussed to illustrate the fact that what matters is whether the conduct helps a person to develop moral virtues. If belief in life after death helps to promote the growth of virtue, it could not be described as 'wrong'.

FURTHER READING

If you would like to study some general readers which explore the themes in the connections paper, you could look at the following introductory texts on philosophy of religion and ethics. All of them contain chapters that discuss some or all of the themes in the connections paper:

1 Brian Davies, *An Introduction to Philosophy of Religion*, Oxford, Oxford University Press, 2003.
2 Michael Palmer, *Moral Problems in Medicine*, Cambridge, Lutterworth Press, 1999.
3 Peter Vardy and Julie Arliss, *The Thinker's Guide to God*, Hants, John Hunt, 2003.
4 Peter Vardy and Julie Arliss, *The Thinker's Guide to Evil*, Hants, John Hunt, 2003.
5 Peter Vardy and Peter Grosch, *The Puzzle of Ethics*, London, Fount, 1999.

Glossary

A posteriori
A statement which is knowable after experience.

A priori
A statement which is knowable without reference to any experience.

Abortion (procured abortion)
The termination of a pregnancy by artificial means.

Absolute
A principle that is universally binding.

Absolutism
An objective moral rule or value that is always true in all situations and for everyone without exception.

Act Utilitarianism
A teleological theory that uses the outcome of an action to determine whether it is good or bad.

Active euthanasia
The intentional premature termination of another person's life.

AI (artificial insemination)
The injection of sperm into a woman.

Analytic statements
Statements which are true by definition.

Anthropocentric
An approach to the environment that places human interests above those of any other species.

Apparent good
Something which seems to be good or the right thing to do but which does not fit the perfect human ideal.

Aretaic ethics
Another name for Virtue ethics, from the Greek word *arete*, which simply means any kind of excellence or virtue.

Assisted dying/suicide
When a person takes their own life with the assistance of another person. When the other person is a doctor, it is called physician-assisted suicide.

Authoritarian conscience
Our sense of moral right and wrong formed in us by authority figures whom we want to obey.

Autonomous moral agent
Someone who can make a moral decision freely; someone who is totally responsible for their actions.

Autonomy
Self-directed freedom, arriving at moral judgement through reason.

Benevolence
Butler saw this as wanting the well-being of others.

Biocentric
An approach to the environment that considers the biological nature and diversity of the Earth to be of supreme importance.

Biodiversity
The variety of living things on Earth.

Blastocyst
A fertilised egg at about four to five days of development.

Cardinal Virtues
Originated in Plato – prudence, justice, temperance, courage. Added to with three theological virtues of faith, hope and charity.

Categorical imperative
A command to perform actions that are absolute moral obligations without reference to other ends.

Celibacy
Not having sexual relations with another person.

Christian Realism
The belief that Christianity may use violence to bring about the Kingdom of God and secure peace on Earth.

Cloning
A form of genetic engineering by which a plant, an animal or a human is created with the same genetic identity as another.

Compatibilism
The belief that it is possible to be both free and determined, as some aspects of our nature are determined, but not our ability to make moral decisions.

Conscience
Our sense of moral right and wrong.

Conscientia
Aquinas called this the actual ethical judgement or decision a person made.

Consciousness
Awareness of self as an independent being, the ability to feel pain and pleasure.

Consequentialism
The rightness or wrongness of an act is determined by its consequences.

Consequentialist
Someone who decides whether an action is good or bad by its consequences.

Conservation ethics
The ethics of the use, allocation, protection and exploitation of the natural world.

Copernican Revolution
Belief that the solar system revolves around the sun.

Cultural relativism
What is right or wrong depends on the culture.

Deep ecology
An approach to environmental ethics that sees all life forms as of value and human life as just one part of the biosphere. It rejects anthropomorphism.

Deontological ethics
Ethical systems which consider that the moral act itself has moral value (e.g. telling the truth is always right, even when it may cause pain or harm).

Descriptive relativism
Different cultures and societies have differing ethical systems and so morality is relative.

Determinism
The view that every event has a cause and so, when applied to moral decisions, we do not have free will.

Divine Command theory
Actions are right or wrong depending on whether they follow God's commands or not.

Divine Law
The Bible – this reflects the Eternal Law.

Doctrine of double effect
An action where the main intention is to do good, but which may have a bad side-effect. The good intention makes the action right.

Dominion
The Judaeo-Christian idea that humans have a special place in the natural world and have responsibility for it.

Duty
A motive for acting in a certain way which shows moral quality.

Ecosophy
A word formed by contracting the phrase 'ecological philosophy'. It refers to philosophies which have an ecocentric or biocentric perspective such as deep ecology.

Embryo
The developing bundle of cells in the womb up to eight weeks' gestation.

Emotivism
A theory which says that moral statements are just expressions of feelings.

Ensoulment
The moment when the soul enters the body – in traditional Christian thought this was at forty days for boys and ninety days for girls. The Church now believes that life begins at conception.

Eternal Law
The principles by which God made and controls the universe which are only fully known by God.

Ethical naturalism/ethical cognitivism
A theory that moral values can be derived from sense experience.

Ethical non-naturalism/ethical non-cognitivism
A theory that ethical statements cannot be derived from sense experience.

Eudaimonia
The final goal of all human activity – happiness, well-being, human flourishing.

Euthyphro Dilemma
The dilemma first identified by Plato – is something good because God commands it or does God command it because it is good?

Feminism
A way of thinking that seeks to emancipate women in society and give them equal opportunities.

Foetus
An organism in the womb from nine weeks until birth.

Gaia hypothesis
A theory of James Lovelock.

Gender
Cultural and psychological characteristics which determine whether a person is male or female.

Genetic engineering
The technology involved in cloning, gene therapy and gene manipulation.

Geocentric
An approach to the environment which considers the geological nature and diversity of the Earth to be most important.

Germ line engineering
Changes in the parent's sperm or egg cells with the aim of passing on the changes to their offspring.

Golden Mean
The balance of extremes of virtues and vices. A balance between *excess* (having too much of something) and *deficiency* (having too little of something).

Good will
Making a moral choice expresses a good will.

Hard determinism
The belief that people do not have any free will and that all moral actions have prior causes. This means that nobody can be held morally responsible.

Harm principle
The belief that an act or consequence is morally permissible if no harm is done.

Hedonic calculus
Bentham's method for measuring the good and bad effects of an action.

Hedonism
The view that pleasure is the chief 'good'.

Hippocratic Oath
Written in the fifth century BCE, it became the basis for doctors' ethics. Other promises now replace it, but it is specifically against abortion.

Holistic
An approach to the environment that considers a range of factors, including the importance of balance within the ecosystem.

Human genome
A map of the human genes.

Hypothetical imperative
An action that achieves some goal or end.

Incompatibilism
The belief that determinism is logically incompatible with free will. Thus some incompatibilists will say that determinism is a fact and so we are not free, but most take the opposite view that free will is a fact and so determinism is false.

Instrumental value
Something's value lies in its usefulness for others.

Intellectual virtues
Characteristics of thought and reason – technical skill, scientific knowledge, prudence, intelligence and wisdom.

Intrinsic value
Something's value lies in itself.

Intrinsically good
Something which is good in itself, without reference to the consequences.

Intuitionism
A theory that moral truths are known by intuition.

Involuntary euthanasia
This term is used when someone's life is ended to prevent their suffering, without their consent, even though they are capable of consenting.

IVF (in-vitro fertilisation)
The procedure by which sperm and eggs from a couple are fertilised in a laboratory dish (in vitro = in glass; test-tube babies).

Jus ad bellum
Justice in the decision to wage war.

Jus in bello
Justice in the conduct of war.

Jus post bellum
Justice in the ending of the war.

Just War theory
The belief that war is morally justified if it meets certain criteria.

Kingdom of Ends
A world in which people do not treat others as means but only as ends.

Law
Objective principle, a maxim that can be universalised.

Libertarianism
The belief that determinism is false and people are free to make moral choices and so are responsible for their actions.

Logical positivism
The view that only those things which can be tested are meaningful.

Maxim
A general rule in accordance with which we intend to act.

Meta-ethics
The analysis of ethical language.

Moral absolutism
There is only one correct answer to every moral problem.

Moral objectivism
Truth is objectively real regardless of culture.

Moral relativism
There are no universally valid moral principles and so there is no one true morality.

Moral virtues
Qualities of character such as courage, friendliness, truthfulness.

Natural Moral Law
The theory that an eternal, absolute moral law can be discovered by reason.

Naturalistic fallacy
The claim that good cannot be defined.

Normative ethics
A term used to describe different moral codes of behaviour; rules by which we make moral decisions (e.g. Utilitarianism, Natural Moral Law, Kantian ethics, Virtue ethics).

Ordinary and extraordinary means
According to Natural Law moral duties apply in ordinary situations. A patient may refuse certain treatments on the grounds that they are 'extraordinary' (i.e. over and above the essential).

'Ought implies can'
The idea that someone cannot be blamed for what he could not do, but only for what he was capable of doing but did not do.

Pacifism
The belief that violence is wrong.

Passive euthanasia
Treatment is either withdrawn or not given to the patient in order to hasten death. This could include turning off a life-support machine.

Personhood
Definition of a human being as a person – having consciousness, self-awareness, ability to reason and self-sufficiency.

Phronesis (practical wisdom)
According to Aristotle the virtue most needed for any other virtue to be developed. Balancing self-interest with that of others. Needs to be directed by the moral virtues.

Predestination
The belief that God has decided who will be saved and who will not.

Preference Utilitarianism
Moral actions are right or wrong according to how they fit the preferences of those involved.

Prescriptivism
A theory that ethical statements have an intrinsic sense so other people should agree with the statement and follow it.

Primary precepts
The fundamental principles of Natural Moral Law.

Proportionality
In war, weapons should be proportionate to the aggression.

Purpose
The idea that the rightness or wrongness of an action can be discovered by looking at whether or not the action agrees with human purpose.

PVS (permanent vegetative state)
When a patient is in this condition, doctors may seek to end their life. The relatives have to agree and usually the patient must be brain-stem dead.

Qualitative
Looking at the quality of the pleasure.

Quality of life
The belief that human life is not valuable in itself; it depends on what kind of life it is.

Quantitative
Looking at the quantity of the happiness.

Queer theory
The idea that there can be no fixed rules about what is or is not a legitimate sexual relationship. Being queer is the freedom to define oneself according to one's nature.

Real good
The right thing to do – it fits the human ideal.

Realism
Normal moral rules cannot be applied to how states act in time of war.

Relativism
Nothing may be said to be objectively right or wrong; it depends on the situation, the culture and so on.

Rule Utilitarianism
Establishing a general rule that follows utilitarian principles.

Sanctity of life
The belief that human life is valuable in itself.

Secondary precepts
These are worked out from the primary precepts.

Self-love
Butler thought of this as wanting the well-being of self or enlightened self-interest, not selfishness.

Sentience
The ability to feel pleasure and pain.

Sex
Biological characteristics that determine whether a person is male or female.

Shallow ecology
The Earth is cared for to make conditions better for humans.

Situation ethics
The morally right thing to do is the most loving in the situation.

Slippery slope
This means that when one moral law is broken others will also be gradually broken and there will be no moral absolutes.

Soft determinism
The belief that determinism is true in many aspects, but we are still morally responsible for our actions.

Somatic cell engineering

Changes in somatic (body) cells to cure an otherwise fatal disease. These changes are not passed on to a person's offspring.

Stem cell

A 'master' cell that can become any kind of material.

Stewardship

A way of interpreting the use of dominion, which sees humans as caretakers of the natural world.

Subjectivism

Each person's values are relative to that person and so cannot be judged objectively.

Summum bonum

The supreme good that we pursue through moral acts.

Super-ego

Freud's idea is that the super-ego reinforces ideas of correct behaviour implanted in us when we were young.

Synderesis

Aquinas' idea of what he termed 'right' reason by which a person acquires knowledge of basic moral principles and understands that it is important to do good and avoid evil.

Synthetic statements

Statements that may be true or false and can be tested using experience or senses.

Teleological

Moral actions are right or wrong according to their outcome or *telos* (end).

Teleological ethics

The morally right or wrong thing to do is determined by the consequences.

Theory of justice

Principles underpinning law. Two main theories: right of the individual (Thomas Hobbes), and rights of the community (Marx, Rawls).

Therapeutic cloning

A method of producing stem cells to treat diseases such as Alzheimer's.

Universalisability

If an act is right or wrong for one person in a situation, then it is right or wrong for anyone in that situation.

Utilitarianism
Only pleasure and the absence of pain have utility or intrinsic value.

Utility
The theory of usefulness – the greatest happiness for the greatest number.

Viability
Where a foetus is considered capable of sustaining its own life, given the necessary care.

Vices
The direct opposite of virtues – habitual wrong action.

Virtue
Habitually doing what is right – being good requires the practice of a certain kind of behaviour.

Voluntary euthanasia
The intentional premature termination of another person's life at their request.

Zygote
A 'proto-embryo' of the first two weeks after conception – a small collection of identical cells.

Bibliography

PUBLICATIONS

Ahluwalia, L. *Foundation for the Study of Religion*, London, Hodder & Stoughton Educational, 2001.

Anscombe, E. 'War and Murder', in *Moral Problems*, Palmer, M., Cambridge, Lutterworth Press, 1991.

Aquinas, T. 'Summa Theologiae', in *Basic Writings of Thomas Aquinas*, Pegis, A.C. (ed.), Hackett, IN, Random House, 1997.

Aquinas, T. *Summa Theologiae II–II q.40* (Dominican translation), London, Burns & Oates, 1936.

Aristotle. *Nichomachean Ethics: An Introduction to Aristotle*, McKeon, R. (ed.), Ross, W.D. (trans.), New York, Random House, 1947.

Ayer, A.J. *Language, Truth and Logic*, London, Penguin, [1936] 2001.

Baelz, P. *Ethics and Belief*, New York, Seabury Press, 1977.

Barclay, W. *Ethics in a Permissive Society*, London, Collins, 1971.

Bellioti, R. *Good Sex: Perspectives on Sexual Ethics*, Kansas, University Press of Kansas, 1993.

Benson, J. *Environmental Ethics*, London, Routledge, 2000.

Bentham, J. *Introduction to the Principles of Morals and Legislation*, Harrison W. (ed.), Cambridge, Cambridge University Press, 1948.

Bentham, J. and Mill, J.S. *Utilitarianism and Other Essays*, London, Penguin, 1987.

Blackburn, S. *Being Good: A Short Introduction to Ethics*, Oxford, Oxford Paperbacks, 2002.

Blackburn, S. *Ethics: A Very Short Introduction*, Oxford, Oxford University Press, 2003.

Blackburn, S. *Lust*, Oxford/New York, Oxford University Press, 2004.

Bolt, R. *A Man for All Seasons*, London, Methuen, [1960] 1996.

Bowie, R. *Ethical Studies* (2nd edn), Cheltenham, Nelson Thornes, 2004.

Butler, J. *1726 Fifteen Sermons*, London, Bell, 1964.

Catechism of the Catholic Church, London, Geoffrey Chapman, 1994.

Coates, A. *The Ethics of War*, Manchester, Manchester University Press, 1997.

Cook, D. *The Moral Maze*, London, SPCK, 1983.

Coppieters, B. and Fotion, N. (eds) *Moral Constraints on War*, New York/Oxford, Lexington Books, 2002.

Crisp, R. and Slote, M. *Virtue Ethics*, Oxford/New York, Oxford University Press, 1997.

Davies, B. *Philosophy of Religion: A Guide and Anthology*, Oxford, Oxford University Press, 2000.

Davies, B. *An Introduction to the Philosophy of Religion* (3rd edn), Oxford, Oxford University Press, 2003.

Deane-Drummond, C. (ed.) *Brave New World*, London/New York, T & T Clark, 2003.

Deane-Drummond, C. *Genetics and Christian Ethics*, Cambridge, Cambridge University Press, 2005.

Deidum, T. 'The Bible and Christian Ethics', in *Christian Ethics: An Introduction*, Hoose, B. (ed.), London, Cassell, 1998.

Dominion, J. *Passionate and Compassionate Love: A Vision for Christian Marriage*, London, Darton, Longman & Todd, 1991.

Dregson, A. and Inoue, Y. (eds) *The Deep Ecology Movement: An Introductory Anthology*, Berkeley, CA, North Atlantic Books, 1995.

Fletcher, J. *Situation Ethics*, Philadelphia, PA, Westminster Press, 1963.

Foot, P. *Virtues and Vices*, Oxford, Blackwell, 1978.

Gensler, H. *Ethics: A Contemporary Introduction*, New York/London, Routledge, 1998.

Gensler, H., Earl, W. and Swindal, J. *Ethics: Contemporary Readings*, New York/London, Routledge, 2004.

Gill, R. *A Textbook of Christian Ethics*, London/New York, T & T Clark, 1995.

Glover, J. *Causing Death and Saving Lives*, London, Penguin, 1990.

Glover, J. *Humanity: A Moral History of the Twentieth Century*, New Haven, CT, Yale University Press, 2000.

Graham, G. *Living the Good Life*, New York, Paragon House, 1990.

Graham, G. *Evil and Christian Ethics*, Cambridge, Cambridge University Press, 2001.

Graham, G. *Eight Theories of Ethics*, London, Routledge, 2004.

Grayling, A.C. *What Is Good? The Search for the Best Way to Live*, London, Phoenix Press, 2004.

Grisez, G. and Boyle, J. 'The Morality of Killing: A Traditional View', in *Bioethics: An Anthology*, Kuhse, H. and Singer, P. (eds), Oxford, Blackwell, 1999.

Gula, R. *Reason Informed by Faith*, New Jersey, Paulist Press, 1989.

Hare, R.M. *The Language of Morals*, Oxford, Oxford University Press, 1952.

Hare, R.M. *Freedom and Reason*, London, Clarendon Press, 1963.

Harman, G. and Jarvis-Thompson, J. *Moral Relativism and Moral Objectivity*, Oxford, Blackwell, 1995.

Hinman, L. 'Ethics Updates', available online at http://ethics.acusd.edu/.

Hodge, R. *What Is Conscience for?*, London, Daughters of St Paul, 1995.

Holloway, R. *Godless Morality*, Edinburgh, Canongate, 1999.

Holmes, R. *On War and Morality*, Princeton, Princeton University Press, 1989.

Holy Bible: New Revised Standard Version (anglicized), Cambridge University Press and Oxford University Press, 1996.

Honderich, T. *How Free Are You?*, Oxford, Oxford University Press, 1993.

Hoose, B. (ed.) *Christian Ethics: An Introduction*, London, Cassell, 1998.

Hope, T. *Medical Ethics: A Very Short Introduction*, Oxford, Oxford University Press, 2004.

Hughes, G. 'Natural Law', in *Christian Ethics: An Introduction*, Hoose, B. (ed.), London, Cassell, 1998.

Hume, D. *Treatise of Human Nature*, London, Penguin, [1740] 2004.

Hume, D. *An Enquiry Concerning Human Understanding and Concerning the Principles of Morals*, Oxford, Oxford University Press, [1748] 1975.

Hume, D. *Dialogues Concerning Natural Religion*, London, Penguin, [1779] 1990.

Hursthouse, R. *On Virtue Ethics*, Oxford, Oxford University Press, 1999.

Hursthouse, R. 'Virtue Theory and Abortion', in *Ethics in Practice: An Anthology*, Lafollette, H. (ed.), Oxford, Blackwell, 2002.

Jarvis-Thompson, J. 'A Defense of Abortion', in *Bioethics: An Anthology*, Kuhse, H. and Singer, P. (eds), Oxford, Blackwell, 1999.

Jones, R. 'Peace, Violence and War', in *Christian Ethics: An Introduction*, Hoose, B. (ed.), London, Cassell, 1998.

Kant, I. *Lectures on Ethics*, Heath, P. and Schneewind, J.B. (eds), Cambridge, Cambridge University Press, 1997.

Kant, I. 'Groundwork of a Metaphysics of Morals', in *The Moral Law*, Paton, H.J. (trans.), London, Routledge, 2005.

Keenan, J. 'Virtue Ethics' in *Christian Ethics: An Introduction*, Hoose, B. (ed.), London, Cassell, 1998.

Kirkwood, R. 'Ethical Theory' in *Dialogue*, Special Issue.

Kuhse, H. 'Why Killing Is Not Always Worse – and Sometimes Better – than Letting Die', in *Bioethics: An Anthology*, Kuhse, H. and Singer P. (eds), Oxford, Blackwell, 1999.

Kuhse, H. and Singer, P. (eds) *Bioethics: An Anthology*, Oxford, Blackwell, 1999.

Lafollette, H. (ed.) *Ethics in Practice: An Anthology*, Oxford, Blackwell, 2002.

Leopold, A. *A Sand County Almanac*, Oxford/New York, Oxford University Press, 1968.

Leopold, A. 'The Land Ethic', in *Ethics in Practice: An Anthology*, Lafollette, H. (ed.), Oxford, Blackwell, 2002.

Louden, R. 'On Some Vices of Virtue Ethics', in *Virtue Ethics*, Crisp, R. and Slote, M. (eds), Oxford, Oxford University Press, 1997.

Lovelock, J. *Gaia: A New Look at Life on Earth*, Oxford, Oxford University Press, 1979.

MacIntyre, A. *A Short History of Ethics*, London, Routledge, 1968.

MacIntyre, A. *After Virtue*, London, Duckworth, 1985.

Mackie, J.L. *Ethics: Inventing Right and Wrong*, London, Penguin, 1990.

Macquarrie, J. and Childress, J. *A New Dictionary of Christian Ethics*, London, SCM, 1986.

Maguire, D. *The Moral Choice*, New York, HarperCollins, 1979.

Maguire, D. *Death by Choice*, New York, Image Books, 1984.

Mahoney, J. *Seeking the Spirit: Essays in Moral and Pastoral Theology*, London, Sheen & Ward, 1981.

Mill, J.S. *Utilitarianism*, Indianapolis, Hackett, [1861, 1863], 2002.

Moore, G. 'Sex, Sexuality and Relationships', in *Christian Ethics: An Introduction*, Hoose, B. (ed.), London/New York, Cassell, 1998.

Niebuhr, R. *Moral Man and Immoral Societies*, New York, Scribner, 1932.

Norman, R. *Ethics, Killing and War*, Cambridge, Cambridge University Press, 1995.

Norman, R. *The Moral Philosophers*, Oxford, Oxford University Press, 1998.

O'Connell, T. *Principles for a Catholic Morality* (revised edn), New York, HarperCollins, 1990.

O'Neill, O. *Autonomy and Trust in Bioethics*, Cambridge, Cambridge University Press, 2002.

Palmer, M. *Moral Problems*, Cambridge, Lutterworth Press, 1991.

Palmer, M. *Moral Problems in Medicine*, Cambridge, Lutterworth Press, 1999.

Peters, T. *Playing God? Genetic Determinism and Human Freedom*, London, Routledge, 1997.

Plato. 'Euthyphro', in *The Last Days of Socrates*, Tredennick, H. (trans.), London, Penguin, 1969.

Plato. *The Republic*, Lee, D. (trans.), London, Penguin, 2003.

Pojman, L.P. *Ethical Theory*, Toronto, Wadsworth, 1989.

Pojman, L.P. *Ethics: Discovering Right and Wrong*, Toronto, Wadsworth, 2002.

Preston, R. 'Conscience', in *A Dictionary of Christian Ethics*, Macquarrie, J., London, SCM, 1967.

Rachels, J. 'Active and Passive Euthanasia', in *Bioethics: An Anthology*, Kuhse, H. and Singer, P. (eds), Oxford, Blackwell, 1999.

Rachels, J. and Rachels, S. *The Elements of Moral Philosophy*, New York, McGraw-Hill, 2007.

Ramsay, I. *Christian Ethics and Contemporary Philosophy*, London, SCM, 1966.

Rawls, J. *A Theory of Justice*, Harvard, MA, Harvard University Press, 1971.

Ridley, M. *The Red Queen: Sex and the Evolution of Human Nature*, London, Penguin, 1994.

Ridley, M. *Genome*, London, Harper Collins, 2000.

Robinson, J. *Honest to God*, London, SCM, 1963.

Rosenstand, N. *The Moral of the Story* (5th edn), New York, McGraw-Hill, 2006.

Ross, W.D. *The Right and the Good*, Oxford, Clarendon Press, 1930.

Rulan, V. *An Ethics of Global Rights and Religious Pluralism*, San Francisco, CA, University of San Francisco Press, 2003.

Sacred Congregation for the Doctrine of Faith. 'Declaration on Euthanasia', in *Bioethics: An Anthology*, Kuhse, H. and Singer, P. (eds), Oxford, Blackwell, 1999.

Scruton, R. *Kant*, Oxford, Oxford University Press, 1982.

Sidgwick, H. *Methods of Ethics*, Indianapolis, Hackett, 1981.

Singer, P. *Practical Ethics*, Cambridge, Cambridge University Press, 1993.

Singer, P. (ed.) *A Companion to Ethics*, Oxford, Blackwell, 1994.

Singer, P. *Rethinking Life and Death*, Oxford, Oxford University Press, 1994.

Singer, P. 'All Animals Are Equal', in *Ethics: The Big Questions*, Sterba, J. (ed.), Oxford, Blackwell, 1998.

Slote, M. *Morals from Motives*, Oxford/New York, Oxford University Press, 2001.

Smart, J.J.C. and Williams, B. *Utilitarianism: For and against*, Cambridge, Cambridge University Press, 1973.

Song, R. *Human Genetics: Fabricating the Future*, London, Darton, Longman & Todd, 2002.

Stevenson, C.L. *Ethics and Language*, Oxford, Oxford University Press, 1945.

Stroll, A. *Did My Genes Make Me Do It?* Oxford, Oneworld Publications, 2006.

Taylor, P. 'The Ethics of Respect for Nature', in *Ethics: The Big Questions*, Sterba, J. (ed.), Oxford, Blackwell, 1998.

Thompson, M. *Ethical Theory*, London, Hodder Murray, 2005.

Thompson, M. *Teach Yourself Ethics*, London, Hodder Arnold, 2006.

Van Inwagen, P. *An Essay on Free Will*, Cambridge, Clarendon Press, 1983.

Vardy, P. *The Puzzle of Sex*, London, Fount, 1997.

Vardy, P. and Grosch, P. *The Puzzle of Ethics*, London, Fount, 1999.

Walker, J. *Environmental Ethics*, London, Hodder & Stoughton, 2000.

Ward, K. *The Development of Kant's View of Ethics*, Oxford, Blackwell, 1972.

Warnock, M. *An Intelligent Person's Guide to Ethics*, London, Duckworth, 1999.

Warren, K. 'The Power and Promise of Ecological Feminism', in *Ethics: The Big Questions*, Sterba, J. (ed.), Oxford, Blackwell, 1998.

Warren, M.A. 'Abortion', in *A Companion to Ethics*, Singer, P. (ed.), Oxford, Blackwell, 1991.

Warren, M.A. 'On the Legal and Moral Status of Abortion', in *Ethics in Practice: An Anthology*, LaFollette, H. (ed.), Oxford, Blackwell, 1997.

Wilcockson, M. *Issues of Life and Death*, London, Hodder & Stoughton, 1999.

Wilcockson, M. *Sex and Relationships*, London, Hodder & Stoughton, 2000.

Williams, B. *Morality: An Introduction to Ethics*, Cambridge, Cambridge University Press, 1993.

Williams, B. *Ethics and the Limits of Philosophy*, London, Routledge, 2006.

Wink, W. *Jesus and Nonviolence: A Third Way*, Minneapolis, Abingdon Press US, 2003.

WEBSITES

http://www.newmanreader.org/works/grammar/index.html

http://www.pbs.org/wgbh/questionofgod/ownwords/future2.html

http//www.jcu.edu/philosophy/gensler/et/

http://www.angelfire.com/ms/perring/baier.html

http://www.oup.co.uk/academic/humanities/philosophy/viewpoint/hursthouse/

http://plato.stanford.edu/

http://gadfly.igc.org/e-ethics/Intro-ee.htm

http://erg.ucd.ie/arupa/references/gaia.html

http://www.religion-online.org/

http://www.utilitarianism.com/mill1.htm

http://www.victorianweb.org/philosophy/utilitarianism.html

http://www.uri.edu/personal/szunjic/philos/util.htm

http://www.utilitarian.org/utility.html

http://www.hkbu.edu.hk/~ppp/Kant.html

http://www.rep.routledge.com/article/DB047

http://www.nobunaga.demon.co.uk/htm/kant.htm [Kant's works online]

http://www.faithnet.org.uk

http://www.newadvent.org/

http://www.rsweb.org.uk/ [Useful for all A level RS – Newman on conscience]

http://www.newmanreader.org/works/grammar/chapter5-1.html

http://www.bbc.co.uk/religion/ethics/

http://www.religioustolerance.org/

http://www.srtp.org.uk/

http://www.justwartheory.com/
http://www.importanceofphilosophy.com
http://online.sfsu.edu/~rone/Environ/Enviroethics.htm
http://en.wikipedia.org/

Index